FAST MINDS

FAST MINDS

How to Thrive If You
Have ADHD
(Or Think You Might)

Craig Surman, M. D.
Tim Bilkey, M. D.

with Karen Weintraub

BERKLEY BOOKS, NEW YORK

THE BERKLEY PUBLISHING GROUP
Published by the Penguin Group
Penguin Group (USA) Inc.
375 Hudson Street, New York, New York 10014, USA
Penguin Group (Canada), 90 Eglinton Avenue East, Suite 700, Toronto, Ontario M4P 2Y3, Canada
(a division of Pearson Penguin Canada Inc.) • Penguin Books Ltd., 80 Strand, London WC2R 0RL,
England • Penguin Ireland, 25 St. Stephen's Green, Dublin 2, Ireland (a division of Penguin
Books Ltd.) • Penguin Group (Australia), 707 Collins Street, Melbourne, Victoria 3008, Australia
(a division of Pearson Australia Group Pty. Ltd.) • Penguin Books India Pvt. Ltd., 11 Community
Centre, Panchsheel Park, New Delhi—110 017, India • Penguin Group (NZ), 67 Apollo Drive,
Rosedale, Auckland 0632, New Zealand (a division of Pearson New Zealand Ltd.) • Penguin Books (South
Africa), Rosebank Office Park, 181 Jan Smuts Avenue, Parktown North 2193, South Africa • Penguin
China, B7 Jiaming Center, 27 East Third Ring Road North, Chaoyang District, Beijing 100020, China

Penguin Books Ltd., Registered Offices: 80 Strand, London WC2R 0RL, England

This book is an original publication of The Berkley Publishing Group.

Copyright © 2013 by Harvard University.
Interior text design by Tiffany Estreicher.

FIRST EDITION: February 2013

Library of Congress Cataloging-in-Publication Data

Surman, Craig.
Fast minds: how to thrive if you have ADHD (or think you might) / by Craig Surman, M.D., and
Tim Bilkey, M.D., with Karen Weintraub. — First edition.
pages   cm
Includes bibliographical references and index.
ISBN 978-0-425-25283-3
1. Attention-deficit hyperactivity disorder—Popular works.   2. Life skills—Popular works.
I. Bilkey, Tim.   II. Weintraub, Karen.   III. Title.
RC394.A85S87   2013
616.85'89—dc23   2012040937

PRINTED IN THE UNITED STATES OF AMERICA

10 9 8 7 6 5 4 3 2

PUBLISHER'S NOTE: Neither the publisher nor the author is engaged in rendering
professional advice or services to the individual reader. The ideas, procedures, and suggestions
contained in this book are not intended as a substitute for consulting with your physician. All matters
regarding your health require medical supervision. Neither the author nor the publisher shall be liable
or responsible for any loss or damage allegedly arising from any information or suggestion in this book.

ALWAYS LEARNING   PEARSON

*To my parents, Lezlie Anne Humber Surman, R.N.,
and Owen Stanley Surman, M.D., who gave me the chance
to thrive and taught me the power of empathy.*
CS

*To Holli, who provides immeasurable support and
creativity in all of our projects; and our son, Geordie, who
was and is our inspiration for writing this book.*
TB

*To Rita, whose challenges and humor kept it real, and to
my family, who can now have their dining room table back.*
KW

*To the many people who have entrusted us with
their personal stories, and taught us the principles
we convey in the pages that follow.*
CS, TB, AND KW

ACKNOWLEDGMENTS

A book is always the work of many more people than are named on its cover. In this case, a few people have provided particularly invaluable assistance, including Dr. Julie Silver, our editor at Harvard Health Publications; Denise Silvestro, our editor at The Berkley Publishing Group; Linda Konner, our agent; David Emslie, Dr. Bilkey's research and communications officer; and Holli Bilkey, who both supported FAST MINDS every step of the way. Geordie Bilkey provided extensive input and critique.

Thanks, too, to our publicist Leslie Wolfe Arista, and the staff at The Berkley Publishing Group and Harvard Health Publications, including Natalie Ramm and Meredith Giordan, as well as graphic artist Scott Leighton.

This book is also deeply indebted to the collective work of professionals who pioneered the understanding and treatment of Attention Deficit Hyperactivity Disorder in adults. We are grateful to these pioneers and to the many colleagues and mentors who trained us and have collaborated with us. In particular, we are indebted to the staff and resources of the Massachusetts General Hospital Clinical and Research Program in ADHD.

Finally, we want to thank our families, whose constant support made this book possible, and the people who opened up their lives to us so we could adapt and tell their stories here—without identifying their real identities.

CONTENTS

PART III: BUILDING THE LIFE YOU WANT

FOREWORD

My name is Howie Mandel and I am an actor and comedian. But what you may not know is that I also suffer from Adult ADHD. I'm sure I had it as a child but I was not diagnosed until I was an adult. I got into trouble in school due to my ADHD impulsive behavior. At that time, I had no idea I had this disorder.

As I became an adult, I sought out help and for treatment of this condition, and was diagnosed with ADHD. I am trying to bring awareness to adults that ADHD is real for them, although many do not believe it is a true disorder. Throughout my life, it has been very difficult for me to sit down and read a book or concentrate during normal conversation. I was even thrown out of school for acting on my impulses and as a result did not continue my education. It was too difficult to control my behavior. Some people say ADHD is a gift, and I say if it is, I'd like to return it, even with all my success in show business. What I am trying to do is bring awareness to this condition so that people will not be afraid to go for help as soon as they feel they have any symptoms.

My advice to anybody who thinks that they have ADHD is to have their doctor find a specialist and go for help. Medication is not the end all and be all, but it can help. So can coaching and or therapy.

—Howie Mandel

INTRODUCTION

So you've picked up this book called FAST MINDS. It caught your eye; you are curious about what this is. FAST MINDS is an acronym that we use to identify a medical condition that we've known about for more than one hundred years. About 4 percent of adults may have this condition—and many who don't have the full condition have many of its traits.

FAST MINDS stands for:

Forgetful
Achieving below potential
Stuck in a rut
Time challenged
Motivationally challenged
Impulsive
Novelty seeking
Distractible
Scattered

If people have enough of these traits, they may have a condition known as Attention Deficit Hyperactivity Disorder (ADHD). But this book is also about and for people who struggle with ADHD-type challenges—people who have FAST MINDS.

Whether you picked up this book for yourself or out of concern for someone you care about, we will help you maintain better focus, manage restless or impulsive behavior, and stay organized. The principles and exercises within allow readers to build *personalized* strategies and empower them to get the most from available tools and professional help.

For the last fifteen years, we have both worked with and learned from thousands of people who have struggled with FAST MINDS challenges and now successfully stay on top of their daily lives. Intensive research has revealed new insights about ADHD in adults. But in spite of these scientific advances, most adults with ADHD—and many more who have only some symptoms of the condition—suffer without knowing that help is available.

Another reason many adults with ADHD and FAST MINDS do not receive help is that there are many versions of this condition, so that two people with the same diagnosis can have very different issues. And people who can cope just fine in one situation may be completely overwhelmed in another. Students who coasted through high school may fall apart in college or graduate school; people who do okay early in life may suffer when they have to manage work, kids, home maintenance, and a marriage at the same time.

This book is for anyone who struggles with these FAST MINDS traits, whether you know you have ADHD, think you might, or are concerned about someone else with these characteristics. This book is intended to help people better recognize the symptoms of Adult ADHD so they can advocate for themselves and have a more fulfilling, productive life. We encourage people who have ADHD or are concerned about traits that we describe as FAST MINDS to seek evaluation and treatment from a professional. However, we find that people get far more out of meetings with doctors, therapists, or professional coaches if they have done the work in this book ahead of time.

We are both physicians who have devoted our careers to understanding and improving the treatment of ADHD in adults. Dr. Bilkey, a psychiatrist, has counseled more than 3,400 patients at his clinics in Ontario, Canada. He developed the original FAST MINDS program to help other physicians recognize, diagnose, and treat Adult ADHD, and as an international lecturer on ADHD he has presented it at conferences around the world. This FAST MINDS program has been accredited through the College of Family Physicians of Canada since 2009.

Dr. Surman is a neuropsychiatrist at Massachusetts General Hospital and an assistant professor of psychiatry at Harvard Medical School. He conducts and coordinates research on a team that is internationally recognized for its contributions to understanding and treating ADHD across the life span. He has also cared for thousands of adults with ADHD or other organizational challenges. His research has expanded our understanding of how ADHD and organizational challenges impact adult life and explored new treatments. His work has been supported by the United States National Institutes of Health, and he has been a consultant, lecturer, and investigator for companies that develop pharmaceutical or nutritional treatments. He also teaches physicians how to identify and treat these challenges, at Harvard Medical School and internationally.

Karen Weintraub is a science journalist who has many friends and acquaintances with FAST MINDS. She has also written extensively about neuroscience and conditions such as autism, Alzheimer's, obsessive-compulsive disorder, and ADHD.

We have all been inspired by the creative and adaptive ways people thrive with FAST MINDS, and we came together to write this book to share those insights. Through their voices and our professional experience, we offer ways to cope both on your own and with the resources available to you. These ideas are presented in the stories and strategies of real people, whose names and personal details have been changed to protect their privacy.

Some books seem written for people who are already organized or who can easily change their habits. Others are written as if every reader has the same challenges. Instead, we offer principles rooted in research and the experience of thousands of people we have worked with that can allow you to develop *your own solutions*. We know medication can be a game-changer for many people with ADHD, altering how their brains operate and reducing FAST MINDS challenges. But it is not always the right solution, and often is not enough. We believe you will function better if you capitalize on your strengths and support your challenges.We think we can help you in that work.

Part I identifies how biologically based FAST MINDS traits may underlie life's struggles; Part II explains common patterns that compound these challenges and offers tools for eliminating or working around them. FAST MINDS traits can get in the way of forming new habits. That is why Part II helps you figure out which changes will help the most for the least amount of effort, and how to stay on the path of self-improvement. Part III presents a practical guide for how to find and make the most of resources, both medical and nonmedical.

So, if you or someone you care about can identify with being forgetful, underachieving, stuck, time challenged, motivationally challenged, impulsive, easily bored, distractible, or scattered—welcome to FAST MINDS.

Dr. Tim Bilkey
Dr. Craig Surman
Karen Weintraub

PART I

Understanding
FAST MINDS

What Are FAST MINDS?

James likes to tell a story that sums up what his life used to be like. He was speeding to make it to a sales team meeting on time. He lit a cigarette and opened the window of his sport-utility vehicle for some fresh air. His cell phone rang and as he tried to find it in the pile on the passenger seat, his cigarette disappeared. Answering the phone and distracted, he thought briefly, *It must've blown out the window.*

A few minutes later, still chatting, he happened to glance in his rearview mirror and saw flames shooting up from the backseat. Swerving off the road, he jumped out and yanked fast-food containers, empty cigarette cartons, product samples, and scorched work papers from the backseat and tossed them into the roadside dust. When the fire was out, James didn't know whether to laugh or cry at what had happened. But he did know he was tired of not being on top of his life, and something had to change. There were too many such fires in his life, both actual and metaphorical. And he finally admitted he couldn't put them all out on his own.

James has traits we describe as FAST MINDS. Although these show up in many different ways in people's lives, the core challenges include difficulty with focus, controlling behavior, and/or disorganization. One in twenty-five adults across the globe struggles enough with these traits to have the clinically recognized condition Attention Deficit Hyperactivity Disorder.* The diagnosis of ADHD has been identified in children for decades, but in the last dozen years, scientists have acknowledged that the condition continues into adulthood for more than half of children who have it. The condition is also often missed in women, probably because when they were girls they were less likely than boys to act in disruptive ways. They were less likely to fit the stereotype of the impulsive, hyperactive troublemaker or class clown. Instead, most girls and women we see with ADHD quietly struggle to focus and behave according to society's rules.

Doctors and therapists use formal criteria to identify ADHD: The person must have a certain number of symptoms of inattention or impulsivity/hyperactivity that have been present since childhood and can't be explained by another diagnosis. These characteristics must cause significant problems in more than one area of life—thwarting success at school, at work, and/or in relationships. We see many people who don't meet the full criteria for diagnosis—this includes people who have only some of the required characteristics, had challenges starting later than childhood, have symptoms that are due to another condition, or have difficulties that impact only one area of their life. We find that the strategies, approaches, and exercises in this book can help anyone impacted by FAST MINDS traits, whether they meet the full technical criteria of ADHD or not.

We see many people who fulfill all of the criteria for ADHD and have talked with other clinicians but have never been diagnosed or

---

*Throughout the book, we will use the term *ADHD* to indicate the full clinical condition, in its inattentive, impulsive, or hyperactive forms.

treated. We believe this occurs for two major reasons: Many clinicians do not understand the condition or are not comfortable treating it, and it takes longer than a typical twenty-minute clinic visit to understand how a person functions day to day well enough to recognize the pattern of ADHD. We wrote this book so that people can understand whether they have the condition or traits of it, and to empower them to get the help they need.

A clinical diagnosis of ADHD should be made only when there is impairment from FAST MINDS–type traits in the pattern described here. Often when clinicians sit down with people like James to diagnose ADHD, they look for obvious signs of impairment such as being dismissed from jobs or poor grades at school. But this focus on external consequences misses what it's like to live with these characteristics every day. It fails to capture the most common burden of FAST MINDS: the extra time and effort it takes to compensate for its traits— such as late hours at work making up for the constant distractions during the day, or last-minute cramming on projects that won't get done without deadline pressure. People with FAST MINDS who seem successful to others may, from their own perspective, just be "getting by" or "living by the seat of their pants." They may be living with the constant stress of being reactive rather than proactive—handling demands at the last minute, under stress, rather than being prepared and feeling confident. They may spend their time constantly double-checking themselves to make sure they haven't made a mistake. This extra effort may get them by at work or school but leaves little time and energy for themselves or a social life. They may suffer demoralization, anxiety, or other distress because of the impact of FAST MINDS traits on their lives. Yet often, only those closest to them know how hard they work to succeed.

We wrote this book to help people put a name and solutions to the varied struggles of FAST MINDS. Specialists in ADHD are not common, so we want people to become their own experts—to understand what helps or hurts their personal patterns of FAST MINDS challenges.

FAST MINDS Explained

The original FAST MINDS program has been presented at lectures, seminars, and conferences around the globe for clinicians, educators, mental health care workers, and families affected by ADHD. The acronym can also help people identify ADHD traits in themselves and people they care about—the first step in getting a diagnosis, receiving more help, or understanding why someone acts a certain way.

FAST MINDS is an acronym for the characteristics of the condition, but it also speaks to how some people feel: as if their brain sometimes works too fast for their own good, as if they can't get out of their own way. The symptoms may not reveal themselves as dramatically as we saw with James and his backseat combustion at the beginning of the chapter. But the people to whom we will introduce you throughout this book all felt overwhelmed by their FAST MINDS traits and blocked from reaching their potential. We helped many of them seize control of their lives to function better at home, school, and work. That's why we think we can help others do the same.

Not everyone will relate to all of these traits. Some people with ADHD are fidgety and active; others are much more sedentary and have trouble getting started. Some can't stop playing video games at work; others are superstars when the pressure is on but have trouble filling out necessary paperwork.

When reading the following traits to see if they reflect your experience (or those of someone you care about), think of them in the context of the boring stuff of life—not the exciting moments when adrenaline is pumping. ADHD characteristics are much more evident when a person is doing things that don't seem particularly compelling.

RECOGNIZING YOURSELF

Note which of these traits affect your day-to-day life, so you can reflect on them as we proceed in this book:

☐ **FORGETFUL:** Do you forget what people have told you? Do you forget where you put things? Do you need reminders for every day things? Do you miss appointments?

☐ **ACHIEVING BELOW POTENTIAL:** Do you feel you underachieve for how well you can do in your life? Do you feel you should be getting better grades than you do at school, or should have made it further than you have in your career?

☐ **STUCK IN A RUT:** Are you having a hard time moving ahead in your life? Do you feel like you're trapped trying to keep your head above water, playing catch-up instead of living how you want to? Are you stuck in important areas of your life, such as at work or in school?

☐ **TIME CHALLENGED:** Are you often late? Do you often underestimate the amount of time that things take? Does time drift away? Do you have trouble figuring out how long a task is "supposed" to take?

☐ **MOTIVATIONALLY CHALLENGED:** Are you a procrastinator? Do you do things at the last minute or need the pressure of a deadline to get things done? Do you have a hard time getting started on tasks? Do you get partway done with many tasks but have trouble completing them?

☐ **IMPULSIVE:** Do you do things without anticipating consequences (making decisions, shopping, driving, sex, drugs)? Do you blurt things out in conversation? Do you engage in risky sexual behavior? Do you make purchases without considering the cost or your budget?

☐ **NOVELTY SEEKING:** Are you often bored? Do you seek out new,

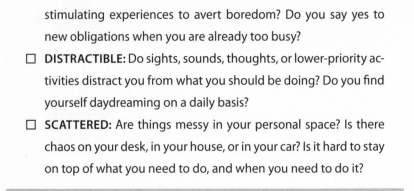

stimulating experiences to avert boredom? Do you say yes to new obligations when you are already too busy?

☐ **DISTRACTIBLE:** Do sights, sounds, thoughts, or lower-priority activities distract you from what you should be doing? Do you find yourself daydreaming on a daily basis?

☐ **SCATTERED:** Are things messy in your personal space? Is there chaos on your desk, in your house, or in your car? Is it hard to stay on top of what you need to do, and when you need to do it?

Let's take a closer look at the FAST MINDS traits.

FORGETFUL: Forgetfulness disrupts life in many ways, from leaving things behind at home, to failing to make an important phone call, to neglecting important e-mails. Someone we know thought his car had been stolen until police located it in a commuter parking lot— and only then did he remember that he had ridden the train the day it "went missing."

ACHIEVING BELOW POTENTIAL: "Could've done better," "Not working up to potential," or "Makes too many careless mistakes": This is the kind of feedback adults with ADHD often got as kids and how they still think about themselves now. They, and the people in their lives—parents, teachers, bosses, spouses, and friends—feel they have underperformed and missed out on opportunities that should have helped them thrive.

STUCK IN A RUT: For people with ADHD, feeling stuck is not just mild and temporary; it is a life pattern. FAST MINDS traits drain energy and increase the effort it takes to succeed at school or work or to reach other personal goals. It's about feeling stuck in a job that doesn't match your strengths; stuck in a school, not knowing where you are headed and underachieving; stuck in your parents' basement, still financially dependent on them. This sense of imprisonment leads to a pervasive feeling of being demoralized and losing hope for what could be a bright future.

TIME CHALLENGED: Many people with ADHD underestimate the amount of time that tasks take. They lose track of time when they are doing something that stimulates them, leading to chronic lateness and rushing through things at the last minute. They often lack a sense of how much "should" be accomplished in a day, so they never know whether they've done enough.

MOTIVATIONALLY CHALLENGED: Most people procrastinate on tasks such as paying bills, cleaning the bathroom, or going to the gym. But for some people with ADHD, the phone service has to get cut off before they pay the bills; the clutter makes it hard to find everyday items; the gym membership remains unused year after year. It's not just tough to get started on certain tasks—it seems nearly impossible.

IMPULSIVE: Impulsivity has many faces. It's being verbally impulsive, cutting people off in conversation; it's spending money you don't have; it's constantly changing your mind and making decisions without anticipating consequences; it's blindly jumping into a job or quitting a job. It could take the form of bingeing on alcohol, drugs, or food, or driving carelessly. Even a little bit of impulsivity in an adult's life can have significant consequences.

NOVELTY SEEKING: The trait of novelty seeking is about craving the new. Being unable to manage boredom, the mind always jumps to the next "shiny" thing. This can make it extremely difficult to complete tasks. Obligations pile up that can't be fulfilled. Sometimes even sticking with a relationship can be a challenge. Boredom is also a toxic state because of what people do to avert boredom—oversleeping, overeating, spending hours playing video games, losing themselves on Facebook or YouTube instead of getting work done. For some, novelty seeking and poor impulse control are an entry to drugs, alcohol, or other high-risk activities that can ruin lives.

DISTRACTIBLE: Distractibility may be the most common of all the FAST MINDS traits. Many people with ADHD have trouble paying attention. They may focus for hours on something of particular interest but be unable to tune in for more than a minute or two to other facets of life. Their minds sometimes fill with so many different thoughts simultaneously that it is impossible to follow just one. The sights and sounds of normal life can make it impractical to work in a busy office or study anywhere without complete silence.

SCATTERED: People with ADHD can be disorganized, though not all are. Like James, their cars and living spaces can be filled with clutter—becoming tripping hazards, fire hazards, and relationship hazards. Scattered people finish projects at the last minute, or even later. And their minds jump from one subject to the next, making accomplishments and conversations a challenge.

The Many Faces of FAST MINDS

Everyone in the FAST MINDS category has their own pattern, their own way of expressing these traits. For some people with FAST MINDS, being time challenged or disorganized may be a dominant motif; for others, it's not much of an issue at all. People should determine their individual challenges, so they can accommodate them.

A person's version of FAST MINDS also depends on their particular strengths and any other challenges they have. Unfortunately, brain conditions often come in pairs, or more. People with ADHD are likely to have other mental health conditions, too, such as anxiety, mood, or substance problems; social challenges such as Asperger's; or learning disabilities such as dyslexia. Traits typical of ADHD—including problems with focus, follow-through, and restlessness—are common in other mental health and chronic medical problems, so a clinician should help clarify whether FAST MINDS traits are due to ADHD or another condition.

A person's experience with ADHD depends on whether the condition was identified in childhood. Most of the adults we see are diagnosed for the first time as adults. Some of them come to see us because they find the challenges of their own children all too familiar—ADHD runs strongly in families. When parent-teacher conferences and conflicts at home echo their own childhood, adults may realize that they continue to struggle in the same way. Others come in because a new role or responsibility strains their abilities, creating new struggles. Although awareness has grown, even now, many children with ADHD go unrecognized. Some of them are not disruptive and so never attract attention—often because they are more daydreamy than hyperactive. Women are much less likely than men to have been diagnosed in childhood, though at least in Dr. Bilkey's clinics, half of those who seek diagnosis or treatment are women.

Though these aren't part of any formal criteria, we see two other major patterns that influence what people with FAST MINDS need to do to thrive: how easily they adopt new habits and stick with them, and how much control they have over their emotions.

UNHEALTHY DAILY RHYTHMS

Many adults with ADHD can imagine useful routines they wish they had—such as putting clothes and dishes away, keeping keys in one spot, or regularly sitting down to plan for the coming day or week. But they can't seem to deliver on this vision. They try many new strategies once or twice and then quickly neglect them. Trouble with routines also can extend to how adults with FAST MINDS take care of themselves. Dr. Surman, Dr. Bilkey, and other researchers have discovered that adults with ADHD are often either out of sync or inconsistent in routines that are critical for well-being, such as regular sleep, eating, and exercise. Some books suggest new habits that they expect readers to easily adopt. We don't assume in this book that readers will adjust to change so simply. We discuss the key principles for getting daily habits into line with productivity and health, including how to counteract the tendency to fall back into less useful, default rhythms of activity and self-care.

EMOTIONAL CONTROL

Recent studies confirm that many adults with ADHD do not have as much control over their emotions as people without ADHD. Researchers have found that more than half of children and adults with ADHD are quicker to anger and get frustrated than individuals who do not have ADHD. Many adults with ADHD also experience a less stable sense of well-being than their peers, with regular dips into dismay or sadness and back again. These problems with emotional control are different from diagnosable disorders such as depression or bipolar disorder, because they are briefer, are reactive to situations, and occur even during normal times. Dr. Surman's work also shows that the combination of ADHD and poor control of emotional expression can run in families, leaving patterns that span generations.[1] Relationships with others may be very vulnerable to these traits.

WHAT CAUSES ADHD?

It used to be thought that ADHD was a kids-only problem. Just give them enough time and they'll grow out of it. Now we know that roughly 4 percent of adults meet the criteria for ADHD.[2]

We aren't sure exactly what causes ADHD, though scientists believe it's a combination of genes and environment. Many insults disrupt the exquisitely choreographed development of the brain, such as lead poisoning or smoking during pregnancy. Although demands of modern life put a premium on focused, sitting work, international studies suggest that the frequency of ADHD in children is not much different between more and less developed regions of the world.[3] There's not a lot of support for the idea that television or media or modern life causes ADHD, though present-day demands to perform and unlimited distractions on the Internet can highlight people's limitations. But technology also offers new opportunities for adapting, with online calendars and downloadable tools. We describe ways of using many of these resources in the second section of the book.

ADHD is often carried in the genes. Twin studies are a classic method for determining whether a condition is inherited or due to experiences—and they give striking evidence for the genetic nature of ADHD. In more than three-quarters of identical twin pairs, when one has ADHD, the other does as well—making ADHD one of the most strongly inherited conditions in mental health.[4] If a parent has ADHD, there's a good chance their child will also have it.[5]

So, much of what causes ADHD is hard-wired. There are clear brain differences, visible with brain-scanning techniques that compare tiny differences in structure and real-time pictures of what the brain is doing during mental activities. We come back to these in later chapters.

Attention and *hyperactivity* get top billing in the formal diagnosis of ADHD; they emphasize problems controlling attention and overactivity. But up to half of adults with ADHD may also have differences in brain capacities for other "executive functions"—the "boss" capacities of the brain.[6] These include the ability to prioritize, plan, be aware of time, and stop one thing and start another. As we explore in later chapters, these biological differences contribute strongly to the organizational struggles, the difficulty forming habits, and the unhealthy daily styles of life mentioned earlier. In the section that follows, we identify both these patterns and the specific supports needed to limit their effects.

In our experience, medication is a cornerstone in the treatment of ADHD. Medication often makes it easier to control focus and behavior, but it takes adopting new habits and applying strategies for a person to thrive. Volumes of research show that medication works by increasing levels of neurotransmitters already present in the brain. But other science, including Dr. Surman's work with his colleagues at Massachusetts General Hospital, part of Harvard Medical School, shows that a combination of awareness, useful strategies, and effective support can transform the struggle of ADHD into a life well lived.

There are plenty of successful people with ADHD in many fields: actors and singers, such as Howie Mandel, Adam Levine;[7] sports stars, such as swimmer Michael Phelps,[8] hockey player Cammi Granato,[9] and quarterback Terry Bradshaw;[10] and business leaders such as Jet-Blue Airways founder David Neeleman[11] and Kinko's founder Paul Orfalea.[12] A painter we know says her ADHD behaviors boost her creativity in the studio.

Having FAST MINDS traits can mean there is a mismatch between the way the brain works and the demands of life. It's a way of thinking and being that makes it harder to function in today's world. This book is intended to make that journey easier.

WHAT YOU CAN DO

The path to having a successful, engaging life with FAST MINDS is different for everyone. For many people with ADHD, it will be much more challenging to fulfill personal goals without medication—but there is a reason that we choose to wait until Chapters 10 and 11 to discuss the place of medication among other resources for ADHD. We feel it is critical for you to first identify what you want to work on in your life and to highlight changes you'd like to make. Then you can make an informed decision about what tools you want to seek out to get there. The brain—with or without ADHD—is an incredibly flexible organ. It has multiple ways to accomplish the same goals.

As you read this book, keep these ideas in mind:

FAST MINDS and ADHD call for different strategies to thrive. With the right understanding and resources, life may be different—but just as fulfilling with ADHD as without.

Information That Can Help Clinicians Evaluate Whether You Have ADHD

These are some questions that a specialist thinks about to diagnose ADHD. Bring your answers to these questions with you if you seek professional assessment.

- Which FAST MINDS symptoms do you have now?

- Do you have problems in multiple areas of life because of FAST MINDS symptoms (at work, in school, in social interactions, with family, behind the wheel, etc.)?

- How long have you had these symptoms? Is there evidence that they've been around since childhood? Were you held back by hyperactivity, impulsivity, and/or distractibility? (Did your early report cards include comments such as "poor attention span," "does not apply himself/herself," "could do better"?)

- Have you been diagnosed or treated for other psychiatric conditions that could produce FAST MINDS–type symptoms, such as anxiety, mood disorder, or addictions?

- Do you have other medical disorders such as seizures, brain injury, or sleep disorders that may account for FAST MINDS traits?

Gather evidence of what is and isn't working. Do relationships, family, friends, and job expectations help or get in the way? Being in a flexible work or school setting and having an accepting partner can make all the difference.

Keep track of challenges. Being aware of difficulties can help focus attention. But don't allow them to become overwhelming and paralyzing. Everyone has problems they must cope with.

Build a *personal* set of strategies. Solutions must bubble up from personal experiences and creativity. They have to work organically, not because someone else says they should.

Success comes from using strengths and finding effective resources. No one else can "fix" the challenges except the person who has them.

Over the course of the book, we lay out four basic self-help principles, which we abbreviate to *ADHD*, to help you keep your eyes on the prize of a more fulfilling life:

AWARE: Be aware of your emotions, behavior, and habits as the first step in changing them.

DECIDE: Choose your own priorities and figure out the steps you need to get there.

HELP: Provide yourself with tools that meet your needs and people who "get" you.

DESIGN: Build a life with structure and accountability that will help you thrive.

JAMES: LEARNING TO CHANGE

What frustrates James (whom you met earlier) the most about his FAST MINDS characteristics is how they limit his relationships.

"When I was single, it didn't matter as much if I took extra time to do things, had to correct mistakes or search for things. Now, there are more people riding on my everyday habits." Susan, his wife of sixteen years, has always been understanding, but when James first sought help for his FAST MINDS traits, he worried he was a lousy husband and father. He kept forgetting his eight-year-old daughter's hockey games and when and where he was supposed to pick her up. Susan was getting exhausted from pulling far more than her fair share at home—because he couldn't be relied on to get the groceries, wash the dishes, or finish projects he started around the house. He struggled to stay focused in talks with his daughter, too. "Dad, are you paying attention?" she'd ask repeatedly.

"He's just not tuned in to the same channel as everyone else," Susan said on the couple's first visit to a doctor's office. "He listens but doesn't seem to hear. He looks but he doesn't seem to see." In spite of these difficulties, Susan appreciated James's good heart and how much fun he was to be around. But she saw how his day-to-day misfires lowered his self-esteem and caused stress in their relationship.

James chose to start medication for his ADHD, finding that it helped many of his tendencies to tune out and get distracted. But he still had to put in significant, careful effort to rework some major patterns in his life. With Susan's help, he became more aware of where his FAST MINDS traits were interfering with his life.

James decided to tackle his paperwork issues first. Every time James sat down to do paperwork for his small business, he would end up doing twenty-five other things instead. He knew he was best at doing such tedious tasks if the room was quiet, with few distractions and some soft music playing. After giving it some thought, he realized his home office was too chaotic—geared for sales calls, not paperwork—so he carved out a spot on the desk in the guest bedroom. He slowly became more aware of when his at-

tention drifted, and when he recognized he was getting distracted, he got better at reminding himself that finishing his paperwork was his top work priority. After a few weeks of effort, he was astonished to find that it took only fifteen minutes to rid himself of the paperwork that used to haunt him all day long.

Today, James still has ADHD with FAST MINDS traits, but they are just one aspect of who he is; they do not define him. And the clutter and disorganization in his life no longer creates "fire hazards."

THOUGHT EXERCISE

For James, paperwork was hard because he was so distractible, scattered, and novelty seeking that sitting down to fill out forms felt like physical torture. In his case, he didn't have any other issues such as depression to get in his way, but his struggles to keep up had become emotionally charged, and he never felt comfortable with routines. Once he decided to take charge of his paperwork problem, he was able to make improvements fairly quickly. He was able to make the process less emotional by creating the best possible context for himself, telling himself that he was up to the challenge, and getting help from his wife to see it through. Then, each success reinforced itself until the paperwork ceased to seem like a huge burden.

Your issues may be more complex, but the process is the same. We'd like you to think of three tasks or situations that you really wish could flow better, that disrupt your quality of life, or that you will be upset about in the coming months and years if you aren't able to resolve. They might be a problem at home, work, or school; a fraying relationship that you wish could work better; a work skill you desperately want to learn; a dream you don't want to give up on. Keep these priorities in mind as you read through the rest of the book and think how each strategy and each piece of new information can help in your pursuit of these goals. Write these three briefly in the spaces that follow, so you'll remember them and be able to refer back to them in later chapters:

1. _____

2. _____

3. _____

James's story shows, and we hope you will take away from this book, that people with ADHD can adapt and learn to function better in the world. Each individual has their own specific best way of doing this. But we can give you principles, ways to think about yourself and questions to ask, so that you have a better understanding of your own personal brand of ADHD. This book is intended as a companion for the kind of life you care about; a life that's based not just on being distracted by whatever is "shiny" in the moment, but on what *you* decide really matters.

Acknowledging FAST MINDS is a big step. Most people are relieved and energized when they get a diagnosis. They always knew something was getting in their way, but now, they've learned that there's a name to what's causing them distress—and that it is not their fault. That recognition can be powerful. One woman we worked with said it best: "My diagnosis gave me a heads-up on what I was dealing with and a starting point toward positive change."

KEY POINTS

■ Many people have FAST MINDS traits without needing a full diagnosis of ADHD.

■ Everyone's constellation of FAST MINDS traits is different. Accommodating those traits requires a personalized approach.

Tune In to Your FAST MIND

E ddie is a champion procrastinator. In the old days, when the home office called demanding his paperwork, he'd say he'd already put it in the mail and then scramble to get it out the door. Then came fax machines and e-mail, dramatically cutting down on the time he had to work once the ultimatums came in. The years he had a "battle-axe" of a secretary were the best. He found her slightly terrifying, so when she told him to get something done, he'd scurry off and do it. "If she controlled the paperwork and my agenda and everything else, I was very, very effective," he says. Otherwise, he tended to get lost amidst the reams of paper. "I have to wonder what I could have done if I'd actually read that stuff."

In school, Eddie wrote every paper the night before it was due and studied for every test at the last minute—he skated by but never felt like he was really learning. He never managed to finish the thesis he needed for graduate school. And the thousands of dollars he lost by not paying bills and taxes on time? He sometimes fantasizes about the trips he could have taken and things he could have bought with it all. "I could have been better at everything I've done if I'd been better organized," he says. "I have lots of regrets."

But Eddie is far from a failure. He shines when the pressure is on. For one job, he used to stand up in front of 1,200 middle schoolers and deliver off-the-cuff speeches—he loved that. "They'd stick a micro-phone and TV camera in front of me and I'd perform. My mind cleared and I'd remember things from years earlier," he says. His bosses always supported Eddie's creative ideas and new approaches, and he always pulled through enough at the last minute to get done what was needed.

He's also been a wonderful father to his two sons, now in their twenties. He says he thinks he was able to hyperfocus on fatherhood because he had his children late and because it was so important to him to be around more than his own father had been. "When I was a kid, I went to a lot of father-son hockey banquets alone, and I remem-bered that." Eddie was involved enough in his sons' lives to win cus-tody when his marriage fell apart and to raise them largely alone for the next decade. "I gave parenting everything I had," he says. "I was very aware that I couldn't put my kids in a pile like my paperwork and come back to them later."

One of the frustrating aspects of ADHD is how it seems to bestow gifts with one hand and yank them away with the other. Many people thrive in one aspect of their lives, as Eddie does with his parenting and public speaking and as others do in video games, sales calls, down-hill skiing, or writing. And then those same people are completely off their game in other settings, creating struggles that overshadow their successes.

These strengths and weaknesses can also change over time or in different contexts, so someone like Eddie, who never once read to the end of a book in grade school, can grow up to become an avid reader—now that he can choose the book for himself.

In this chapter, we'll describe the experiences of Eddie and another adult with ADHD, a woman we'll call Tiegan. Their stories show that although ADHD has some common threads, the differences among people with it can be huge. An extroverted person may be able to skate through school on the strength of his personality; a shy girl may get passed on to the next grade without the teacher noticing she was capable of more.

And context matters. As one man you'll meet later says, if he had grown up in the same Italian town his father did, where everyone worked with their hands from dawn to dusk, he would have fit in fine and wouldn't have had the kind of frustrations he endured in school.

RECOGNIZING YOURSELF

- ☐ Are you struggling or did you struggle to make it through school?
- ☐ Did you manage okay when you were younger but start to fall apart when you had less structure—and less parental support?
- ☐ Are you overwhelmed with the responsibilities of parenthood, marriage, work, and maintaining a household?
- ☐ Are you often lost in your own thoughts?
- ☐ Do friends, colleagues, and family members complain that you space out or disappear on them?

Changes over the Life Span

Certain times of life present particular challenges for people with FAST MINDS traits. People who were hyperactive and impulsive as children often look somewhat different as adults: Instead of bouncing off the walls, they may be fidgety, need to move on to the next thing, talk excessively, and act on impulse. Inattentive daydreaming often persists into adulthood, but instead of tuning out the teacher and forgetting what was asked of them, people tune out in conversations or miss meetings.

We also find that people who have a "scattered" organizational style and those who have trouble keeping to productive and healthy routines tend to struggle more as adults than they did as children. The structure and routine of a six-hour school day are gone. Parents and teachers are no longer as involved in daily life. Friends no longer have the same routine to use as a model. Demands, distractions, and complexities also increase after high school. Sometimes, people who managed okay through their teen years fall apart as they face the greater organizational demands of adulthood.

As mentioned, Dr. Bilkey has developed a nationally accredited medical education program for physicians to help them recognize ADHD. He identifies common traits exhibited by people with ADHD, and although every person is unique in how FAST MINDS affects their life, he found it helpful to describe certain profiles that doctors can easily recognize. There's "**The Struggling Student**," which sums up Eddie's experiences during university and graduate school. A second category of people we often meet in our offices are—to evoke the old sitcom—"**Married with Children**." Mary, whom you'll meet in the next chapter, fits this description. Her energy, smarts, and creativity propelled her through school and her early twenties, but now she's married and must manage a job, a household, children, and a spouse; her kids have ADHD, too, so they're a challenge to parent well. People like Mary thrive in some contexts but are now overwhelmed by the tasks of adult life. A third sort, "**The Distractible Daydreamer**," seems spacey, forgetful, disorganized, time challenged, and likely to procrastinate.

We see people who fall into all three categories, as well as others, but these are good examples of what leads to underachievement with FAST MINDS traits. Support from family and co-workers can hide the impact of FAST MINDS traits, at least for a while. Eddie had his secretary, who helped him stay organized; when his role changed at work, his lack of organization became a problem for him. At home, where he never had that support, bills piled up and taxes went unpaid. We find that students who aren't natural organizers are particularly challenged by university, where unstructured days and long-term assignments are the norm. Spacey people often miss out on opportunities for advancement, wandering through life without direction or purpose. They spend so much time in their own heads that often they miss the world going by until suddenly they're overwhelmed by demands and needs.

The Gender Gap

Studies suggest that ADHD is more common in males than females. About twenty-one boys and men are diagnosed for every ten girls and women.[1] Women tend to get diagnosed with ADHD later than men and may be more likely to receive other diagnoses, such as depression, before being diagnosed with ADHD.[2] The condition is underrecognized in girls because boys are more likely to behave disruptively. Women show the more subtle signs of distractibility, forgetfulness, and disorganization. They may quietly underachieve and struggle, not coming to anyone's attention. As with men with ADHD, adult women are likely to have other conditions, as well. Dr. Surman and his colleagues have demonstrated that in some women, ADHD may be associated with a higher risk of the eating disorder bulimia nervosa for instance.[3]

Impulsivity in young women with ADHD can also lead to major consequences, such as sexually transmitted diseases and unwanted pregnancies.[4] Research has shown that first-time expectant mothers with ADHD were less likely to be married, were less likely to have a university education, were less likely to have wanted the pregnancy, and had fewer expectations about their role as a parent.[5] Dr. Bilkey explores this idea more in his well-received documentary on women with ADHD, *Her FAST MIND.*

Many women are diagnosed when they bring their children in for help. In addition to the challenges of being "Married with Children" or "The Distractible Daydreamer," women are often expected to be the emotional and social center for their family. Yet simply getting dinner on the table is already a challenge for some. "The only part of Martha Stewart I understand is the jail part," says one woman we'll introduce you to later. Not fulfilling societal expectations makes it harder for a woman to feel good about herself.

Take a minute and think about what other people would say about you. We encourage you to do this in many chapters of this book. How you impact other people may be noticeable only to them, not you—kind of like having garlic on your breath.

RECOGNIZE THE IMPACT—DO OTHER PEOPLE SAY YOU:

- ☐ Don't live up to your abilities?
- ☐ Should "try harder"?
- ☐ Should turn things in earlier?
- ☐ Are on top of some things but not others?
- ☐ Need help staying on top of things?

It's Not an Attention Deficit

As anyone who has ADHD—or interacts with someone who has it—knows, the name of the condition doesn't fit well. It's not that people with FAST MINDS can't pay attention. They can spend hours playing video games or being incredibly successful at things they do well. But everyday tasks are often tripping hazards—the drive to work, laundry, time sheets, term papers, even simple conversations.

We prefer to think of ADHD not as an attention disorder, but as a problem maintaining consistent engagement. Even when a project is important, such as filing your taxes, FAST MINDS traits make it hard to consistently engage. "No matter what I start on my to-do list," one engineer explains, "I know that whatever is shiniest will be what I end up spending the most time on." Unfortunately, most people with ADHD seem to get stuck on these short-term interests rather than long-term goals. For them, even caring deeply about something is not enough to get them or keep them engaged in doing it.

Everyone tends to drift—to become disengaged—when a meeting, conversation, or class lecture drags on, but the ADHD brain tunes out more easily and more often. It is as if boring things are more boring, and distracting things are more distracting.

The traits of ADHD stem from one fundamental truth about the human brain: We are wired to focus on what we need to survive. The tiger that is chasing us is inherently interesting. We all have excellent systems for producing focus—the system that helps us go on red alert. All of our senses instantly become sharper when we catch a glimpse of the tiger. Our hearts start racing, our breathing gets shallow and fast, our eyes begin scanning for escape routes while we keep tabs on the beast. We are primed for action, and we pay careful attention. But when the situation isn't as scary or novel, our brain has more work to do to choose what to focus on. Put another way, if a task is not naturally engaging, such as filling out tax forms, we must make a conscious effort to engage.

Research over the last twenty years has confirmed the existence of an "engagement" system in our brains that enables us to control what brain faculties we engage and thus what we do—whether it involves thinking, feeling, sensing, or acting. Several regions of the brain work together as a circuit to manage attention. This engagement system functions unconventionally in people with ADHD. Imaging and genetic studies demonstrate differences in the physical structure of this engagement system in some people with ADHD. Sometimes the biological machinery that allows the brain to control focus and behavior doesn't work well. In other people, the brain chemicals dopamine and norepinephrine, which regulate this machinery, operate differently.

FAST MINDS Traits May Have Posed an Evolutionary Advantage

Evolution, the theory goes, preserves traits that serve a purpose. Studies from large populations suggest that the signs of ADHD are common across the population, occurring at varying levels on a continuum—meaning that there is a chance of having few, some, or many traits, with individuals with ADHD falling at one extreme.[6] It has been proposed that these ADHD traits survive in the general population because they presented an evolutionary advantage. The theory goes that our ancient ancestors would have benefited from having group members with heightened awareness of their surroundings, an ability to quickly respond to threats or prey, an extreme level of energy to sustain long-distance travel, and an extra edge during the hunt or combat.[7] Just as changing human contexts over the ages may have shifted which traits are most useful, people today with FAST MINDS traits may fit better in roles where their attributes are valued.

Brain Differences

Studies often find differences in the biological machinery and/or chemical messengers of ADHD brains, but the pattern of these differences varies. Many of these differences occur in regions responsible for control over attention and behavior, such as the following:

- **Prefrontal cortex**, which is critical to most of what makes us human, including control of behavior, emotion, and social connection

- **Cingulate cortex**, which research suggests may be involved in processing thoughts and feelings and management of effortful activity

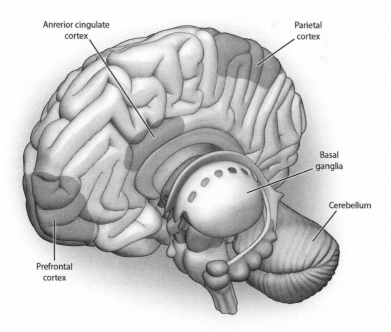

Anrerior cingulate cortex

Parietal cortex

Basal ganglia

Cerebellum

Prefrontal cortex

■ **Parietal cortex**, a major area for processing sensory and spatial information; this area is so involved in awareness that damage to the right parietal area eliminates awareness of the left side of the body

■ **Basal ganglia**, a region that ADHD medications target, and which is thought to work in concert with the prefrontal cortex during learning of a behavior or habit (we discuss this more in Chapter 8)

■ **Cerebellum**, long thought to be a motor coordination center and now known to contribute to nonmotor functions including attention

Modern imaging techniques have demonstrated differences between the ADHD and non-ADHD brain, in size, activity, and communication, in regions that make up this network. For example, a recent study by Dr. Surman's colleagues at Massachusetts General Hospital suggests that the cortex of adults with ADHD may be thinner in the regions critical for attention management.[8]

Dr. Surman's colleagues have shown that the cingulate cortex is anatomically different in people with ADHD,[9] that it functions differently during a task requiring attention in people with ADHD than those without, and that it acts more like the non-ADHD brain when on ADHD medication.[10]

Different Skills, Different Challenges

People with ADHD respond in distinct ways to these biological differences, which accounts for the many versions that we see. Some thrive in hospital emergency departments, on stock-trading floors, or in high-drama relationships—in situations that are stimulating and demanding—so stressful that the tiger is nearly always in the room, as it were, and it's easier for them to stay engaged. Other people crave high-stimulation activities such as speeding, gambling, or drug or alcohol use. Others simply spend their time switching among different activities, getting little accomplished.

People with FAST MINDS traits are less able to direct their mental effort at will, so they may avoid activities that are difficult or put them off until the last minute, when deadline stress provides the missing tiger. We know people who can tell a beautifully organized story for an audience, for instance, but couldn't write it down if their lives depended on it, as well as people who have memorized all sorts of details about their favorite professional sports team but regularly struggle to hold on to important details at work.

Sometimes neuropsychological tests, the kinds of tests that are used as part of IQ tests or for learning disabilities, reveal differences in brain function. They show that some people process information more slowly, for example, though they have excellent verbal and math abilities. Such inconsistencies—strong in some areas, but not able to perform well day to day—can derail advancement at work and undermine trust in relationships.

It may seem that someone has FAST MINDS traits because they are irresponsible or lazy or don't care—but that is not true. Instead, these traits are a result of how the brain does or doesn't devote itself to what is important in the moment. What someone pays attention to comes down to how intuitively interesting the options are, or the ability to get one's brain interested in them.

TIEGAN: WEARING THREE HATS

Tiegan used to be a "Struggling Student," but now she's "Married with Children." In between deciding to skip university and striving to raise two ADHD kids with an alcoholic father, she's had a successful career with an insurance company. But it hasn't been easy.

Tiegan knew she was different from an early age. As a teen, she was always questioning why the other girls seemed so much more mature than she was. All her report cards described her as "chatty" and complained that she couldn't get down to work or finish projects. She barely made it through high school and opted for art school instead of college, but she floundered there. A skills test to help her figure out what to do next caught her by surprise, suggesting she should pursue a career in high finance or banking. "I never even passed math," she says.

But it has turned out to be a good suggestion. Her client-focused jobs fit her well, because she can rely on her verbal and social skills. Her supervisors appreciate her ability to be productive when the stakes are high. The clear roles, expectations, and goals of the corporate world also help her. She's bounced around from job to job, finding positions where the pace and responsibility are stimulating and where other people handle the paperwork. Moving up with each jump, she is now an account manager at a giant financial services firm.

Tiegan's troubles started when she had to manage work, marriage, and a challenging home life all at once. Her son was diagnosed first with Tourette's syndrome, then ADHD and Obsessive-Compulsive Disorder (OCD). When the doctor who diagnosed him with ADHD was explaining the condition to her, Tiegan lost focus and started watching a bird out the window (recall our description of "The Distractible Daydreamer"?). Noticing her lack of concentration, the doctor advised Tiegan to get herself screened for ADHD, too. She says her diagnosis was a revelation—and medication and other things she used to control her ADHD made a quick and dramatic difference.

"Once I started treatment, it was unbelievable, the focus and

self-security I had," she says. "If I had been diagnosed and treated
earlier, I think I would have achieved much more. I would have
had the security of self to do some things I didn't." The medication
also helped her with verbal impulsivity. "I would have been able to
keep my mouth shut in certain situations. I would have made it
through school. . . . Instead, I made some mistakes along the way
that would have been nice not to have made."

Distinguishing FAST MINDS from Other Conditions

As we've mentioned, FAST MINDS traits also show up in other conditions, such as mood and anxiety disorders and addictions. You may
need to address these other conditions before you are ready to deal
with your FAST MIND. Not all health care professionals are equally
experienced at distinguishing between ADHD and other conditions,
so you may have to help them help you. The following are some conditions that overlap with ADHD and symptoms that specialists consider
when they're trying to clarify the diagnosis.

MAJOR DEPRESSION: Depression is a mood disorder that includes a combination of sadness, tending to be easily angry or upset,
guilty thinking, loss of interest in things that are usually enjoyable,
low energy, problems thinking or concentrating, poor sleep, desperate
thinking, and poor appetite or weight gain. People with FAST MINDS
traits are often demoralized by their struggles, but depression is diagnosed when there is a broader pattern of physical and emotional
distress.

BIPOLAR DISORDER: People with bipolar disorder have, at some
point in their life, experienced depression and partial or full *mania*—
including a sustained high, giddy, or irritable mood accompanied by
some combination of poor judgment, grandiosity, higher sex drive,

lack of need for sleep, racing thoughts, increased talking, problems with thinking or concentration, and "strange" ideas or thoughts. Periods of mania often last a few days or more. If you've ever experienced such an agitated state, paranoia, delusions, or hallucinations, you should tell a medical professional before trying a medication treatment for ADHD, as the drugs may reactivate or intensify these problems. Grandiosity, elevated or expansive feelings, and changes in thinking are not a part of ADHD. However, FAST MINDS traits and ADHD are common in people with bipolar disorder and may be a risk factor for worse forms of bipolar disorder. Dr. Bilkey contributed to a study that looked at adults with both ADHD and bipolar disorder and found that they were more likely than people with bipolar disorder alone to have problems with drugs, alcohol, and panic and anxiety disorders.[11] Treating bipolar disorder sometimes reduces FAST MINDS traits, but organizational problems often persist and may benefit from many of the strategies we address in this book.[12]

ANXIETY: Anxiety disorders consist of worry, panic, fear, or physical discomforts such as sleep disruption, stomach upset, and muscle tension. Symptoms may occur in particular situations or be burdensome much of the day but are more extreme than make sense for the circumstances.

ADDICTIONS: There are different levels of addiction, but the common theme is that your life centers in an unhealthy way around using a substance. The habit is out of control and has consequences. Specialty help, twelve-step programs, and other sobriety group programs can be found on the Internet and are a major resource.

OBSESSIONS AND COMPULSIONS: Obsessive-Compulsive Disorder (OCD) involves rituals or obsessive thoughts that take up time or impair ability to function. Many people with ADHD are concerned about making mistakes (again), so they check their work compulsively. If you are checking far more than is needed or than peers are doing, consider whether this disorder is a factor.

The television personality Howie Mandel has spoken and written about having both ADHD and OCD. In an interview with *Psychology Today*, Mandel said he impulsively "outed" himself as having OCD during an appearance on Howard Stern's radio show.[13] He was devastated by his impulsive comment—until he left the studio. "Out in public, after I did the show, people came to me and said, 'Me, too.' They were the most comforting words I've ever heard. Whatever you're dealing with in life, know that you're not alone," Mandel told the magazine.

PERSONALITY DISORDERS: Personality disorders are diagnosed when someone has an enduring pattern of behavior, emotional expression, or thinking that differs significantly from social norms. Often, they show up in how a person thinks about or treats other people. Examples include those with self-centered disregard for others (narcissistic personality disorder) or dramatic changes in feelings toward themselves or others (borderline personality disorder). Impulsivity is common among people with personality disorders and may lead to poor decisions and unanticipated consequences.

LEARNING DISABILITIES: People with the reading disability dyslexia and other learning disabilities are at higher risk of having ADHD, and vice versa. If you avoid schoolwork or have problems focusing in class, neuropsychological testing may reveal whether the reason is a learning disability. Treatment of ADHD may make it easier to both learn and to use compensation strategies for learning disabilities.

SOCIAL SKILL DEFICITS: Problems understanding nonverbal communication or the "rules" of social interaction occur in autism and Asperger's disorder, but less dramatic social skill challenges are also sometimes seen in children and adults with ADHD. We discuss managing the social challenges that can occur with FAST MINDS traits in Chapter 9.

EDDIE: LEARNING TO ENGAGE IN WHAT MATTERS

Eddie first suspected he had ADHD when listening to a lecture a friend was giving on the subject. The friend had asked Eddie to critique his performance, but Eddie got sucked in, recognizing his then-seventeen-year-old son in slide after slide about FAST MINDS traits. Then suddenly he realized that he recognized himself, too.

He started on medication, which he says cleared up his head. He quickly completed his long overdue paperwork and filed two years of taxes. He got better organized, realizing that if he put things in piles, he'd never deal with them.

He also saw for the first time what had probably doomed his relationship with his wife and many other women: Although he might have been hyperfocused on them briefly in the beginning, something else always came along that seemed more interesting. "The women in my life were on the back burner," he says. "If they wanted to be involved in my life, they had to go along for the ride. They always did—for a while. And then they'd call me on it. They had the nerve to think they should be the priority in my life. I lost some wonderful relationships because of it."

He also has some powerful reasons to keep him focused on improving his organization and efficiency and finding a woman he can love—his main priorities right now. "At sixty-one, you've only got so many good years left. I'm aware of my mortality now—I'm hoping to use that as my incentive. I'm running out of time to make excuses."

If Someone You Care About Has a FAST MIND

We now understand that ADHD is a brain-based condition that manifests itself differently in different people. You can help the person you care about by understanding that their inconsistencies and idiosyncrasies are just part of who they are, not an intentional effort to annoy, disrespect, or disappoint you.

You can also help by working with them on the exercises at the end of every chapter, identifying when and where their FAST MINDS traits can get them into trouble. Your supportive perspective will be essential to them as they embark on this journey.

You can be a witness for what works for them and what appears challenging. When were they at their best? What would you say the different challenges are? How many seem to be about steering in the right direction, engagement, and focus? This information will help the person track their behavior and identify patterns, habits, and strategies that mean the most for them.

WHAT YOU CAN DO

FOCUS ON THE FLOW

We like to ask people to tell us about moments of success, when their interests and actions are aligned and they feel like they're firing on all cylinders. These are periods we think of as full engagement, or what some psychologists call *flow*. For Eddie, it was giving speeches in front of giant crowds; for Tiegan, it's chatting up clients.

Think about how you felt the last time you were doing something you truly love: You were in the moment, not criticizing yourself or worrying that you might be doing something wrong. You just did it. Hold that thought. We want you to briefly note at least three of these moments: Maybe they happen when you're running, or solving a tricky problem, or working with your hands, or teaching someone else what you know.

1. _____

2. _____

3. _____

Then, dig into those experiences a bit to better understand what helped them work, what context got you firing on all cylinders. If your glorious moments come when playing the violin, do you perform best when you're alone at home or when you have an audience; when you've had a busy day or at the end of a long, relaxing weekend? When your interests are high and distractions low? In the summer when there's lots of sunlight or in the winter when the cold may keep allergies at bay? When the material is somewhat challenging but not overwhelmingly so?

We want you to record the *whens* and *wheres* of these experiences so you can start thinking about the *whys*. Pay particular attention to the question, "How did you make it happen?" Consider, for example, how the event or situation was different from ones that were less successful. Did the context play to your strengths? Your interests? Did it minimize challenges?

SUCCESSFUL EVENT #1

What was it? _____

When was it? _____

Who was there? _____

Where did it happen? _____

How did you make it happen? _____

SUCCESSFUL EVENT #2

What was it? _____

When was it? _____

Who was there? _____

Where did it happen? _____

How did you make it happen? _____

SUCCESSFUL EVENT #3

What was it? _____

When was it? _____

Who was there? _____

Where did it happen? _____

How did you make it happen? _____

Once you've recorded three positive experiences, look for patterns. What do you notice about how your interests, strengths, or challenges influence where you are successful? For example, a person may do their best when doing something new, standing in front of an audience, working collaboratively on a team, or alone late in the day. Keep this list of factors that support your strengths in mind as you progress through the rest of this book.

Our main goal is to help you become aware of your patterns and figure out how to use the engagement system of the brain to your advantage. Successful people with FAST MINDS use what naturally engages them to find environments, people, and strategies that support what they want to do.

In the next chapter, we'll talk about the emotional barriers to success that can build with years of struggling with FAST MINDS traits.

KEY POINTS

- People do not have FAST MINDS traits because they are irresponsible or lazy or don't care. They have these traits because that is the way their brain operates.

- FAST MINDS show up differently in different contexts: think Struggling Student, Married with Children, Distractible Daydreamer, and so on. Understanding your pattern is a key to adapting.

- Your ability to engage—to be in "flow"—is probably better in some roles and situations than others. To make more of your life, understand what helps these moments happen.

FAST MINDS Made Me Do It

M aria remembers when the nervous excitement she felt in start- ing college slowly gave way to sadness. She recalls sitting week after week in her first huge lectures at college, feeling lost—not just in class, but in the sea of new people and new things to try. She fell be- hind in her work, despite long hours trying to read more than she had ever been asked to do in her life. Finding a spot where she wouldn't disturb her roommates, she drank gallons of coffee to write last- minute papers late into the night—the only one in the dorm awake, and so tired. She didn't even know she could ask for an extension, because she wasn't used to asking for help. Everyone else just seemed to be getting their work done.

Her family helped her decide to take time off from school after that first semester, and she accepted a job with a family friend. She learned to follow her colleagues when she missed a point in meetings, staying late to get quarterly reports together in time, needing the deadline pressure to perform. By her midtwenties it was almost a reflex when someone came to talk to her to presume she'd have to apologize for something—enough so that her office mate took her aside a few times to ask her why she always blamed herself unnecessarily.

By the time she turned thirty, Maria was resigned to being unfulfilled at work but was disappointed with her inability to stay on top of things she cared about at home. Although she always took care of her family, she felt that her challenges were making them suffer, too. She was barely keeping up: remembering at the last minute that she had forgotten to put an appointment in her calendar, coming across a bill she had meant to pay, or having to turn around to get something required for one of her children's activities. Her husband reassured her that she was a wonderful mother and told her that the only person she was neglecting was herself. He recognized how critical she was of herself for everyday lapses such as the dishes in the sink, piles of dirty laundry, and unpaid household bills.

When Maria was thirty-four, her eight-year-old son was diagnosed with ADHD. Listening to the doctor describe her son's signs, she realized he might as well have been describing her own. As she learned more about ADHD, Maria began to realize it was the condition, not a flaw in her character, that explained her lifetime of disappointments. The diagnosis gave Maria permission to blame ADHD—instead of herself—for most, if not all, of her struggles and to become a better friend to herself. "There's been good reason my whole life not to feel right about myself," she says. "I have had lots of goofs, slipups, things I said that I wish I could take back. But it is so important for me to remind myself that I was struggling for good reason—there was something different about me that I didn't have the tools to make right."

———————————

Would someone feel like a terrible person if their nose got stuffy during allergy season? If they needed glasses to see the blackboard or a street sign? ADHD is a medical condition that is not your fault.

No one asks for or wants FAST MINDS traits—they're just stuck with them.

Sometimes, a little self-blame can be productive. Worried about their performance, people push themselves a little bit harder, work a little more diligently. But many people with ADHD find themselves burdened with a lifetime of feeling unsuccessful and failing to meet their potential. It's a weight that often interferes with improvement.

The goal of this chapter is to break the cycle of self-blame for having a FAST MIND. We will explore some of the states of mind that commonly limit the vision, hopes, and actual mental ability of people with ADHD.

RECOGNIZING YOURSELF

Do you often say things to yourself like:

☐ Things will never work out for me.

☐ I am such a disaster/mess.

☐ Why do I always get stuck like this?

☐ I should have started earlier. Why am I in this situation again?

☐ People must think I'm really stupid.

☐ What's wrong with me?

Understanding the Self-Blaming Mind

Research has consistently shown that ADHD damages self-esteem. Experiencing a string of disappointments, regardless of the reason, is demoralizing. While some people with ADHD are remarkably resilient and positive about themselves, lingering self-doubt is common in adults with ADHD.

The cause of low self-esteem in ADHD may be the accumulation of blows to the ego from years of failing to finish projects, missing important instructions, and feeling different, or it may be from brain differences that come along with ADHD—or some combination of both. Regardless, this blend of ADHD and low self-esteem causes suffering. It may lead people to experiment with risky behaviors such as having sex at a younger age (putting teens at higher risk for pregnancy and sexually transmitted diseases),[1] or earlier use of drugs and alcohol (increasing risk of addiction and long-term consequences).[2] The results of these extra risks then compound feelings of inadequacy. Even short of severe outcomes, how we feel about ourselves clearly creates or limits the horizon of possibilities we see in our lives.

People who are diagnosed with ADHD in adulthood are particularly likely to blame *themselves* for their problems, rather than their ADHD. And doing that puts them at higher risk for self-esteem problems, depression, and anxiety issues, research shows. Self-blame seems to make people feel stuck with their challenges and less able to do something about them—while blaming something outside themselves empowers them to make change.[3] We think this is why people should give up on self-blame: It's a waste of time and energy. Putting effort into learning is far more productive than putting it into self-blame and guilt. We are not saying it is easy, but we have worked with many people who found that with practice they could redirect their thoughts and emotional energy in more productive ways.

We're not suggesting that smiling and acting chipper will solve ADHD. It is crucial for people to be real with themselves about their strengths and weaknesses, to look for FAST MINDS issues, and to evaluate for themselves which approaches are likely to be most effective and lasting. But self-blame gets in the way of personal growth. Attitude makes all the difference between someone who is willing to risk addressing challenges and someone who remains stuck in old patterns.

Take a minute and think about what other people say about you, and what that may tell you about how you think about or treat yourself.

RECOGNIZE THE IMPACT—DO OTHER PEOPLE SAY YOU:

- ☐ Are too self-critical?
- ☐ Have low self-esteem?
- ☐ Often seem overwhelmed and demoralized?
- ☐ Talk as if life is never going to work out for you?

Grief

Many people diagnosed with ADHD in adulthood talk about feeling overcome by grief. They are distressed about having to work harder than others just to keep up. They deeply mourn their lost opportunities; if only they'd known earlier that their problems were part of a diagnosable condition, maybe they would have made it through school, made that relationship work, or not lost that job. They grieve for their sad childhood, the feelings of failure, the loss of success.

As psychiatrists, we recognize that coping with this grief is an important part of coming to terms with your ADHD. The first step is noticing it and allowing it to happen. It's okay to spend some time putting your history into new context, paying tribute to that younger version of you who suffered playground bullies, took home disappointing report cards, and endured withering looks from parents who couldn't understand. Close friends, an ADHD support group, or a therapist may help you with this process. We think that getting outside perspectives is the least you owe yourself.

Trading Self-Blame for Self-Gain

There are two major schools of thought about how to address self-esteem problems. One says that people should stop beating up on themselves—once the self-blame stops, they will feel better. The other says that people need to *be* effective to feel effective. We embrace both. How you think and feel will determine how you behave, and the success you have will determine how you think and feel. A key to success in either effort, as we see it over and over in our work, is *to feel comfortable with who you are and accept your challenges*. If you are comparing yourself to anyone but yourself, you will suffer.

It's not your fault if you have ADHD, just as it is not someone's fault if they have allergies or need to wear glasses. We understand that ending self-blame is easier said than done, but we've helped so many people do it that we're pretty sure we can help you, too. Over the course of the work in this book, you will learn which ADHD traits you may have to accept as being unmovable and which you can change. We show you how to react with rational thought instead of negative emotions, freeing your mind to use solutions you already have and those you will learn in the rest of this book. If negative attitudes are clouding your mind, it is time to start removing them.

People with ADHD may have a particularly hard time stopping these negative thoughts. After all, you may have had decades of practice not living up to your own or others' expectations. But it's important to think about which challenges are due to how you are wired (which it's pointless to feel bad about) and what you can do to compensate for this wiring. A computer programmer we know has trained himself to ask a simple question when he starts to beat up on himself for something he's done: "Is this something I can control?" If the answer is no, then he knows there isn't much use getting upset about it. If he could have done something about it, then he makes a plan to do so next time a similar situation comes up.

If you are feeling upset or limited, ask yourself if it's a FAST MINDS problem. If so, are you reacting rationally, or is there a way to redirect your energy? Cognitive Behavioral Therapy (CBT) techniques can help you practice such redirection.

Cognitive Behavioral Therapy

CBT is a form of talk therapy based on the theory that how we think and feel are interrelated and affect how we behave. By changing how we think about ourselves, for instance, we can change our behavior. Cognitive Behavioral Therapy has repeatedly been found effective in treating a range of psychiatric ailments including depression and eating disorders. Dr. Surman was part of a groundbreaking study of CBT led by Dr. Stephen Safren that was published in the prestigious *Journal of the American Medical Association*. Their research demonstrated that CBT reduced ADHD symptoms more than a relaxation technique for people on medication.[4]

Several approaches that we teach in this book are derived from the findings of that and related studies.[5] With simple exercises to help practice redirected thoughts, CBT helps you change your counterproductive thinking.[6] A 2009 British study showed that CBT successfully boosted self-esteem in people with ADHD.[7] In the study, sixty-one adults taking medication for their ADHD were placed in a cognitive behavioral program that involved three one-day sessions spread over three months. At the end of the program, attendees reported that they better understood their ADHD, their self-esteem was higher, and they were less depressed and anxious compared to a similar group on the program's waiting list. The change in self-esteem, the authors wrote, could be the result of a deeper understanding that they were not to blame for their ADHD.

If Someone You Care About Has a FAST MIND

Do they often:

- Apologize when it's not their fault?

- Say they feel different and misunderstood?

- Make self-deprecating statements such as "I am no good at this?" or "Why do I always screw things up?" or "What's wrong with me?"

- Have fragile self-esteem?

- Make a lot of excuses?

If you answered yes to several of these questions, realize that the person is probably having many negative thoughts about themselves. This is common when people have difficulty controlling their focus or behavior. It hurts to notice someone you care about feeling this way, but it often helps to know that they can learn to have a better self image. If it feels appropriate and the person welcomes your participation, you might help them recognize the cause of their negative feelings and thoughts and join them in working through the "thought record" exercise described later in this chapter.

WHAT YOU CAN DO

When people with FAST MINDS blame themselves for the mistakes they make, it compounds the struggle they face every day. Whether because of negative feedback they received growing up or a tendency to notice the negative, there is abundant opportunity for someone with FAST MINDS traits to gather evidence that they fall short of their potential. This creates a vicious cycle in which a jaded

outlook leads to low expectations and worse performance. Many people don't realize their self-expectations are low until their thought
pattern is pointed out to them. All of us can use tools to short-circuit
self-defeating ideas—replacing them with self-supporting, grounded
perspectives and pragmatic efforts to adapt. Instead of thinking that
each problem you face is a tragedy, you can use the creative side of
your brain—which is likely to benefit from your FAST MINDS traits—
to figure out a solution. Separating fact from emotion can allow you
to focus on the real challenges you face, instead of attacking things
you imagine to be worse than they are.

MARIA: COOLING OFF "HOT THOUGHTS"

*Maria would often say aloud to herself: "I am so screwed!" The
feeling of fear and disappointment that accompanied this statement was enough to shut her down, making it harder to solve her
problems. Once, she ruined her husband's best shirt by including
a new bright pink sock in the wash with it. As usual, when she
discovered her mistake, she followed her thoughts of fear and self-
blame to an extreme and dramatic end: "Now he won't be able to
wear it to his job interview next week and he won't get the new job
and he'll blame me for it and we'll get divorced."*

*Once her therapist introduced her to some CBT techniques, she
began nipping such negative thoughts in the bud, skipping the at-
tacks on herself, and quickly moving on to a plan for solving the
problem—and for making sure it didn't happen again.*

*How did Maria eliminate her reflexive catastrophizing? She
used thought records and became aware of how she was mentally
distorting reality. She spent a few weeks practicing and talking
with her therapist about how she did.*

*One night in the middle of this process, she made a mistake:
She realized only after she'd already cooked and drained enough*

pasta for dinner that she'd forgotten to buy sauce. Normally, this sort of thing would make her feel miserable and ruin the evening. This time, before she even told her husband or son what she'd done, she decided to write a thought record about her mistake.

In her thought record, she noted how critical she was feeling toward herself and came up with a supportive, rational statement: "Sometimes I overlook details and am forgetful, but I handle most things well in the end." Then she was in a better mind-set to brainstorm ways to solve the problem: "We do have olive oil, cheese, and fresh vegetables, so I can serve pasta primavera instead of spaghetti and meat sauce for dinner."

Improvisation is a way of life for many people with ADHD—some people laugh about the sticky situations their creativity has allowed them to escape. But creativity requires the right frame of mind. It's harder to think of solutions when one is busy being critical, seeing narrowly, and missing what is possible. For Maria, learning simple ways to blame ADHD and not herself allowed her to escape self-hatred and enabled her to quickly put her revised plan into action. On the sauceless night, no one noticed her mistake, and her family even complimented her on her cooking.

These kinds of successes feed on themselves, just as negative talk leads to a downward spiral. At first, this shift in thinking requires a lot of conscious effort. Like anything else, with practice it becomes more natural and instinctive. Instead of thinking, "I am so screwed," and allowing a simple mistake to ruin her family's dinner and her entire evening, Maria now reflexively thinks: "Okay, here's another challenge, just the kind I am an expert in. I have handled my share and the house is still standing." Then she is able to handle the challenge in a constructive way, further reinforcing her positive self-image.

THOUGHT RECORD

A *thought record* is a basic CBT strategy that can help you start becoming more aware of the attitudes you bring to challenges. Attitude makes a major difference in performance. Most elite athletes say that peak performance happens only when they think it's possible. Working at changing negative self-talk puts you in the best mind-set to improve *your* performance, too. A key goal of a thought record exercise is to identify patterns of thought that are not productive and actively refocus mental effort productively. It is okay if you find this exercise challenging—identifying and changing thought patterns takes practice. Working on it with someone else, such as a mental health professional, could help.

Start by writing a few words or sentences about three situations that you have been upset about, in which things didn't go your way—such as times you did not perform well at work or at home.

1. _____

2. _____

3. _____

Next, note what was going through your head at the time. What were you saying to yourself about the mistake and your role in it? To help generate a list of thoughts, put yourself back in the situation you are considering, and try completing sentences with the first thought that comes into your head, such as "I did that because _____" or "That happened because I am _____" or even just "I _____."

_____

_____

_____

_____

_____

Write down as many of these as you can, then pick one statement that is the "hottest," most emotionally charged, negative thought of the statements. Also jot down the feelings that go along with these thoughts. Do you feel guilt? Frustration? Anger? Fear? Sadness? Or something else?

Then, rate the intensity of these thoughts on a scale of 0 to 10 (with 10 being the most intense). For example, "I screwed up dinner because I am a lazy, forgetful person" was Maria's "hottest" thought the day she forgot the sauce. As she said this to herself, she rated her feeling of sadness at 7 out of 10.

Now, step back from your feelings and ask yourself some questions to figure out what parts of the situation were and were not under your control: Could this have happened to anyone? Was it out of your control? Were there factors that made the problem hard for you, in particular, to avoid? Is having ADHD one of these factors?

Make notes about these uncontrollable factors here. For example, Maria noted that she was frequently forgetful, so it made sense that she had forgotten to get everything from the supermarket that she needed for meat sauce:

_____

_____

_____

_____

_____

Now think about what you realistically could have done to avoid the situation—is this a lesson for what you might work on in the future? Maria considered the possibility of keeping a running list of what she needs for her next trip to the store—and keeping it in her purse so she doesn't have to remember it—or buying extra jars of sauce the next time she's at the store. For your situation, note what you could do differently next time:

_____

_____

_____

_____

_____

Knowing what you can control about the situation and looking at it rationally, come up with the most useful statement to tell yourself the next time a situation like that occurs. It may help to think about what someone who cares about you would say to coach you through the situation, or what you would say to someone else. This might go something like, "Because I make mistakes when _____, I can work to avoid these mistakes by _____, but when they happen, the way to be kind to myself is to say _____."

_____

Many people find that stepping back like this can cool the internal distraction of emotional thinking. Where you are not already doing so, learning to coach yourself through situations rationally uses your energy more productively than simply getting upset. We understand, however, that doing a thought record takes effort—as does the practice of trying alternative attitudes. Be kind to yourself as you try this and other exercises in this book. Where they are hard for you, take note that they may be more useful with practice or professional help. (In Appendix B, under "Thought Record," we have included a list of questions you can ask yourself to practice rational rather than emotional thinking.)

Another CBT technique that can help people come up with more productive thought patterns is to identify how self-critical thoughts mismatch the facts. These "thinking errors" are also called *cognitive distortions*, and they include things such as overgeneralizing, foreseeing only the worst possible outcome (also called *catastrophizing*), and taking on other people's problems as your own. Everyone has these kinds of patterns, but a life full of missteps and challenges makes many people with ADHD more prone to them.

If you tend to say things like, "I never complete anything," that is a sign of *all-or-nothing thinking*. If you say, "This is what *always* happens when I try to get something done," that is an example of *overgeneralizing*—you are generalizing from a specific example and assuming that it pertains in every situation. If you *personalize*, you might blame yourself for other people's reactions: "She didn't ask me to help because she knows I don't get things done." People who *catastrophize* think everything—even a minor problem—is going to be a disaster, such as Maria's thought that accidentally discoloring her husband's shirt was going to get him fired and lead them to divorce.

When you see a pattern like one of these types in your negative thoughts, try to come up with a kind phrase to tell yourself preemptively, to remind yourself that you are in emotional thinking territory. A quick comment like, "There I go again, pretending I can predict the future," can be very grounding. Thought records can also be a powerful way to identify ways of self-talking through emotional mindsets, as we explore in Chapter 6.

JOHN: GETTING ORGANIZED

The transition from high school to college has been tough for John. He always faced challenges at school, but in his hometown he was surrounded by support—teachers knew he was hardworking and gave him extra attention, his parents reminded and encouraged him to keep up with assignments, and his friends and sports left him feeling good about himself even though he was troubled by how hard he had to work to keep up with schoolwork.

But at college, he had to get all that support from within himself. Although he made some friends, they spent much less time than he did doing schoolwork. John struggled in particular to write long papers for two of his classes. By the middle of the first semester, he felt pretty down on himself. Writing essays was always a problem for him, and it just didn't seem that he could do it well enough to get by in college. He felt overwhelmed even thinking of sitting down to write them—so he stopped thinking about them. As for many people with FAST MINDS challenges, John's decision to avoid doing work that was emotionally difficult for him made things worse.

Luckily, John sought help. He met with a counselor who sug-

gested that whenever he was feeling demoralized or overwhelmed, it meant he was wasting mental energy. Instead of spending that energy feeling poorly about himself, he should use that energy to tackle the problem at hand. For writing, that meant breaking the assignments down into manageable steps that he could focus on one at a time. For his English paper, he asked his teacher and a fellow student to talk through his ideas with him and list the themes they heard him mention. He used the teacher and friend as "peripheral brains"—an idea we talk about more in the next chapter—to find the organization in what had felt to him like a jumbled mess. Once he had an outline based on themes he identified himself, he broke his work down into steps that he could complete in one sitting—so he felt a sense of accomplishment as he tried to write the paper.

DRAINING OUT THE EMOTION

Some research suggests that emotion disrupts the ADHD brain more than the non-ADHD brain.[8] In a study of children with and without ADHD, brain scans showed that in children with ADHD, brain areas involved in memory and attention reacted more powerfully to emotionally charged images than neutral ones. As an adult, ADHD may mean that negative emotions have a stronger pull on you than on others.

You probably have circumstances that overwhelm you and cause you stress. Feeling overwhelmed can make a task that much harder. Just as John and Maria grounded themselves in more productive perspectives, you can, too.

Here is a summary of how we coach people to end the self-blame and lighten emotional situations:

1. Discover patterns of negative emotional thinking that are not rational, for example, where you blame yourself or catastrophize. Practice recognizing these thought patterns quickly so you can replace them with a more positive mind-set where you can focus on solutions. Try to predict ahead of time when you are likely to fall into negative thinking and catch yourself.

2. Practice a more adaptive mind-set. Find a phrase that you can tell yourself as soon as you start to feel overwhelmed, ideally one that comes with moments of humor and feeling kind to yourself. It might be a rational thought you came up with in a thought record, or a lighthearted phrase to keep yourself in a productive frame of mind: "Here I go again!," or "Time to take a scenic detour around these roadblocks," or Maria's "I've done it before, so I can do it again." A simple phrase can defuse the problem's emotional power and make you smile instead of fill with dread. Give yourself credit for making the effort to reduce these negative attitudes.

Use these two steps even as you work through this book. You may have self-critical or overwhelmed feelings and thoughts as you look at your challenges and work on solutions. Take the attitude you are practicing in this chapter to explore the rest of this book with an open mind. We help you channel your thoughts and energies into actions you can be proud of, into your becoming your best version of you.

Where you get overwhelmed is a good guide to where you need to direct your effort. This isn't easy—every skill, such as driving or playing a sport, requires practice. But we've seen these strategies work for many other people with FAST MINDS, so we're confident they can work for you. Thought records are one of several ways that people work toward productive mind-sets. We explore other methods, such as practicing mindfulness, later in this book. However you choose to take charge of your mind-set, we feel strongly that it is crucial for you to stop any cycle of self-blame. Being kind to yourself is essential for getting the most out of the rest of this book—and life!

KEY POINTS

- Adult ADHD and FAST MINDS are brain-based; they're not your fault.

- Blaming FAST MINDS gives you something to work with—blaming yourself wastes energy.

- Cognitive behavioral techniques can help people with FAST MINDS maximize rational thinking to help generate solutions—solutions you can create for yourself in the rest of this book.

PART II

A FAST MINDS
Operating Manual

4

Use the Prefrontal Checklist

Alicia's report cards were consistent from year to year. In fourth grade she was told to pay more attention in class; in seventh, to focus her attention on the lesson; in ninth, that she was "not making good use of class time." By her senior year, she was described as "a capable student who must work harder to achieve her potential."

Again and again we hear about adults like Alicia who struggled in school and were told they could succeed if they only tried a little harder, paid a little more attention, and goofed off less. When they become adults, their loved ones, employers, and colleagues may say similar things about them. People with FAST MINDS traits often get off track despite wanting and trying to accomplish things they care about. In this chapter, we explore the major factors that derail people, the brain system responsible for staying focused, and how to create the conditions under which this system works best.

Planning and Controlling Behavior

Differences in the function of the prefrontal cortex appear to contribute to ADHD. Brain-imaging studies have shown that the prefrontal region is a key part of the circuit that governs our ability to engage in tasks. In some people with ADHD, this circuit may be less active during organization and attention tasks than it is in those without the condition.[1]

The prefrontal region has been described as a mental "sketchpad," because this is probably where plans are made for thoughts and actions. This region goes through substantial development in adolescence and early adulthood as we become more able to organize and plan our lives independently. Differences in "maturation" of the prefrontal region may explain why the attention and behavior problems of ADHD persist into adulthood in some people and not others.[2]

Medication is thought to be effective for ADHD because it increases levels of the brain chemicals norepinephrine and dopamine, which activate brain machinery—including prefrontal regions—that control focus and behavior. At the right levels, the brain operates better. Stress can also increase norepinephrine levels, and rewarding activities increase dopamine. Some people with ADHD function well under stress or intensely rewarding experiences—such as working on a stock-trading floor or in an emergency room. But such lifestyles can be draining, and many everyday tasks are hard to make as stimulating or rewarding.

Much of our behavior requires active control. The prefrontal cortex allows us to make—and stick with—a pattern of behavior, such as continuing to read this book rather than calling a friend, or countless other things. Brain-imaging studies show that some people with ADHD have clear impairment of their prefrontal function. Even if someone has good prefrontal function, the presence of FAST MINDS traits puts their ability to control their behavior in high demand—the prefrontal region may have to work harder to allow a person to keep reading this book if they are easily distracted.

Three factors commonly impair the operation of our center for planned behavior: lack of clear plans to follow, internal distractions (such as emotions, thoughts, or stress), and external distractions (sounds, sights, or demands from the offices and other environments around us).

RECOGNIZING YOURSELF

Imagine that you are in an everyday situation, such as a classroom, conversation, or job:

☐ Do you often get sidetracked while doing tasks?

☐ Does your mind feel busy or clouded?

☐ Do you find that thoughts and ideas pop up and leave you daydreaming or distracted?

☐ Do you keep thinking about other things you need to do?

☐ Does sound and activity around you make it hard to work or converse?

UNCLEAR PLANS

The brain's behavior control center operates best when there is a clear plan of what the behavior should be. If you've ever watched a group of young teenagers trying to decide where to go, you've seen how unproductive it is to operate without a plan. Chaos is inherently distracting. Anyone is more productive when they know what step to take next than when they don't—but for someone with FAST MINDS traits, it's even more important that the next action can be easily held in mind.

INTERNAL DISTRACTIONS

PHYSICAL DISTRACTIONS: The brain's control center doesn't function well if someone is unhealthy, poorly nourished, or tired—making it hard to concentrate and learn. Illness, pain, or lack of sleep can all undermine brain performance.

EMOTIONAL DISTRACTIONS: Excitement or dread can be distracting—think of the night before a big trip, a performance, meeting future in-laws for the first time, or starting a new job. Everyone has many different states of mind, even in the course of one day, some of which are counterproductive to doing effortful mental work. The intensity and changes in emotion are themselves a kind of internal distraction, as thoughts shift with feelings.

PACE: Some people with FAST MINDS also seem to have an internal restlessness—like a metronome constantly ticking—that keeps them needing a fast pace or moving on from one thing to the next.

Does ADHD Impact Emotional Behavior?

For many years pioneer researchers in ADHD, such as Dr. Paul Wender and Dr. Russell Barkley, noted that many adults with ADHD struggled to control how they express their emotions. Those initial insights have been confirmed by more recent research showing that many people with ADHD are more likely to express anger or upset toward others,[3] and that these traits run in their families.[4]

The prefrontal region of the brain helps control reactions to emotions, which may be due to connections with emotional regions of the brain such as the amygdala. The amygdala contributes to emotional reactions, and recent research suggests it may communicate differently with the prefrontal cortex in some people with ADHD.[5]

Others talk about constantly being distracted by their own ideas; before they've had a chance to complete one thought, another one pops into their head and they drop the first to pursue the second.

GERRY: POPCORN PROBLEMS AND VIRTUAL DISTRACTIONS

Gerry, a stock trader, says that while he's focusing on something—maybe in the middle of reviewing a trade—"pop!" a new thought bursts into his head, and then another. Sometimes it's a related thought, and sometimes it's a completely different one, such as "What will I do after work today?" To keep his original focus, Gerry has to ignore each new idea—which quickly gets exhausting. He has struggled in the past with noisy work environments and often found it hard to tackle one client's problem at a time. He describes a mind that is either full of distractions or looking for them. "Either the popcorn thoughts are popping up, or I notice all the other things I could be doing." We like to call the endless list of other things that one could potentially be doing virtual distractions—because they are based on ideas . . . making a call, sending an e-mail, running another errand. Since Gerry began taking medication for ADHD, he has felt that his mind is quieter and it's easier to stay on track. But the distractions still happen, and it takes some strategizing for him to stay on course.

STRESS: Stress is a common form of internal distraction. Some people seem to focus better under pressure, which awakens the behavioral control parts of the brain.[6] One man we know struggled with graduate school yet thrived in a job in a war zone. Many others can't finish projects without the pressure of a looming deadline. "It is as if I will fill all available time with who-knows-what before something is due, and then pull it off at the last minute," a college student told us,

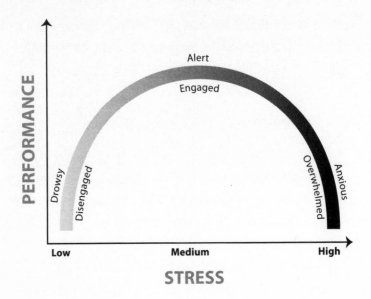

sounding a lot like Eddie from Chapter 2. Stress, then, can be productive in the short-term and in moderate amounts.

But we also know that too much stress can be counterproductive and even dangerous. Researchers have described a stress-performance curve as an upside-down U, in which too little alertness or stress leads to too low engagement and little productivity. The highest productivity comes in a zone where the prefrontal cortex is awake and vigilant, but not under too much stress. Any stress above this zone reduces adaptive flexibility and productivity.[7]

Stress can be caused by many things, and people have individual thresholds for how much stress is enough and how much is too much. So, people can fall into a Catch-22 in which they need stress to perform but too much stress limits their performance.

RECOGNIZE THE IMPACT—DO OTHER PEOPLE SAY YOU:

☐ Should listen better or are easily distracted?
☐ Are not present or seem preoccupied?

☐ Seem scattered, stressed, or overwhelmed?

☐ Take a long time to get things done or are easily sidetracked?

EXTERNAL DISTRACTIONS

Some people can tune out environmental distractions better than others, but we all get distracted by some things. The sirens and flashing lights of ambulances, police cars, and fire engines were designed to create the kind of distractions that everyone must notice.

External distractions are often things that trigger the senses—sights, sounds, even smells—and they can take many forms. Working in a glass-walled office on a main corridor can be distracting. A loud, chatty person at the next desk can be distracting. Even a library can be distracting if people are whispering or the book titles seem appealing. Certainly, today we have innumerable potential distractions in the Internet and social media. Distractibility is one of the most common traits in ADHD. In a study comparing adults with and without ADHD, Russell Barkley, a clinical psychologist and leading ADHD researcher, found that distractibility was among the traits most strongly associated with a diagnosis of ADHD.[8]

The hyperawareness of the sensory environment that is common among people with ADHD suggests that their brains have trouble filtering the importance of the sensations everyone takes in—trouble telling the foreground from the background. Frontal regions of the brain help determine what is important and what is not. Research suggests that frontal regions in ADHD may be operating differently as they control what sounds and sights to attend to.[9]

This same hyperawareness of surroundings can also be an advantage at least some of the time. People with ADHD may notice more of what is going on around them, from things they see in passing on the street to what a co-worker is working on. A salesperson may make a

If Someone You Care About Has a FAST MIND

Here are four things you can do to help someone capitalize on how their brain works best to help them engage and minimize distraction. This should be framed as constructive help, not criticism:

1. You can help them identify where they get distracted by external factors, thoughts, or feelings.

2. You can create written, step-by-step agendas for conversations or activities between the two of you, and each work to stick to it.

3. You can help them think of ways to clarify the steps to their goals, achieve a calmer state of mind, and eliminate distraction when they need to focus.

4. You can help them brainstorm ways to stay engaged when you need them to. So, if your husband always monopolizes end-of-the-day conversations, you might come up with a plan to let him talk first about his day for twenty minutes, and then you get twenty minutes to do the same.

connection with a client by noticing the kinds of photos on their wall; a parent may find a teachable moment when passing a construction site. This heads-up way of going through the world can make someone a great explorer, and in some people it seems to contribute to a broad knowledge of their environments and the world.

WHAT YOU CAN DO

As we discussed in Chapter 2, you likely have times when you are naturally engaged, or in "flow." In those moments, your prefrontal cortex is managing to keep you on track and effective. Those are times when you probably have a clear vision of what you are doing and are less distracted.

But when you want to improve engagement—for tasks where flow is elusive—we suggest you check whether conditions are optimal before tackling a task. Review the Prefrontal Checklist.

THE PREFRONTAL CHECKLIST

- Is the next step vivid and clear in my mind?

- Am I internally distracted? (Are thoughts, feelings, or my mental or physical state preoccupying?)

- Is my environment distracting? (Note sensory and virtual distractions, reminders of other tasks.)

The rest of this chapter is a guide to capitalizing on these three questions to maximize your engagement.

MAKING TASKS MATTER

If what you are doing matters to you, it will be easier to engage. Knowing what matters to you—what you care about, what you value—can help you see the worth of the hoops you need to jump through to fulfill long-term goals. Obviously every job, every class, and every relationship—no matter how great—will have aspects that you just have to slog through. A painter has to make sure the supply cabinet is stocked, a human resources person has to write negative job reviews, a journalist must double-check facts. That's when it's important to keep your long-term goals in mind.

Carlo, whom you'll meet again in Chapter 12, likes nothing more than spending his evenings in the basement, tinkering with his latest invention. His wife, on the other hand, gets annoyed when he fails to come upstairs to eat the dinner she's worked hard to prepare. This created a lot of tension in the first few months of their marriage, but now, on most nights, Carlo forces himself from his "man cave" to eat dinner with her. He has a clear vision of the step he needs to take—dropping what he is doing and getting upstairs—and why it matters: to sustain his marriage. A happy home life is more important to him than anything he might dream up during an extra evening in the basement. His wife still needs to remind him to come up to dinner, but now he quickly does.

Understanding your long-term motivators can clarify the short-term steps toward them. Being there for your kids? Getting a promotion at work? Sustaining your marriage? Those motivators should be in line with your priorities day to day. Look back at the ones you wrote down back in Chapter 1, if you need to remind yourself what they are.

Once you know your goals, you may need some help breaking down the steps it takes to reach them. Carlo's wife told him how important it was for her that they ate dinner together. By prioritizing their relationship, he could see that making it upstairs to dinner every night was something he needed to do to keep their marriage strong. When he just wants to do one more thing in the basement before dinner, he can pull himself back to this priority, write down the "one more thing" so he'll remember it, and then wash up for dinner.

Think of the most important "roles" you play in life: maybe being a student, a worker, a parent, a partner, or a good friend. Picking among these roles, list tasks you dread or have trouble completing (e.g., paying the monthly bills, doing your monthly expense report at work, cleaning up your desk and filing important papers, ironing that huge pile of wrinkled clothes that's sitting in the corner of the laundry room, listening to your children's stories). List your key roles and some dreaded or avoided tasks that come with them:

ROLE   **AVOIDED TASKS**

1. _____   _____

2. _____   _____

3. _____   _____

Now look at each task and think of how they are part of a greater goal—part of a role, outcome, or principle that is meaningful to you. For instance, feeling put-together, confident, and competent may be an important goal at work. Although ironing clothes can be an onerous, boring task, starting the day having wrinkle-free, ready-to-wear clothes could help you start confidently off on the right foot, getting off to work or school easier and less stressful.

List the kinds of big-picture motivators that make harder tasks worth it, that you can keep in mind.

TASK   **GREATER MOTIVATION**

1. _____   _____

2. _____   _____

3. _____   _____

CHOOSING STEPS YOU CAN WORK WITH

As we said earlier, chaos is inherently distracting. The opposite of chaos is an effective plan, a clear vision for what you need to do, a plan that allows you to run on rails. Our mind's eye can hold only so much of a project in our head at once, and the rest becomes distracting. Therefore it's important to break down an activity or task into **steps**.

We suggest you do this in a way that makes the step **vivid and clear**. You can either note them as a list and check off steps as you go, walk it through in your head, or draw it in a cartoon format with every frame representing a step. Try to match how you think best—if you're visual, go with the cartoon; if you're verbal, say it out loud. A friend, teacher, co-worker, or boss may be able to help you break the task or assignment down into manageable steps, if this is difficult for you.

Here's an example of steps that you can hold in your mind's eye to accomplish a larger project, such as writing a twenty-page term paper:

1. Come up with a preliminary question you want to answer.

2. Make a list of what you need to research to answer the question.

3. As you do research, collect information on each item in the list (you may need to refine your topic question).

4. Write a thesis statement you can explore well with the information you have.

5. Create an outline that reflects the question and answers to the question.

6. The outline might look something like this:
   a. Introduction—with thesis statement
   b. Main Point #1 and how it relates to your thesis
   c. Main Point #2 and how it relates to your thesis

    d. Main Point #3 and how it relates to your thesis
    e. Conclusion

7. Write up each part of the outline in order.

8. Revise the draft, making sure you have transition sentences, have supported all your key points, and have fulfilled the teacher's requirements.

9. Read through for spelling and grammatical mistakes.

10. Hand in your paper and reward yourself for finishing it!

MANAGING A MESSY WORK AREA

1. Select one area of your workspace (e.g., half of your desk, your tool bench).

2. Estimate how much time it will take to organize that single area and set aside the necessary time.

3. Make sure you have trash and recycle bins handy.

4. Sort items, discarding any that are unnecessary or won't be used again.

5. Place any items requiring storage in storage immediately, instead of moving them to another area of the workspace.

6. Place everyday items within easy reach and vision.

7. Once the job is completed, give yourself a reward.

8. Plan to tackle another small area of your workspace the following day at the same time (break it down in chunks: e.g., from 10:00 to 10:15 I will clean an area of my workspace).

9. Leave yourself a reminder (computer, smart phone) to do this task on a daily basis until your work area is organized.

USING A PLANNING SYSTEM

Having a way to plan your day is essential to being organized. Using a planner well can help fulfill the prefrontal checklist by maximizing your vision of next steps and making it easier to manage the "popcorn" thoughts and virtual distractions. The most important thing you can do to make your life more organized is to always **capture priority action items** as they come up *in a manner that protects time for them.*

WHAT YOU NEED:

- One place to plan *what you will do and when*—whether it's a calendar that syncs work and home, or a paper planner.

- Separate to-do lists where you can capture and prioritize action items for roles in your life—*for you, for work, for school, for home*—whether it's in the planner or on an electronic device.

- A **thought-capture record** for things that you can't quickly assign an action time to or put on a list, such as a new project or a kind of software program you need, that come up over the course of the day, so you can retrieve them easily. This may mean leaving a space for each day in the planner, or a file on a phone or electronic device.

HOW TO USE A PLANNER:

Many people who keep to-do lists end up with a long inventory of things to do that crosses multiple roles—parent, spouse, employee, student—and multiple places of action in their lives. The grocery list and things to research before the meeting next Wednesday can end up on the same list. This can only add to the feeling of being overwhelmed. Instead, we suggest that as thoughts of things to do come up, you quickly sort them so they can become action items later:

1. Ask yourself whether the item is a time-sensitive high priority—if so, **put the to-do item in your schedule at the times and places** where and when you will have what you need to get it done in time. For example, if you need to write an e-mail about a proposal, and all the documents are on your desk at work, write "e-mail about proposal" in your planner at a time when you will be at your desk, and have enough time to do the task.

2. If the item is a specific task that is less time-sensitive or a lower priority, ask yourself what category this item falls into, then put it into a list dedicated to role-based to-do items, for example, **for you, for home, for work, for school.**

3. Capture other important thoughts. If the item is an idea or issue that you can't quickly put as an action into your planner or on a to-do list, write it down in a place to capture general thoughts and intentions. You might write "prepare to go back to school" or "figure out job options" or "reorganize the closet." Items on this intention capture list should be things for which coming up with action items will take some thought and planning. Record these in a place so you can break them down into action items in your Planning Time, described next.

PLANNING TIME:

In-the-moment management is important, but another top priority is having a time to plan. This can be at breakfast, before you start your day, first thing when you walk into the office, or at night. Use your **planning time** to schedule for the short term. Critical habits during a planning time include the following:

- **Scheduling** action items from your thought-capture record and to-do lists—for example, to get ready to return to college or graduate school, you could distribute tasks in blocks of times over the next few weekend afternoons, such as researching housing options, checking what credits you need to graduate, choosing courses, and arranging travel.

- **Revising** time estimates—if you have done a task many times, you may have a good idea of how long it will take—but sometimes estimates will be wrong. How long it will take to reorganize a closet may need radical adjustment if it now includes sorting and discarding items that have fallen in the back where you forgot them.

- **Breaking down** action items into steps you can do in a reasonable space of time and focus on. Remember that it is easier to engage in something that can be easily held in mind. So if you are trying to explore job options, consider steps such as "write down what I like to do and what I do well," "make a list of positions in fields that would match those traits," "make a list of resources I can use to find a job— contacts, credentials, references," "pick some positions to apply for."

- **Planning well** for things means that you avoid overloading yourself. If there isn't time to do it, something else has to give. Use your planning times to decide which to-do items are priorities, and set aside enough time to accomplish them. Some people like to schedule out each day hour by hour. However, many people with FAST MINDS find they are more productive if they allow themselves periods of flexible time where they can choose among their to-do list priorities. They might write "tackle at-home to-do list" in their planner for Saturday afternoon, and then choose among the priorities on that list when Saturday comes.

So far our suggestions for lists and using a planner are close to the conventional wisdom and popular organizational methods. But we know from extensive experience that people with FAST MINDS traits need even more adaptations. If you have already struggled to be consistent or use this kind of system well, in the rest of the book we help you understand what is getting in the way.

Managing Internal Distractions

Capture Popcorn Thoughts:

If you are a "popcorn" thinker, try capturing those thoughts. When a random thought pops into your head, quickly make a note of it and then get back to what you were doing. That way, you won't need to take up any mental space remembering it, but you also won't get distracted for too long. If the ideas that pop up are action items, get them in your schedule or on the to-do list instead—or if that will take a while, you might write "plan activity X" and schedule it later. For example, if in the middle of writing a report you remember that it's time to get the oil changed in your car, write on your to-do list: *Call mechanic and make appointment for oil change.* And then get back on task.

You should also give some thought to where to capture your thoughts. One person we know keeps a notebook and pencil in every room of her house, so she can write down important things that pop into her head wherever she is. Keeping track of those notes can be a problem, though. We know people who stick notes on the refrigerator, rewrite them on a whiteboard, or keep a special file in their computer. We strongly encourage having your schedule and thought record on you at all times—in a small planner or electronic device.

As discussed in our guide to using a planner, you should leave time to review these captured thoughts—your planning time is perfect for that. Besides turning the thoughts into action items, this time may provide fodder for your thought record. Take a minute to think about the kinds of thoughts that pop up. Are they self-defeating, worried, or sad as we discussed in Chapter 3? If you feel overwhelmed and are thinking negatively as you face tasks this may be an important clue that you need other kinds of supports for your internal distractions. One investment banker we know was so full of anxious thoughts about how his company measured up against the competition that he had trouble reading financial information about competitor companies. This was counterproductive, because he needed to know what the competitors were doing so he could keep up or jump ahead of them. Using a thought record can help transform these thoughts into more rational, grounded considerations. Whenever he had a thought such as, "Why didn't we do what that company did? I should have thought of that," he was able to redirect it and change it to, "What ideas can I get from analyzing their strategies?"

Defeat Internal Restlessness
Some people we know plan for the rhythm of their restlessness, using their to-do lists to occupy them while they take breaks from work. If you spend a lot of time doing particular tasks, then knowing ahead of time how long you can go without feeling edgy or antsy, stretching, or fidgeting can help you plan for this rhythm. Rewarding yourself with a break every hour and then doing something else you need

to do—following up on a bill, arranging an appointment—will more than justify the lost time if you're extra efficient when you settle back down.

One college student, who had regularly been described by teachers as having "ants in his pants," was having trouble focusing on his homework. He would start studying at the library, and then about twenty minutes later he would get up to talk to another student or e-mail a friend. By the end of a study night, he had socialized wonderfully but not done much studying. Through trial and error, he discovered that he could be much more productive if he went running before study sessions and if he embraced his own rhythm of needing frequent breaks from a particular assignment. He got a big table, spread out notes for three different subjects, and moved around the table to a different subject every ten to twenty minutes as his attention flagged. After each "circuit," he would pace around the library, burning off steam for ten to fifteen minutes, and then go back for another circuit. Though he struggled to make this pattern fit more intensive long-term projects, it worked for him most of the time. He had been on the verge of flunking out of college, but coming to understand what he could expect of himself—how long he could sit, how he had to change from environment to environment for different tasks—gave him some control. "I cope by knowing what's not going to fly," he says.

MINDFULNESS FOR A FAST MIND

We commonly see people distracted by sadness, anxiety, and stress, and sometimes by feeling irrationally upbeat. Noticing your own mood can be challenging, though. Sometimes physical symptoms can be clues. Neck or shoulder pain, headaches, poor sleep, constipation, or shallow breathing may be signs of unhappiness or excessive stress. Changing your mental mind-set may take practice, therapy, and/or medication, depending on its severity and your preferences. Feeling more effective day to day by reducing FAST MINDS challenges can certainly help reduce stress, but sometimes active practice can get your mind into a better state for facing the hard work you need to do.

Emerging research and clinical experience suggests that some simple exercises based on mindfulness meditation may be useful for developing awareness of internal mental states, thoughts, and feelings. A growing body of research suggests that meditation is associated with changes in the prefrontal cortex and emotional self-control.[10] We do not expect mindfulness to cure ADHD, and some people with FAST MINDS won't be comfortable with it. Carlo told us he'd find jumping out of an airplane more relaxing than trying to sit still and meditate for five minutes. There are plenty of other options, some of which we discuss in Chapter 11. But if you can imagine sitting with yourself for a little while, mindfulness practice can be a powerful tool for becoming aware of distractions and unproductive states of mind.[11] With regular practice, it may also give you more control over your emotions.

The exercise we suggest here is adapted from mindfulness meditation:

Sit in a chair somewhere comfortable and quiet, feet on the floor, not too slouched. Begin breathing deeply and easily using your chest, and focus your mind on these slow inhales and even longer exhales.

It is normal for other thoughts to pop into your head—ideas about the exercise, concerns of the day, fuzzy feelings without words. Let them go without concern or self-criticism, and return your focus to your breath. Do this for one minute to start (or even less!) and gradually increase the time to a few minutes at a time as you gain more control. Set a timer so you don't need to think about time passing.

You may discover as you do this how busy your mind is—and how much your brain is constantly filtering and sorting. You may also notice that you get better at letting these thoughts go as you practice this exercise again and again. If this mindfulness exercise resonates with you, there are many versions you might explore to practice strengthening internal awareness and control. We reference such options further in Chapter 11.

Managing External Distractions

Controlling Your Physical Space

Some people need to arrange their offices so that they look out on a peaceful, uncluttered scene; others do their best work in a busy park or café. You need to be aware of your own best situations—and think about how they may change over the course of the day, as you get tired or more energized.

It is ideal to take control of your environment on your own, in a way that maintains your privacy. You may be able to get your school or employer to help change the environment you operate in. We've known people to ask their employers to allow them to work in workrooms instead of cubicles and to change clear glass walls to frosted ones, so they could focus better. We discuss in Chapter 9 how to decide whether it's a good idea to ask for such accommodations at work—because in some environments these requests may not be possible to fulfill.

Some people work much better when their desk is clean and organized, but organization can be a challenge for those with FAST MINDS. One person we know used to feel like she was at war and her office was the battleground. It would fill with junk and she could never find what she needed when she needed it most. An ADHD coach herself, she was losing paperwork, clients, and self-

respect. So she devised a strategy. Now she invites a naturally organized friend over once a month. She turns on some upbeat music and
she and her friend pore over every inch of her office. Working with
someone else who can see the steps to getting it clean helps her,
and she is less distracted by other demands on her time or her poor
feelings about herself. Between cleanings, the mess piles up again,
but she feels better knowing she has a plan for coping with it, and
after a few sessions of cleaning she started to remember better where
she should put things. Not only is her consulting business operating
more smoothly, but her stress level is lower and war metaphors no
longer apply.

Preoccupy Your Restless Brain

Many people with FAST MINDS traits learn that they function best
with just the right sensory environment or activity. The goal may not
be to just limit distraction or stay still; it may also be to occupy the
senses. To return to the idea of a "hunter" brain, it is as if the brain is
constantly scanning the environment for something interesting or
looking for a reason to make the body move. Giving the sensory and
motor parts of our brains something to do—but not too much—can
help. We know several people who find that they can settle into work
using just the right environment. But be careful not to make the
search for the right environment another way of procrastinating, or
to kid yourself about how much you are really getting done. Here are
common factors to think about in deciding which environments
might work for you:

   Sounds: If you are easily distracted by noises around you, seek out
quiet places; try noise-canceling headphones, earplugs, or playing
music or white noise. Many people find that songs with lyrics are too
engaging. Sometimes your favorite music can set the tone for getting
to work—but turning on less distracting music once you start working can help maintain focus. One university student used to quietly

play his iPod during lectures to wash out conversations around him, yet still allow him to hear the speaker.

Sights: If things in your environment distract you, remember the old adage, "Out of sight, out of mind." It can be hard to keep a regular workspace clear of distractions, so pick at least a small space you can clear off for tackling important projects, even a small table, where there are no visible alternatives to the work. If you refuse to keep anything in your workplace except your current project, it won't get crowded with unnecessary papers or distracting objects. On the other hand, the right visuals may actually keep a person more engaged. On a dinner date, for example, you could choose to sit where you see just a wall, or other people in the restaurant, or a television at the bar. For many people who are distracted by not knowing what the sounds and noises around them mean, sitting where they can see the restaurant is a better choice. But if they can see the TV, it might compete with their dinner partner.

Other senses: What people find distracting or comfortable can vary widely. If you are easily distracted by smells, you may want to schedule your trips to the library around your roommate's cooking plans. Comfortable clothing and particular textures may be less physically distracting, while for some having a texture to run fingers over may occupy a restless sensory brain.

Channeling restlessness: Some people find that squeezing stress balls or having small objects they can "fidget" with keeps them seated and working longer. For some, exercise can preempt physical restlessness. Some people actually read better on an exercise machine—or while drumming their fingers or rocking.

Virtual Distractions
The Internet, television, and social media offer an endless array of potential diversions. Some people turn off their e-mail and social media for set amounts of time or while they're working on a particu-

larly taxing project. If you struggle with controlling your online habit, try disconnecting for a short time one day, a little more the next, and so forth. If that's impossible, try working somewhere that doesn't have Internet access, or turn it off for work periods. Some even use Internet blocking services to disable access temporarily.

KNOW WHAT DISTRACTS YOU!

Think again about the areas of your life that you said in Chapter 1 were a top priority for you to address.

1. _____

2. _____

3. _____

Which of the following distractions and mental states are getting in the way of your addressing these areas?

INTERNAL DISTRACTIONS:

Mood? _____

Stress? _____

Thoughts? _____

What kind of thoughts? (Worried, sad, neutral?) _____

Are you thinking about things you need to do? _____

Things you already did? _____

Random thoughts? _____

Restlessness? _____

EXTERNAL DISTRACTIONS:

Sensory? _____

Visual? _____

Reminders of other things you could be doing in your environment?
_____

As you went through the preceding list, you may have noticed some distractions you can avoid or that you can work on keeping at a nonannoying level. For most people with FAST MINDS, distractibility is a way of life, unless medication eliminates it. If there are changes that you know will help, the rest of the book will help you implement them and stick with them. We guide you through what it takes to form new habits and keep them going, and we direct you to resources that can extend the work you will do in this book.

In the next chapter we move from focusing on improving engagement in the moment to improving patterns of behavior, thought habits and systems that can create a less strained, more efficient life.

KEY POINTS

A clear vision and low distraction are essential for better control over mental activity and behavior. We repeat the prefrontal checklist here, as a tool for grounding yourself in moments where you want to maximize your engagement:

THE PREFRONTAL CHECKLIST

- Is the next step vivid and clear in my mind?

- Am I internally distracted? (Are thoughts, feelings, or my mental or physical state preoccupying?)

- Is my environment distracting? (Note sensory and virtual distractions and reminders of other tasks.)

Be Your Own Chief Executive

Nate looks like the ultimate organizer. He's an accountant and earns his living by getting the details right. When he reads a self-help book, he opens an Excel spreadsheet and types out all the key points, so he'll remember them. He lives by his lists, which remind him to take vitamins, buy an anniversary gift, pick up the kids, make dinner, meet various work demands, and more. The system, Nate says, means he is more likely to remember what he needs to and less likely to have to scramble or make a quick decision. If it's Monday morning, Nate knows it's time to pay bills, and he does. "The more I have to think about something, the worse it is," he says.

Michael has a harder time with organizational systems. His to-do lists take on a life of their own, his desk is often distractingly messy, and mail is a daily challenge to his sanity. "I have a kitchen-sized trash bag filled with papers I need to shred," he says. He has trouble planning his day, in part because he struggles to figure out how much he *should* accomplish in one day. "Nowhere is it written, 'This is enough for you to get done in a day.' I think I still struggle with realistic expectations—especially if I have a lot of time at my disposal," he says. "It seems the more time I have, the less able I am to budget my time." He jokes about how his life would go if he were an outdoorsman: He might arrive at a spot convinced that he could chop down enough trees to build himself a cabin by nightfall. Then he would spend too much time trimming branches perfectly, or it would rain heavily, or there would be some other predictable mishap, and by the end of the day, he would have only a small part of one wall ready. "But I thought I'd have a cabin, so I didn't bring a tent."

In the previous chapter, we focused on the factors that allow, or get in the way of, engaging in a task. In this chapter, we discuss how patterns of behavior—what some people call their "systems"—can improve organization and productivity. Most adults with ADHD, in addition to having trouble controlling what they are focusing on moment by moment, have trouble with other so-called executive functions. These are activities that a business executive would need to run a company well, such as organizing, prioritizing, delegating, estimating time and resources needed, and sticking to a schedule. Being able to engage in something is only one facet of these executive functions. In this chapter, we tackle other executive challenges—the ones that leave people struggling to do the right thing at the right time.

RECOGNIZING YOURSELF

- ☐ Do you often have difficulty estimating the amount of time it takes to do tasks?
- ☐ Are you often late?
- ☐ Do you often feel overwhelmed or like you are "flying by the seat of your pants"?
- ☐ Do you have to be rigid in your habits to keep your life from spinning out of control?

☐ Do you live among so many piles and so much clutter that it's hard to find things you need or it embarrasses you?

☐ If you have lots to do, is it hard to know where to start first?

☐ Do you get bogged down in tasks that someone else could do for you?

☐ Do you realize well into the day that you are off track from what you intended to do?

☐ At the end of the day, are your priorities accomplished?

The Executive in Executive Function

As we have been highlighting, a network of brain regions is critical for controlling engagement. Frontal areas like the prefrontal cortex regulate the ability to organize, plan, and handle change. Another area of brain machinery important for control of behavior that we introduced in Chapter 2, a forward region called the anterior cingulate cortex, may be particularly relevant for determining what the brain engages in at a given moment. Research suggests that the anterior cingulate's purpose is to improve the efficiency of goal-oriented thinking and action—keeping the brain on track to a goal.[1] In this sense, the anterior cingulate may be the "executive" of the executive-function regions, responsible for keeping us on course from moment to moment. Multiple studies show that in children and adults with ADHD, the anterior cingulate is less active, smaller, or less connected to other regions.

Focus can get a good boost from ADHD medication, but medication is often less effective for these other executive functions and organizational challenges. Children with ADHD are unlikely to "grow out of" these executive-function difficulties as they transition from childhood into adolescence, according to a 2008 study by Dr. Surman's colleagues at Massachusetts General Hospital.[2] These organizational challenges crop up early, in cluttered rooms and locker mess, and in trouble managing larger school assignments such as term papers. We often see bigger consequences as people move on to high school, college, and beyond; as options and responsibilities increase.

Being Your Own Executive Secretary

Remember Eddie from Chapter 2, who said that his most productive work years were in a position where he had a "battle-axe" of a secretary? This assistant knew what he needed to do and when he needed to do it and made sure he was aware of it, but she also took care of paperwork that he found tedious. She provided skills that he did not have and effectively organized him so he could keep up with the steady demands of his office.

Any busy person can benefit from such assistance—but the organizational challenges of many people with FAST MINDS traits make such a resource even more useful. Since it's not possible to have an executive assistant in every aspect of your life, we encourage you to work through the rest of this chapter thinking about what management practices you can apply to become your own executive assistant.

It takes practice to establish an executive habit—and people with FAST MINDS will always need reminders and extra effort to change behaviors. Here we want you to understand the kinds of habits that may be high yield for you to practice.

PRIORITIZING AND PLANNING

We discussed in the previous chapter how we suggest people use a to-do list and planner. We want to reiterate here that we feel one of the most important times to protect in life is planning time. Without stepping outside the busyness of day-to-day activities to review responsi-bilities and actively plan to meet them, we are perpetually left in a reactive, crisis management, disorganized pattern.

We feel that each time a new priority action item is identified, it deserves a protected place, off your mind, where it can be referred to at the time it should be acted on. This reduces having to remember and protects time to devote to it. There are two critical moments for making sure an action item happens: the moment you record it, and the moment you remember that it is time to do it. So planning should include how you will remember to do it—whether it's regularly check-ing the schedule or alarm reminders.

Having dedicated planning time creates an invaluable habit for being in control of your days. Allocate time for tasks and transitions and checking priorities. Many people like to do this before going to bed, planning for the next day; sleeping on it and reviewing in the morning seems to help cement the agenda. We want to emphasize again that your top priorities should receive the most planning effort—it may never be feasible to plan every action item.

KEEPING CHECKLISTS

Many professions embrace checklists to reduce human error in com-plex or even just routine tasks. Checklists can ensure that a plane is operational before flight, and that medical procedures are performed safely and on the right body part. We believe that routine activities where people get sidetracked, overwhelmed, or even just bored benefit from checklists. Leaving the house, you see a checklist on the door that reminds you to bring your cell phone and your keys. You are packing for a trip and scan a checklist you made for business trips and realize you almost forgot your phone charger. To work, these check-lists should be ones you are likely to reuse—such as for trips, shop-ping, or what you need to bring for your child when you leave the house each day. Unless the checklist is where you can easily use it, it won't get used. Put the list where it makes sense for the task—a packing list could go in the pocket of a suitcase; a morning departure list could be taped to the inside of the front door. An electronic list should be easy to access.

CONQUERING CLUTTER AND MESS: Many people struggle to keep order in their lives. But some people with FAST MINDS take clutter to a different level. Dining room tables, cars, and garages are hot spots; it's not just the occasional piece of paper or laundry on the floor, but having so much stuff that the floor is hard to find. They tidy up only when they have absolutely no choice, like James from Chapter 1, who hurriedly emptied out his backseat onto the side of the highway to keep the flames from spreading. For everyone, there is a critical moment when an item either becomes part of the clutter or gets put in its place (such as the trash can!). The difference comes down to having effective habits. A habit of throwing away junk mail and paying bills immediately, for example, may help many people keep mail clutter down.

KEEPING YOURSELF ON TIME: Some people with ADHD simply aren't aware of time. They are not two or three minutes late for a meeting or to hang out with friends—they run behind by twenty minutes or more. They can have the best intentions to wrap up work and leave on time, and yet every day they are running late. Many people also have a one-last-thing-before-I-go problem, or doggedly try to finish the task they are on instead of transitioning to the next one. Once they realize they're late, the rushing begins, making it more likely they'll forget the kids' lunches, important work papers, or their house keys. At its worst, chronic time challenges can end relationships or get people fired. One of our colleagues, Dr. William Dodson, surveyed adults in his ADHD clinic and noted that most did not wear a watch.[3]

People with FAST MINDS traits often benefit from setting up reminders to help them move from one task to another. Timers, alarms, or asking someone to call at an appointed time can help you stay on schedule. One woman we know sets an alarm to go off fifteen minutes before she is supposed to leave the office for sales calls. This is a signal that she needs to start wrapping up whatever she's working on. A second alarm that goes off ten minutes later means it's time to shut down her computer and pack up her bag so she can leave for the calls.

Later in this chapter we offer additional exercises for helping you keep to a schedule, manage your time, and avoid being chronically late.

MANAGING TRANSITIONS: We find that many people with FAST MINDS traits—even those who do have watches and look at them to see when it is time to leave—have trouble disengaging and moving on to the next activity. They are not flexible in shifting between different activities. This difficulty in shifting means they are likely to have to work hard to avoid making mistakes during transitions. It takes more effort to be on top of the transition—to leave for a birthday party with a present already wrapped, to arrive at the gym with the workout clothes you need—and even more to be prepared for common unforeseen complications, such as getting stuck in traffic en route to an important meeting or needing to solve a computer glitch before a presentation.

The critical moments may occur far before the transition itself—moments when one could have prepared for it better. Improved preparation may include scheduling extra time to get to your destination, packing the night before for a trip, or going to bed instead of staying up late playing video games.

The prefrontal checklist from the previous chapter can help improve the critical moments of a transition. Are there clear steps to the transition? *First I get my work bag and put my lunch in it and bring that to the door* . . . Are there distractions such as trying to finish up a task as you head out the door? Is fatigue a factor, or are thoughts about the next or last activity distracting? Some people describe these transitions as trying to get themselves out of a rut—having to forcibly shift their interest from their current activity to the task at hand.

RECOGNIZE THE IMPACT—WHAT WOULD OTHER PEOPLE SAY?

People with organizational challenges may have a limited idea of how other, naturally organized people live, and so they may not appreciate how their own executive function challenges affect those around them. If they are less aware of time, they may not realize how disruptive they are to people who are timekeepers. These timekeepers may not feel able to rely on those with executive function challenges or may find it difficult to share work or living spaces, because of the clutter. Friends may lose patience when they are kept waiting yet again.

☐ Do other people have to remind you of important things?

☐ Do other people notice your difficulty with time management?

☐ Do you often leave friends or work colleagues waiting for you?

☐ Do you stress people out because you are not reliable?

☐ Does your clutter or mess bother others?

☐ Do you regularly make last-minute requests or have to ask for extensions in deadlines?

Critical Moments

LIVING IN THE PRESENT

Many people with FAST MINDS "live in the moment"—either because they are reactive (addressing problems just as they appear) rather than proactive (prepared ahead of time), or because they are barely keeping their heads above water day by day. Some moments are more critical than others to getting through the day well. It can be critical when clothes don't get picked out the night before or laundry isn't washed in time. Homework, instruments, and sports gear are left behind, and important work papers are forgotten on the breakfast table.

For some, lack of future thinking is a major problem. We know people who "woke up" in a Ph.D. program in which they had no interest—because they hadn't looked ahead and imagined what it would be like to actually study this subject for years, not to mention have a career in it.

Planning ahead involves an awareness of the present, projecting what the new task will involve, and then switching gears to that task. When planning for a child's guitar lesson, for example, the critical moment may come when the parent does or doesn't add the guitar lesson to their calendar; when that calendar is or isn't consulted; when Mom or Dad doesn't leave the office early enough to do pickup and get to the lesson on time; or when there's no designated place to keep the guitar, so a ten-minute hunt is required to find it. Planning, checklists, and alarm reminders all help this challenge.

KEEPING TRACK

Some people routinely misplace wallets, cell phones, even their car— forgetting where they parked it that morning or the night before. Memory retrieval challenges also make people forget about promises they have made or blank out on details.

Remembering a fact (such as where you left something) requires having stored the memory well in the moment. Storage of such a memory requires focusing on the information enough to place it in *working memory*, so it can then be moved into *long-term memory*. It seems that information needs to be held in working memory while it is filed away. Think of how hard it would be to save a file under a useful file name on your computer if you forgot what kind of information was in the document. The brain similarly needs to hold on to information as it stores it. People with ADHD or FAST MINDS traits often have problems with attention and working memory but rarely with long-term memory.

Working Memory at Work

Any human brain can hold on to only a few thoughts at once. Phone numbers are set at seven digits and that is thought to be the average limit of human working memory (of course, many are longer including the area code; through what is known as chunking, a well-known set of numbers such as an area code can be remembered separately). [4] Our brains actively choose what information to take into working memory, filtering out irrelevant information. A study published in 2009 demonstrated, for example, that brain activity controlling accurate working memory performance was lower during a visual task while participants were processing visual information not relevant to the task. [5]

Because ADHD is marked by difficulty controlling what is engaged in a given moment, it would be consistent if difficulty tuning out irrelevant information contributes to the problems holding ideas, thoughts, and facts in mind that are common among people with FAST MINDS.

Storing factual information for later retrieval requires establishing the information in working memory—but using that information or associating it with other information appears to help the storage process. Having to drive to the top of a parking garage or squeezing your car in next to a support beam will make it easier to remember where you parked. (Just don't forget about the beam when you're pulling out!)

If something is interesting, notable, or otherwise engaging, it is easier to attend to and hold in mind. This explains why we often hear stories about people with FAST MINDS who can rattle off all sorts of facts on their favorite topics but can't remember what they were supposed to get at the store or where they left the TV remote.

Problems with working memory also mean that people easily forget what they were about to do. For example, we've heard stories of people who distractedly put important documents on the roof of their car as they fished for their keys, with terrible consequences as they pulled away. Knowing where you are vulnerable to such absentmindedness is critical to developing strategies for keeping important things in mind. It is crucial to have a system in place where you can check the day's priorities to stay on track. Phone apps or online to-do lists can help with this task.

Overloaded and Overwhelmed

People with ADHD often feel overwhelmed by assignments. A research paper can seem totally daunting for someone who doesn't know how to break it down into manageable pieces. Few schools teach organizational skills, and people with ADHD may need more explicit instructions than others to figure out how to tackle a job one step at a time.

Many people with FAST MINDS seem not to anticipate the consequences of their decisions. Some, like Michael in the beginning of this chapter, are too optimistic about what they can accomplish. This may be due to a mental "skimming over the details" of how hard something will be to do. Some people with FAST MINDS are also too quick to say yes to something new or shiny—and accumulate a to-do list that exceeds human capacity.

The moment that you accept an assignment or take on something new is critical. It can lead to more feelings of being overwhelmed or to a reinforcing success. Deliberate planning up front can make the difference.

If Someone You Care About Has a FAST MIND

You can be a great help with your loved one's executive challenges by helping them identify the critical moments when their choices steer them away from a balanced, organized life. Identifying these moments is the first step in building habits or "systems" to manage them. Sometimes that means pointing out the choice the person is making or missing—such as when to go to bed. Sometimes it means helping them think through priorities or brainstorming organizational systems that suit their strengths and habits.

Use these questions to think about organizational critical moments for the person you care about:

- Are they often late?

- Do they underestimate how long things will take to accomplish?

- Do you need to remind them frequently?

- Do they have trouble keeping things where they belong?

- Do you worry that they won't be on top of what they need to do?

- Are you worried that you can't rely on them to follow through?

- Do they have a system to manage their time, keep important papers organized, or get out of the house in the morning?

- Do they keep you waiting or keep you from your own best habits such as going to bed on time?

WHAT YOU CAN DO

Organization is a constant process. It is not something that is ever "solved" but requires constant effort. No one can ever "master" the dishes, the laundry or the mail—they always pile up again regardless of how well you handled them the last time. Don't waste physical, emotional, and mental time trying to be perfectly organized—or beating up on yourself for not being Martha Stewart (who has an army of people doing her shopping, cooking, cleaning, and organizing). Instead, spend your time and energy creating good systems that require minimal steps and keep you ahead of crises. We also appreciate that people with FAST MINDS traits may need to regularly reinvent their systems to keep each one interesting.

As you read through the rest of the chapter, you may think you are revisiting familiar territory—many books on organization recommend how to use to-do lists, calendars, and approaches such as the one-touch system of organizing papers. We think our approach is different because we are presenting principles that can help you build strategies to accommodate *your own FAST MINDS traits*. Because of either the individuality of people's lives or the challenges of their FAST MINDS traits, we don't think off-the-shelf systems work well for a lot of people with FAST MINDS. How many systems have you started and abandoned as too complicated, too annoying, or too time-consuming? This is particularly important if organization and habit making doesn't come easily. You need to target a few simple systems that give you the most bang for your buck. The rest of the chapter is designed to help you figure out what those might be.

GETTING A HANDLE ON CRITICAL MOMENTS

Many kinds of organizational challenges exist, but we feel that common footholds are available for surmounting the "critical moments" we discussed previously. A critical moment is the moment before you might make a bad choice. It could be a thought like "This is too much for me," so you end up not doing what you should. It could be when you do the next thing you think of instead of checking your planner. It could be dropping the mail in a pile instead of paying a bill then and there. Critical moments are like a fork in the road, one way leading to a life that runs well, and the other to disorganization. Executive function challenges make it harder to see the organized path and to follow it even if it is visible. Just how hard it is to engage these principled, organized behaviors depends on a person's strengths.

MICHAEL AND NATE: FINDING—AND DOING SOMETHING ABOUT—CRITICAL MOMENTS

Michael says the biggest challenge for him is staying vigilant for the critical moments that make or break his day. One recent Saturday, he managed a critical moment poorly when he decided to hang out in bed a little while longer. That extra thirty minutes meant the washing machines in his building were already full by the time he dragged his laundry downstairs. He then had to waste time waiting for a machine, which threw off the rest of his day.

He also worries about missing out on key moments in relationships. He knows, for instance, that he should call and offer support to a cousin whose child is facing a medical crisis. But just as quickly as the thought pops into his head, it slips away again, and he forgets to write himself a note about it or make the call. The thought occurs to him again eventually, he says, circling around his brain just as Halley's comet orbits the sun every seven and a half decades. "Stuff just loops around in my head. If I don't write it down, eventually I'll remember, but maybe it's once every seventy-seven years or something."

Michael said he has gotten a lot of good organizational strategies from a CBT program he was involved in a few years ago—though he admits he should revisit the homework from it. He's long had automated reminders for paying bills and making it to regular appointments. He's also gotten some organizational ideas from other self-help books that emphasize prioritization, planning, and having, as his grandmother used to recommend, "a place for everything and everything in its place." His biggest challenge is still breaking projects down into pieces. "I still have problems with blank canvases of time," he says.

For Nate, a critical moment is when he begins drifting away. It makes a big difference if he can catch himself quickly and return to what he was doing. He says he used to basically lead two separate lives, with his head in one place and his body in another. Since his ADHD diagnosis—in his forties—Nate has been able to focus more on "pulling himself together." His systems help keep him on task. A freelance tax accountant, Nate uses a checklist when he's going over a company's taxes, to make sure he follows the proper audit procedure. The checklist takes all the questions and decisions out of the process, and he can do it easily because he knows what's expected.

Showing up for work on time isn't something he can accomplish through a checklist, however. His clients have learned that he'll turn up eventually. Last year, an ADHD coach pointed out that Nate's slow morning habits and casual approach to getting out of the house were hurting his two sons. His sixth-grader racked up nineteen tardies in a single semester. The boy was only ten to fifteen minutes late each time, but starting from behind was still enough to make his school day more challenging. Now Nate makes

more of an effort to get out of the house on time, both to keep his
sons from falling behind and to model good behavior.

Many people like Nate function better when they have a lot of
systems or scaffolds in place to keep them organized. They use
habits and routines such as checklists to make good choices at
critical moments. Nate uses his lists to start the day and lives by
his planner. The path is clear to him, so he knows how to follow it.

Other people, like Michael, have a harder time picking up or
sticking to organizational habits. At work, he manages a lot of
private documents, and instead of having a habit of reviewing
them in a dedicated workspace and shredding the personal infor-
mation as he goes, he lets the papers pile up and they get left for
later. His work life is full of unwanted surprises from tasks that he
didn't bother to estimate the time for, and he keeps doing extra
background research when he should be submitting what he has
already done to co-workers. Once Michael realized how hard it is
for him to be systematic about reviewing his schedule, he was able
to become more aware of the moments when extra effort would
pay off and began working more efficiently.

We believe the most efficient way to build a more organized life is
to trace the problems back to critical moments and then forge better
choices and habits for those moments. The people around you may
recognize those moments better than you do, so enlist their help.

Think back to the prefrontal checklist as you think about moments
where organizational habits can help. Habits that help you have a clear
plan or reduce distraction from productive patterns will help keep you
engaged.

As you read through the common problem moments and habits
below, think of the three problem areas you chose to focus on in Chapter 1 in mind, or other situations in your life that apply.

CLUTTER: The critical moment is not now, when your desk is a mess, but all those other times when you ended up keeping a piece of paper that could have been filed or tossed in the trash. If the mail piles up, threatening to devour your entire dining room table, you might set aside a time every day to sort the mail. Exert mental control so everything gets sorted right then, with the bills into one spot where you'll see them again, and the junk mail where it belongs—in the trash.

MEMORY: The critical moment comes when you don't record information in the best way, such as stuffing an appointment card into your purse instead of immediately recording the appointment in your planner. If you're likely to drive off with your coffee mug or cell phone on the roof of the car, you might make a conscious effort to talk yourself through transitions where you have to put things down. If you're likely to forget things, you might ask, "What am I leaving behind?" before you leave home, work, the doctor's office—anywhere. Many people living with FAST MINDS glance behind them at the chair they were just sitting in as they leave our office—a self-check that sometimes saves hunting for wallets, keys, or paperwork. But better yet, look back at moments when you have left things behind or forgotten to do something and note how you can achieve flow instead. Some people like to keep things where they will trip over them—sometimes literally—such as leaving that presentation poster leaning on the front door or leaving a special tray just inside the door to hold keys, wallet, phone, and glasses.

TIME WARP: The critical moment comes when you don't plan for a stopping or starting point. If you know you have to pick your child up at 5:30, you need to plan to be done at the office no later than 5:00 (or allow for however long the commute will take you), and structure the rest of your day accordingly. Using buffer zones—periods of time where you intentionally avoid planning things—can help if you are running late. Don't plan a "quick" meeting at 4:30 with a co-worker if you are likely to ramble on and forget the time.

TRANSITIONS: As we mentioned earlier, the critical moment that makes a transition more difficult may have happened further back in time than you realize. It might be when you didn't plan ahead for the steps and elements of the transition and then got overwhelmed with the combination of people, places, things, and time involved; when you didn't put something in its rightful place; when you didn't think ahead to what you would need for the next day or next appointment. But FAST MINDS people can also get stuck—*hyperfocused*—in a task. Seeing the transition itself as a task worth effort, envisioning what you need to do next, and reminding yourself of the larger goal of balancing efforts across your daily responsibilities can help.

LIVING IN THE PRESENT: The critical moment may have passed when you didn't think ahead to imagine the consequences if you did or didn't do something. It can also happen when you say something without thinking. You're entitled to have an opinion about a colleague's work, but saying it out loud in front of your mutual boss will have consequences that you should think through before you open your mouth.

OVERWHELMED: A critical moment here also comes when you don't think of consequences—in particular how a decision fits with everything else you need to do. If you tend to get overwhelmed easily, it may be because you don't understand the steps or time necessary to complete a task, or because you said "yes" to more than you can reasonably accomplish. Using a planner to allocate time for tasks is a good way to visually see when you are going to stretch yourself too thin.

Think about the priority areas you established in Chapter 1 or other situations that are not going as you need them to. Note here some thoughts on the critical moments you need better habits for. Note also WHERE, WHEN, HOW, or WHAT it would take to make a better choice in those moments.

CRITICAL MOMENT:

Goal (e.g., spending more time with your spouse):

_____

_____

What did you do counter to your goal (e.g., stayed at work too late)?

_____

_____

Why did that happen (remember, you may have to think back in time a few hours or even a few days—e.g., you procrastinated earlier in the week and then had to make up for it tonight)?

_____

_____

Did anything else get in the way of your doing what you wanted to do (e.g., because you didn't have a system for getting enough work done earlier in the week, it piled up)?

_____

_____

What could you do differently next time (e.g., break the project down into manageable chunks that you can complete without crazy deadline pressure)?

_____

_____

We further explore how to develop better patterns at critical moments in Chapter 8, where we focus on what makes it easier to practice new habits at critical moments and introduce a Critical Moment Planner.

PERIPHERAL BRAINS

If you are not good at something—memory, managing time, planning transitions—the good news is that you can "outsource" aspects of these tasks. Chief executives have executive assistants to keep them on schedule and staff members to handle tasks they don't like or don't do well. You can run your own life like a business, too. Perhaps because of self-esteem issues, people with FAST MINDS sometimes feel guilty or bad about themselves when they need an assist from someone or something else to be organized. If they stopped to look around, they'd realize that everyone's mail piles up on the dining room table if they don't have an effective system for dealing with it, or that most couples divide household chores to play to their strengths and preferences.

We like to call these external supports _peripheral brains_. Many types of peripheral brains can help improve executive functions. Peripheral brains can be systems or other people who help balance your weaknesses. But use this chapter first to make a wish-list of efficient habits.

MAKING YOUR SCHEDULE AND TO-DO LIST A PERIPHERAL BRAIN

Your schedule can serve as a peripheral brain if you use it to prioritize, allocate your time for planning purposes, and add a reminder system. Some people set an alarm on their computer or phone a few times a day to check whether they are sticking with their daily plans. Use an alarm ten minutes before you have to leave for an event, or at night to remind you to shut off electronics and get ready for bed—so you don't stay up until two A.M. and fall apart exhausted the next day. Some people like to set an alarm on their electronic calendar to remind them of a recurring obligation—such as paying monthly bills or picking the kids up at school.

However, alarms going off all the time are likely to just get dismissed—so choose wisely. Start by setting a reminder for one or two tasks. With enough repetition, hopefully those tasks will become habits and you can use the alarm technique for other reminders.

Some people plan out most of their day, but a novelty-seeking brain is not likely to follow a rigid schedule. Many people we work with prefer scheduling in periods in which they have a choice of activities from their to-do list. It is important to assign a time to activities that are a short-term priority or need to be finished by a certain date. But it may improve your engagement to allow yourself some freedom of choice in other work periods—as long as the to-do list and priorities get tackled. Some people simply write down how long they will spend on a given priority in the days ahead and assign it to a time when that day comes.

Prioritization cannot be undervalued. One man we knew had a to-do list that routinely topped thirty items. Of course, with a list that long, he couldn't get anything done. Eventually, his wife agreed to highlight a few key priorities for him every day. Once he had those priorities straight, he could accomplish something. Both she and the list became his peripheral brains. So was the smart phone on which he stored the list, so he'd always have it with him. That way, trying to remember the items wouldn't become an internal distraction.

CHECKLIST FOR EFFECTIVE EXECUTIVE HABITS

Think about an area of your life that you care about but is not going well because of lack of organization. Run through these questions to see if you have the necessary habits to organize yourself:

☐ **1.** Am I holding a clear vision of what I need to do in my mind? Do I have the steps broken down enough to "see" each one; are they written out, drawn out, talked through?

☐ **2.** Can I get information off my mind but accessible? (Write them on a list, or allocate tasks on a planner.)

☐ **3.** Is there a function that I can outsource? (Such as automated alarms for reminders, meeting-planning websites, smart recording pens . . .)

☐ **4.** Am I blocking out time each day for the priorities I need to accomplish?

☐ **5.** Do I have the right physical place—with the fewest alternate activities or least environmental noise—to get it done?

☐ **6.** Am I doing things at the best time? (Think of when you will have the energy and the tools you need.)

☐ **7.** What is going to really happen if I try this the way I am thinking? What problems might get in my way?

Tips for Finding Good "Systems"

A good system is one that provides planned habits for a moment that you are trying to manage. You want to be able to create a mantra for the moment—for example, "bills go here, not there," or "the reminder alarm means drop everything." But pick only one or two habits to practice at a time—put the energy in where it will count the most.

A good system is **ergonomic**—it fits your strengths and context. If you have to stand on a chair to reach the spot where you keep your checkbook, paying bills is probably going to take too much effort to become a routine.

A good system is **reviewed and improved**. Some people, for instance, need to have different strategies for when they get very busy; for holiday periods, when new priorities come up; or for winter versus for summer, as activities change.

Some people specialize in helping others figure out systems, and we cover how to make the most of their help in Chapter 11. The bottom line is that sometimes it takes working with someone else's perspective to come up with your best solutions. And always be prepared to go back and readjust. It's unlikely anyone would get these organizational strategies right the first time, so check in with yourself, a trusted friend, an organizer, or a coach after a few days and talk about what's working with the strategy and what needs to be tweaked.

We'll also talk more later in the book about what makes habits stick—the bottom line is that you can form new pathways in your brain through practice that makes essential habits more automatic.

Know your own abilities and what you can manage. One executive we know checks voice mail only twice a day and e-mail once a day—though his clients know how to reach him urgently. That way, there is a limit to how much new work he can create. Some days he can't follow this system, but because he makes it a habit, those days are the exception rather than the rule.

Overestimate—build in buffer time for the unexpected. Some people we work with always add fifteen minutes to any time allocation they make in their schedule; many successful executives have a set-aside time to manage the issue of the day. They may not be able to always protect it, but being your own executive means managing not only the predictable but the unpredictable.

Establish a system for managing paper, whether it's bills, work files, or schoolwork. This can be as simple as having a notebook with enough sections to fit class notes from every course subject. Of course, you need to always remember to use the first section for math, if that's what you've chosen, and the second for history, and so on. Mixing your notes from different classes is a prescription for lost notes and wasted time.

Create geographical habits. People learn in a "state-dependent" way—recalling memories and details better where they first encountered the information. Having a designated (and clear) spot for doing planning, for managing bills, or for working on a project takes advantage of this fact. A designated spot for bills, complete with envelopes and stamps, for example, also facilitates creating a routine.

Don't forget to throw things away. Part of a good organizational system is learning how to throw things out. People with ADHD frequently have a difficult time with this. Often the critical moment is a person saying to themselves, "I will be able to use this one day." So they keep it, even though they don't have a system for filing it effectively. The result can be spaces citable by the fire department. And truth be told, could you really find it if you needed it anyway?

Knowing why you keep things can help. A thought record can help here, writing down what you say to yourself about the idea of throwing the item out. If it is for emotional reasons, would scanning it or taking a picture serve that purpose? If it is to use later, how likely is that to happen? Can you be motivated by the opportunity to have more free space for something you like to do?

If you know what your challenges are, you can **fake yourself out:** Avert problems by anticipating them. Leaving things by the door for work can ensure that you will trip over them even if you don't remember them. If you're always losing your keys, make a few extra sets. If you are time-challenged, consider doubling your estimate of how long it will take you to get somewhere or complete a task. If you think the job will take you ten hours, leave yourself twenty; if you're certain the drive across town won't take you more than fifteen minutes, leave at least thirty. We know people who set their watch ahead a vague amount of time, or have two alarm clocks in their bedroom with different times—and intentionally fail to keep track of which is accurate.

Some of these methods for averting anticipated problems are better than others. If you know you're unlikely to sit down to pay bills more than once a month, then make sure to take care of all your current bills at the same time. It's far better to pay a few bills early than to incur charges for paying late. A college student we know was always losing pens, so he bought a twenty-pack of them and flung them all over his dorm room—messy, although he always had one nearby.

Evaluate your strategies for coping with critical organizational moments by asking yourself these questions to see if each one is high-yield enough to keep doing:

1. Is it easy to follow? Does it require just a few simple steps?

2. Does it play to your strengths (creativity, memory, desire for order, ability to think on your feet, etc.)?

3. Is there something that will keep you sticking to it other than desire (i.e., can it become a daily habit or is there someone who can check up on you to make sure you're continuing with it)?

In the rest of Part II, we help you further develop habits and strategies for living an organized and balanced life, starting with managing impulsive choices.

KEY POINTS

- Do a self-check for executive function challenges you have—memory, time, organization, setting priorities.

- What are the critical moments that contribute to disorganization?

- Can you outsource memory and organization effort to peripheral brains?

- Get a system that works for you and work it every day.

Don't Just Do It—Think About It!

U go stands impatiently at the doors to the subway car, waiting for them to open. The instant the gap is wide enough, he hurls himself through, sprints straight for the tiled wall, runs up, and flips over backward, landing on his feet. He slips back through the doors before the car takes off again.

A tall, wiry man-boy in his early twenties, Ugo also enjoys jumping off his parents' two-story roof, doing BMX bicycle stunts in a half-pipe, and hitching skateboard rides by hanging on to the bumper of passing cars. Ugo is an adrenaline junkie—and has the scars and hospital bills to prove it. As Ugo heads into a career as a machine operator in a factory, his mother worries that he will disregard safety rules and get himself in even bigger trouble.

Like many people with ADHD, Ugo is impulsive. He does things as soon as they occur to him, without thinking through their consequences. Impulsivity is one of the hallmarks of ADHD, and it can be both a blessing and a curse. People who are impulsive can be loads of fun to be around. There's no question that riding the subway with Ugo is more interesting than with just about anyone else. Impulsive people are also often propelled and driven and may accomplish surprising, novel things.

Zoe Kessler, an ADHD advocate, writer, and comedian (who asked us to use her real name here), is impulsive in a completely different way than Ugo. For her, the accident waiting to happen comes from her mouth. For years—decades even—she would feel the need to apologize for the overly blunt things she said, the friends she offended, the jokes she made at inopportune times.

Zoe says her impulsivity has also brought her just a step away from alcoholism several times, and she doesn't trust herself to keep liquor in the house. "If it's here, it's gone."

She has always lived on an emotional roller coaster. Even before she hit puberty, her mom would complain about her emotional ups and downs. Being a teenager was hell. "I'm the kind of person who could burst into tears at what would seem to be the tiniest of things," she says. She's also easily irritated and quick to get angry, particularly at other drivers who do stupid or annoying things. "I have to consciously tell myself to love my fellow humans."

But six years after her diagnosis with ADHD and start of treatment, she takes great pride in the progress she's made against her natural instincts. "The impulsive blurting is about ninety-five percent under control, which is *really cool*," she says.

FAST MINDS traits, including impulsivity, are due to biological differences in the system that helps people control their thoughts and behaviors and keep them in line with how they really want their daily life to go. Impulsive decisions and behaviors make sticking with a path particularly difficult—including attempts at developing the kinds of high-yield habits we discussed in the previous chapter. Of all the traits of ADHD, impulsivity can pose the biggest dangers. Lack of fore-thought compounds unhealthy habits, whether eating too much junk food, overspending, gambling, driving recklessly, experimenting with drugs, practicing risky sexual behavior, or stealing. It takes only a few poor choices to ruin a relationship, end a job, or cause a fatal car accident.

Ugo and Zoe didn't think much in those moments before jumping off the roof or blurting out an inconsiderate thought. They seemed to lack a pause button, leaping from idea to action with no time for reflection. Even without being as impulsive as Ugo and Zoe, many people with FAST MINDS seem to skip the "thinking through conse-quences" step before they act—a missed step that can cause a lot of pain to both people with FAST MINDS and those around them.

In this chapter, we explore how impulsivity can be transformed into conscious, controlled, thoughtful actions.

Why FAST MINDS Are Often Impulsive

It's crucial to distinguish between unconscious and willful capacities—the ability to inhibit impulses comes from both. Everyone has some unconscious capacity to limit impulsiveness, just as everyone has the capacity to filter out distraction or pay attention. But some people have less natural capacity than others. It is possible to use the con-scious mind to compensate for such an innate shortfall, but the bigger the gap between will and impulse, the harder it is to compensate. So people who naturally struggle to control impulsivity find it harder to use self-control to override impulsive instincts.

For most people, the urge to fire off an angry e-mail to the boss is tempered by consideration of the consequences. But for naturally im-pulsive people, who have a bigger gap between instinct and their pre-frontal cortex's ability to inhibit, it takes substantially more effort to engage this conscious override. Telling someone any version of "try harder" or "catch yourself before you do that next time" doesn't work, because so much of impulsivity is at the unconscious level.

ADHD medication can make some difference in impulsivity, allowing people to take a thought break in the moment. Yet even on medication, many people with FAST MINDS traits make decisions that have them falling off their planned path—to watch TV instead of going to bed, to socialize in the hallway instead of getting work done, to hit the Send or Reply All button on something they should have kept to themselves. Some people describe being able to hold both the right and the wrong choice in their mind, yet impulsively choose the wrong one anyway.

What looks like impulsive behavior on the outside is due to several different processes on the inside. Our brains are wired with "mental brakes"—which create what researchers call *response inhibition*, referring to the capacity to suppress immediate reactions and allow a choice among alternative reactions. This ability improves with age and development. The brain regions thought to be involved in impulsive physical behavior include the following:[1]

- the prefrontal cortex, which is believed to play a role in monitoring behavior and consequences

- the basal ganglia, an area involved in planned motor movement and rich in the neurotransmitter transporters that stimulants attach to

- the subthalamic nuclei, which may stop a premature response when there are multiple possible responses, thus allowing for better decision making

Just as the prefrontal cortex doesn't work as well when it's distracted or stressed, so, too, does emotion appear to limit decision making and the ability to inhibit actions.[2] We have seen a recent surge of scientific interest in the neurobiological connection between emotion and behavioral control, so hopefully we'll understand it better soon.

RECOGNIZING YOURSELF

Are you involved in any of the following impulsive activities? If so, how big a problem are they for you, on a scale from 1 to 5, with 5 being the worst?

- ☐ **1.** Are you impulsive with your decision making?
- ☐ **2.** Do you often speak before you think, cutting people off in conversation?
- ☐ **3.** Are you an impulsive spender?
- ☐ **4.** Do you binge on food, drugs, or alcohol?
- ☐ **5.** Is it hard to contain or control your emotional reactions?
- ☐ **6.** Do you make calls or send e-mails, texts, or photos impulsively?
- ☐ **7.** Do you drive rashly—cutting people off, cursing fellow drivers, making sudden decisions to change lanes or get off at a different exit?

Now ask someone close to you to answer the same questions about you and see if they highlight any issues you didn't. Do you think they may be right?

Think Before You Speak—or Text,
or E-mail, or Blog, or . . .

Impulsivity can be particularly distressing in communications. Talking more than necessary, saying things without thinking, and speaking out of turn are common patterns among people with FAST MINDS. Some describe this as lacking a filter. One person we know said, "In a meeting I keep telling myself to just listen, don't say anything. About once a month I really goof up and tell someone my opinion without being careful how I say it—it could be something that comes across as putting someone down—like saying that my colleague's idea will never work or telling someone I found their friend annoying before remembering they were friends. I've gotten used to apologizing."

And, of course, you don't have to be face to face with someone to have impulsive misfires—electronic communications have made writ-

Emotional Control

As we highlighted in Chapter 1, research, including work that Dr. Surman and colleagues have published in the *American Journal of Psychiatry*, has confirmed that at least half of all children and adults with ADHD have weaker control over their emotions.[3] Those they studied were quick to anger and got easily upset or excited. This poor emotional control seemed to travel in families, so a parent who often seemed angry or irritable often had a sibling with the same challenge. Emotional states such as anger, frustration, or dismay put people off balance, and a little bit of impulsivity leaves them saying things they later regret. Medication and the suggestions we're emphasizing in this chapter may reduce the emotional fuel behind some kinds of impulsivity.

ten and verbal impulsivity much easier and therefore more dangerous. An angry, thoughtless e-mail directed at a supervisor or colleague can mean big trouble at work; the same message at home can end relationships. Voice mail can be misused in the same way. Sexting—sending provocative pictures via text—can destroy relationships, reputations, and political careers.

Loose Steering—Jumping Around and "Multitasking"

Impulsivity also shows up as poor choice of engagement in activities, leading to a scattered pattern of action. We have already talked about the importance of being able to pause to choose—just as a driver would apply the brakes when approaching a fork in the road. Extending this metaphor, the steering in people with FAST MINDS is a little loose. It may not take much—a distracting idea, a person walking by, an outstanding bill—to send someone veering off course onto a new thought or activity. For many people with FAST MINDS traits, getting through daily life means making constant course corrections—regularly pausing and steering thoughtfully.

When we talk with people with FAST MINDS about how their days go, we often hear about an internal struggle to stick with one thing at a time in the face of distracting alternatives. People talk about heading for the fridge to put the milk away, only to see something else on the counter that should go in a cupboard and start to put that away, but then see their cell phone and remember a phone call they have to make. They may have to work hard to remember and complete their first intention of putting the milk away. The same pattern often rules on the desktops of people with impulsive traits—they have multiple browsers open, leave e-mails partially written, and abandon other items midtask. Their workflow is scattered with impulsive choices.

"Waiting for something to download is the worst," one video producer told us. "I can be off on other screens and not even recall what I was trying to download until an hour or more later, or not at all."

This pattern of inefficient choices and being easily sidetracked can apply to the actual roadway as well. Jumping out into traffic or last-second decisions about which way to go may lead to accidents and high insurance rates.

Unhealthy Habits

Taking good care of oneself requires suppressing urges all the time—the urge to eat more, to stay up later, to avoid exercising, to drink too much. Impulsivity often has its riskiest impact when combined with other mental health diagnoses. As we discussed in Chapter 2, one of the main variations on the theme of FAST MINDS traits and ADHD is the presence of additional conditions such as mood disorders, anxiety, and substance use.

We also mentioned Dr. Surman's research on the connection between ADHD and eating disorders. The higher risk of bulimia nervosa that he and other researchers have found in girls and women with ADHD is an example of how FAST MINDS traits may contribute to other serious burdens. One 2009 report on children with ADHD followed into adolescence found that a relatively high number of teenage girls developed bulimia—and those who did were more likely to have been impulsive as young children.[4] Other studies have found that impulsivity influences the severity of eating disorders.[5]

As Zoe's example suggests, impulsive, novelty-seeking behaviors may also be a risk factor for addictions. A strong connection exists between ADHD and substance abuse risk, as well as between impulsivity in childhood and risk for substance dependence in adolescence or adulthood. One study found that children with ADHD and executive function challenges who also had a mutation on a specific dopamine receptor gene were more likely to become alcoholics.[6] Furthermore, many people who are in recovery from substance abuse demonstrate higher rates of impulsivity. So the impulsivity may strike twice: when the person first gets involved with addictive substances, and then as the substance impairs their ability to control their own behavior.[7] It's as if a person is impulsive by nature, and then, by adding drugs and alcohol, is pouring gasoline on the fire.

In general, the combination of impulsivity and another mental health challenge can be particularly unhealthy—because it takes thoughtful effort and energy to work against depression, substance abuse, binge eating, and other compulsions. Although appropriate therapies exist for many of these mental health diagnoses and challenges, as we highlight in Chapter 11, it is important to understand whether patterns of impulsivity are contributing factors that need special attention.

RECOGNIZE THE IMPACT—WHAT WOULD OTHER PEOPLE SAY?

- ☐ In what ways would other people think you are impulsive?
- ☐ Do other people say you act without thinking?
- ☐ Do people find you unpredictable or have trouble relying on you?
- ☐ Do other people think that impulsive decision making has caused problems for you?
- ☐ Do other people think you are verbally impulsive and that you cut them off in conversations?
- ☐ Has impulsivity put you at risk physically, sexually, or financially?

UGO: A RANGE OF IMPULSIVE BEHAVIORS

Much of Ugo's impulsivity is the unconscious kind, but he also allows his life to be ruled by nearsighted thinking and his search for novelty. He is easily bored, including in relationships, and often abruptly drops girlfriends. Sexual impulsivity has led to two unplanned and unwanted pregnancies with two different girlfriends. He buys things impulsively—often without having the money to pay for them. He impulsively texts people and sometimes posts cell phone photos to the Web, and later regrets it.

Ugo's impulsive speeding and lane changes have contributed to several accidents and increased insurance rates. He likes to tap his right foot while he drives, listening to hip-hop, and his friends say the speed of the vehicle changes with the beat. Few of them will ride with him anymore because his driving makes them too nervous.

Ugo also binge drinks, and once he is drunk, he spends money he doesn't have, mainly on his friends. In school, Ugo always left his studying until late in the evening. If he got a call from a friend asking him to come down to the local pub, instead of resisting the impulse, he would invariably say, "Sure," and the studies would remain undone. When he drank alcohol, he became even more impulsive. One night, at a friend's house, he dove out a second-floor window straight into their pool. He narrowly missed the edge, because he couldn't see it in the dark. Another drunken night, he impulsively accepted a ride from some strangers and was attacked, sustaining serious injuries.

If Someone You Care About Has a FAST MIND

The best thing you can do is not to judge the person for their impulsiveness. They are not doing it on purpose; their biology makes it extremely hard for them to act any other way. That's why telling people to think before they act isn't useful. If they could, they would. Instead, try to get them interested in their own habits: "Have you noticed that you always go on a spending spree after being challenged by your boss?"

Offer to do some of the exercises in this chapter with them—acting as a resource to help them find more engaged ways of making a choice at a critical moment rather than following impulse. Impulsive actions are often nearsighted, novelty seeking, or emotional. If you can help the person practice seeing the big picture or defusing the emotion, you will help them tremendously.

To figure out whether impulsiveness is really a problem for your loved one, ask yourself the following questions:

- Do you often ask yourself, "What were they thinking?

- Do they interrupt or cut you off in conversation?

- Have impulsive decisions put them (or you) at risk physically, financially, or sexually?

- Are their emotional reactions intense or unexpected?

- Do they do things they regret?

WHAT YOU CAN DO

The self-help sections of these chapters are meant to build on each other, so we hope that as you read about working through impulsivity, you will keep in mind that knowing yourself and your priorities are still crucial, and that attention to the prefrontal checklist from Chapter 4 can help you stay in better mental control and less likely to act on impulse. Managing the "popcorn" thoughts by writing them down so you can act on them later can change impulsive ideas into plans: "Call Judy" becomes part of a list instead of spending half an hour speaking with her in the middle of a busy day.

So what else can you do to keep impulsivity under control where it matters? It may help to think of an unfolding day as a movie—a series of scenes. With experience, you can anticipate some scenes as ones where impulsivity is likely to have consequences. You can anticipate and plan for scenes where the stakes are high, such as discussions with someone you don't know well yet, e-mail communication with a demanding boss, or meetings with important clients. Those scenes will take extra planning or effort to ensure that your will overrides your impulse; we suggest you think of a mental pause button as one solution. With some anticipation, you are more likely to say, "I'm going to let that idea go and see if I still want to do that after a pause."

Medication may make pausing much easier. Emerging evidence shows that capacities for self-control can be harnessed through mindfulness and other mental-awareness or mind-body practices, which we discuss in Chapter 11. Exercise can also be effective for burning off extra energy that can otherwise manifest itself in daredevil jumps or impulsive actions. Plus, a workout is a good time to think through decisions you have to make or to plan the rest of your day.

In the previous chapter, we introduced the idea that there are critical moments where new habits can lead to better life organization. We find that there are three major kinds of impulsive critical moments:

Emotional decision making: Strong moods can distort anyone's ability to make decisions.

Nearsighted thinking: Focusing on the immediate leads to an unplanned life.

Novelty seeking: Always chasing the new shiny thing may offer a temporary rush, but it can also ruin relationships and careers.

Letting these three horsemen rule your decisions means traveling into emotional, unsustainable, and risky contexts.

Planning is the antidote to all three. Someone with an overly critical colleague might plan their next presentation with that colleague's complaints in mind, anticipating and preempting most concerns. Getting out ahead of the problem by preparing well and anticipating challenges helps defuse emotion. Planning ahead can overcome nearsighted thinking and help people keep their larger goals in mind, instead of following the next shiny thing that comes along.

THOUGHT RECORD

Using a thought record[8] can help you recognize the types of critical moments that can get you off track. We introduced thought records in Chapter 3, and a blank one can be copied from Appendix B. Here, we add some elements specific to impulsivity to the thought record. First review the three categories of impulsivity with a distressing situation in mind:

- **Emotional decision making:** Would you make a different decision if you were not feeling so strongly?

- **Nearsighted thinking:** Because the quickest, easiest, most reflexive path is often one that is not fully envisioned, ask yourself, would the choice seem as good if you could fast-forward the outcome in your mind?

- **Novelty seeking:** Are you chasing something shiny? Would you make a different decision if you paused to consider what you truly care about, all the roles and obligations you already have?

Look back at the issues you said in Chapter 1 were most important for you, and choose one where impulsivity has been getting in your way. Or think of a recent time when you seriously regretted your actions. Write down a quick **summary** of the situation and when it happened.

_____

_____

_____

_____

_____

Now try to remember what was going through your head as you impulsively chose to do this thing—were you thinking about getting even, or how much you wanted that new toy, or what a jerk your boss was? There may have been a trigger that set you off emotionally. If so, write it down.

TRIGGER:

_____

_____

Catalog your mood and how intense it was. On a scale of 1 to 10, were you angry enough to hit an 11? Were you feeling insecure about your looks? Did your boss just compliment a colleague, which made you feel left out and unrecognized?

INTENSITY (1–10): _____

Note whether any of the three *styles* of impulsivity—emotional decision making, nearsighted thinking, or novelty seeking—were contributing to how you were making the decision.

We introduced the idea of thinking errors in Chapter 3. Here we expand the list of types of thinking errors, because they often underlie impulsive thinking and communication. Most (but not all) negative thoughts fall into a category of thinking error. For example, sometimes your boss really is being a jerk, and your harsh response is appropriate; a "thinking error" is when you assume she is being mean without weighing the evidence. Here are some classic thinking errors:

All-or-nothing thinking: You say to yourself that every aspect of a project has to be finished perfectly and immediately or you're a complete failure.

Overgeneralizations: You see a single negative event as part of a never-ending pattern. Because your boss got annoyed at you once, you assume she hates you.

Disqualifying the positive: You disregard every compliment you ever got but dwell endlessly on every slight or criticism.

Jumping to conclusions or mind reading: You assume your boss doesn't like you because he complimented your colleague and not you.

Magnification or minimization: You exaggerate the importance of problems, such as a modest mistake, or minimize things such as your own strengths.

Catastrophizing: You predict horrible consequences for minor infractions, assuming, for instance, that every tiny mistake will lead to your getting fired.

Emotional reasoning: You assume that your negative feelings reflect reality—if you don't like yourself, you assume everyone else thinks you are unlikeable, too.

Personalization: You see negative events as indicative of a personal failing. A company downsizing seems aimed directly at you and not the result of a lousy economy or a poor business plan.

Note here which of these **"thinking errors"** compounded the situation, rather than defusing it.

_____

_____

_____

_____

_____

Now, in the thought record you are creating in these pages, write down a **more rational, less emotional response** that you can keep in mind for the next similar situation.

_____

_____

_____

_____

Instead of responding to your boss in anger, maybe a more rational response would have been to delay answering until you had thought about it for twenty-four hours. If your impulsivity problem relates to buying clothing or electronic toys, you could decide to wait until your birthday to buy the latest design, ask a parent or spouse to give it to you for your birthday, or set up a hard-and-fast rule that you can't buy anything worth more than $100 without sleeping on it for at least one night. Leaving credit cards at home and limiting yourself to one at a time may hold you more accountable, too.

Rather than upsetting a key player at your job, you might take the time to consider how hard it will be to find another job of similar pay, quality, and status (or whatever is important to you); detail the pros and cons of your current position; and try to figure out another solution that is consistent with how you value your position. Here, your ADHD creativity may come in handy.

SAMPLE THOUGHT RECORD:
#1:

Brief description of the situation
Chased down another driver on the road, screaming and barely avoiding an accident

Context: When, where, how did it happen? What were the triggers?
He cut me off and made me have to slam on the brakes, which was scary.

How intense are your thoughts and feelings as you imagine the situation again (1 to 10)?
10

Irrational forces at play (Emotional decision making? Nearsighted thinking? Novelty seeking?)
Emotional, nearsighted decision making

Did you make any thinking errors? Which one(s) (All-or-nothing, catastrophizing, personalization, etc.)?

Personalization—"He did that to me on purpose."

Describe a more rational thought and response to the situation. Was it part of a pattern to work on?

Other drivers often do unsafe things. I could have decided he was a careless driver and then turned the radio on to calm myself down and think about something else.

Did you drain out some of the emotion? Think now of how intense your unproductive emotional thoughts are as you think of the situation. Rate them from 1 to 10.

6

#2:

Brief description of the situation

Spent $400 I didn't have on an outfit

Context: When, where, how did it happen? What were the triggers?

On the way home from a bad day at work, I passed a store and was tempted.

How intense are your thoughts and feelings as you imagine the situation again (1 to 10)?

7

Irrational forces at play (Emotional decision making? Nearsighted thinking? Novelty seeking?)

Emotional, nearsighted, novelty seeking

Did you make any thinking errors? Which one(s) (All-or-nothing, catastrophizing, personalization, etc.)?

Emotional reasoning: I thought I was a lousy person and that I looked shabby.

Describe a more rational thought and response to the situation. Was it part of a pattern to work on?

I react this way a lot. I could have noticed that I often feel poorly about myself at certain times of the month and/or after having a hard day at work, and thought of other ways to spend or save the money.

Did you drain out some of the emotion? Think now of how intense your unproductive emotional thoughts are as you think of the situation. Rate them from 1 to 10.

4

#3:

Brief description of the situation

Upset my boss by denying his request rudely

Context: When, where, how did it happen? What were the triggers?

In the middle of a busy day, he asked me to do something he knows how to do himself.

How intense are your thoughts and feelings as you imagine the situation again (1 to 10)?

6

Irrational forces at play (Emotional decision making? Nearsighted thinking? Novelty seeking?)

Emotional, nearsighted

Did you make any thinking errors? Which one(s) (All-or-nothing, catastrophizing, personalization, etc.)?

Magnification—it really was a small request, but my emotional thinking made it into a mountain.

Describe a more rational thought and response to the situation. Was it part of a pattern to work on?

> *My boss and I often don't see eye to eye. I could have asked for a moment to respond more calmly, and explained to him that midday requests like that really reduce my productivity.*

Did you drain out some of the emotion? Think now of how intense your unproductive emotional thoughts are as you think of the situation. Rate them from 1 to 10.

> *3*

ZOE: LEARNING TO PAUSE

Zoe Kessler says she still needs to work on learning to say no when someone asks her to do something. She recently agreed to work extra shifts at her part-time job at a time when she'd planned time off to write a book. "My employer said we really need everyone, and I'm like, 'Okay'—and why? There goes my two-week writing retreat. I literally feel sick about it. I should've said no," she says.

She didn't say no because she was using emotional reasoning. As a child, she "was seen to be this bad girl acting out all the time," she says. "My self-esteem was so pummeled that even at fifty-two, I'm trying to please people and be a good girl and be a frigging saint."

Zoe has greatly improved her "nearsighted" impulsivity, though, since her ADHD diagnosis six years ago. She's figured out how to insert a small pause between the thought popping into her head and blurting out of her mouth—a pause long enough for her to consider whether it's really a good idea to say that.

She realized long ago that the impulsive comments she made didn't always land the way they were intended. "I might do something and someone might look at me with horror or fear—obviously there was a disconnect," she says. But she didn't know what the disconnect was about or that she had any control over that moment. "My reaction would be 'Oh my God, I screwed up again!' Then I would start with the self-flagellation and the whole downward cycle. I would get anxious and nervous, and the potential for digging myself in deeper would really be ramped up."

Now Zoe takes medication and is also consciously aware of the need for a pause and the need to consider the consequences of her words. She coaches herself through these dangerous moments. Each time she avoids saying something that could get her into trouble, she mentally pats herself on the back and gains confidence that she'll be able to do it again. "It's practice, and all those things that everybody already knows but that are so so important. If I don't have a good night's sleep, it's going to be a lot more difficult to stay on top of it and manage behaviors. Good food, good sleep, happy frame of mind."

She was anxious when she first started medication that it would take off her edge, that she'd lose her funny thoughts and turn into a boring person. But that's not what happened.

"The creativity still bubbles up and now I can catch those creative bubbles and grab them and go with more of the ideas, because I'm not as scattered or as disorganized. I'm organized enough to actually take an idea and run with it and write a blog post or put it in my stand-up comedy piece, whereas before, I was just too overwhelmed and couldn't really bring anything to term."

And that's the best part for Zoe of gaining control over her impulsivity: She can make great use of its good side.

"Now, my risk taking is by choice, which is really exciting because I am a renegade," she says. "I like being eccentric. I like putting stuff out there."

USING THE PAUSE BUTTON

There are many ways to build in pauses or make good use of them before letting a scene unfold impulsively. If practiced over time, choices can become habits. We talk more about developing new patterns in the next chapters. If you have a predictable or avoidable critical moment of impulsivity, think whether the following habits will help you pause and make more engaged choices:

■ Avoid the trigger! If possible make barriers between you and whatever is your downfall. For instance, don't keep all your snacks in the kitchen; keep some farther away, such as in the basement; or avoid buying junk food altogether. Don't use wireless at home; plug in only for Internet service, so it's slower and harder to get online, giving you time to question whether you really should be surfing so late at night.

■ Delay the choice until a better time when you can effectively engage your prefrontal cortex.

■ Plan a distraction to get you laughing instead of screaming. We know someone who keeps a silly rubber clown doll in his car, which he waves in frustration when people do stupid or annoying things on the road, without the other driver noticing. He usually ends up smiling at himself instead of cursing the other guy.

■ Make the decision in a more engaged, more rational way. Some suggestions for doing that:
   Fill out a thought record.
   Talk it over with someone or imagine what they would say.
   Write a pro-con list to lay out the choice rationally.
   If you're a visual thinker, try drawing out the different possibilities.

Invent a game to help you make the decision. Track it, score it, collaborate with others on it, or make it into a joke.

Consider whether you would make a different decision on a different day—for instance, when you are better rested, in a better mood, or less restless.

STRATEGIES FOR COMMON IMPULSIVE SCENES

Here are examples of how some people have dealt with different types of impulsivity by incorporating the preceding suggestions. You will likely have better ideas for helping yourself—our goal here is not to tell you what to do but to prime the pump, to give you a starting place for coming up with plans that work for you.

Your goal in all of these strategies should be to buy yourself some lead time—a pause so you can think and be in control of the next scene of your day.

It is vital to notice when impulsive actions happen and what is behind them—are they emotional, nearsighted, or novelty-seeking. Then you can break the pattern by replacing it with a new, more constructive habit. This probably won't be easy, particularly at first. That's okay. Give yourself permission to take some time to practice and learn new habits. If you launch into another spending binge but stop after charging only $200 instead of a larger sum, that might be a major victory for you. Celebrate it—but *not* by buying yourself a present!

THOUGHTFUL COMMUNICATION: If this is a problem for you, you may want to set up some rules about how long to wait before you decide how to communicate. You may also want to make sure you compose your communication—such as by sending a well-considered e-mail rather than calling someone, or by sending a handwritten note rather than a text or e-mail. Often it's easier to understand someone's meaning when you're speaking face to face. Instead of firing off an e-mail, consider walking down the hall to have a conversation.

TOUGH DECISIONS: For major decisions, you may want to institute a policy, such as having a friend or family member review your pro-con list. Then prohibit yourself from making a decision until you've had time to talk it over with them.

MANAGING IMPATIENCE: If you can predict a period of frustration where you will get impatient, such as waiting in a doctor's office, pack things to occupy yourself (and your child). Bring your MP3 player and some music that calms you down, an e-reader, games on your smart phone, or a list of phone calls you can make anywhere.

UNHEALTHY HABITS: There are unhealthy choices, such as eating an extra piece of candy, and then there are *really* unhealthy ones. People with addictions, alcoholism, and eating disorders should absolutely prioritize getting support specifically for their habit.

IMPULSIVE SPENDING: Making only a week's worth of cash available at a time works for some people, as does leaving credit cards at home or setting rules such as requiring a twenty-four-hour waiting period before any purchase over $100. Planning an alternative behavior, such as taking pictures of what you want to buy, and talking about it with friends first or researching the product online can help reduce

---

Avoiding Impulsive Choices

- What critical moments of impulsivity can I anticipate?

- Might novelty seeking, emotionality, or lack of foresight get in the way?

- What thinking errors am I at risk for?

- What rational attitudes or responses can I practice ahead of time?

- What habits can I practice for pausing and making a good choice?

a habitual buying reflex. Some friends will encourage restraint; others will encourage you to buy more than you can afford and aren't the best ones to consult. Considering the contribution of moods and emotions, as we note in the preceding thought record example, can also help you see how this and many other patterns can have their roots in emotional distress.

CRITICAL IMPULSIVE MOMENTS AND HABITS LIST

List some of the recent critical moments that you have thought about as you worked through this chapter:

_____

_____

_____

Which of the kinds of habits discussed, or others you can think of, would help you stay in control and choose better in these moments?

_____

_____

_____

KEY POINTS

- Impulsivity is common among people with FAST MINDS traits.

- Know your impulsive risks (communication; spending money; bingeing on alcohol, drugs, or food; sexual activity; driving).

- Consider how emotional thinking may fuel your impulsive choices.

- Practice habits that allow you to pause and make better decisions. Don't just do it—think about it.

Find Where and How You Thrive

When Holly was a freshman in high school, her mother was called in for a conference: "Your daughter is not university material," the guidance counselor said. "We'll do what we can to get her through the rest of high school, but her future will be limited." Holly's mother told her what the guidance counselor said, and Holly took it to heart, assuming she wasn't smart. Still, she managed to get through high school and into college, where her grades were all over the map—as low as a D and as high as an A+.

As Holly struggled through a master's program in psychology, another counselor recommended that she get an IQ test. Her scores were so high that she qualified for Mensa, an international society for people who rank in the top 2 percent on intelligence tests. "When I learned I wasn't dumb as a stick, well, it was a shock," she said. "All this time, I thought I was stupid, so I mostly kept my mouth shut and kept to myself. I never asked any questions because I thought then everyone would know how dumb I really was. But now? I'm asking a whole bunch of questions."

Holly had focused her master's degree on learning how people learn. After getting her scores, she decided to use her academic training on herself. She figured out she had FAST MINDS traits and needed to keep herself busy to stay engaged. Being busy also provided her the structure she needed—a lot to do and a limited time to get things done. Now she has a full-time job, she is pursuing her Ph.D., and she coaches people with ADHD on the side. "The best thing you can give someone with a very busy mind is more and more structure, a shorter leash," she says. "It's not telling them what to do, but helping them make informed choices about what they do."

She also learned to be more understanding of herself, and to teach her clients to do the same for themselves. "It's not about being a Pollyanna or blowing plastic sunshine," she says in her characteristically blunt way, "but genuinely recognizing strengths and challenges and finding the most appropriate environment. It's about going *with* the current rather than against."

———————

The people we know who function best with FAST MINDS are those who have figured out where they fit in the world. They know what they're capable of, and they put themselves in environments where they can thrive—environments where it is easier to practice and stick with the adaptive strategies that we present in this book. A helpful environment supports personal strengths and assists in tackling challenges, fosters useful habits, and makes staying on course remarkably easier.

Elusive Habits

Time and again people tell us their lives are off track, their goals unfulfilled, their New Year's resolutions left behind on January 2. As we emphasized in Chapter 1, FAST MINDS traits can make it harder to adopt or keep up with habits, even ones people know would help.

Take the dishes. Some people (mainly those *without* ADHD) are in the habit of washing the dishes every night right after dinner. They reason that doing the dishes will be harder if the food dries, and they prefer to get the chore out of the way. To them, it's straightforward: There is no other option but to wash the dishes. Some people with FAST MINDS also quickly adopt that "there's no other option" approach. But for others, there are too many distractions in the moment and too few rewards for getting the dishes done. "Why bother with these couple of dishes?" they think. "I'll just wait till the whole sink is full, which will be more efficient." By the time they consider the dishes again, every plate, bowl, and fork in the house is dirty, and many have caked-on food, which is much harder to get clean. This is just one example of how people who don't naturally assume organizational habits can unintentionally make life harder for themselves.

Not having organizational habits means it takes an extra effort to do every task. It's not much of a challenge to remember to brush your teeth when it's an ingrained routine every morning and before going to sleep. It doesn't take up much decision-making or mental energy. But when something isn't a habit, people need to expend more effort to remember to do it and to get it done. As this chapter explains, following key principles makes better habits easier to learn.

Staying on the Road: The Importance of Habits and the Right Kind of Stimulation

Learning to drive is extremely difficult at first: remembering to check mirrors, figuring out the amount of foot pressure needed to accelerate or slow down. Which side is the turn signal on again? But after a while, driving becomes second nature. It would be unusual to have to think "up for left, down for right" when moving the turn signal; in fact, it's hard to even consciously remember how turn signals work—you just "know."

Young-adult drivers don't have these routines down yet, and it may be part of why driving is more dangerous in young adulthood—particularly for young adults with ADHD. But the higher risk for car accidents among adults with ADHD appears to be related to their difficulty maintaining vigilance and their mental wandering. In 2007, Dr. Surman contributed to a study with colleagues at Massachusetts General Hospital and the Massachusetts Institute of Technology in which the researchers put young adults with and without ADHD into a driving simulator.[1] Along long empty boring stretches, those with ADHD were more likely to crash.

How ADHD drivers respond to boring driving shows the critical differences between productive and unproductive ways of managing boring conditions—both on and off the road. Data demonstrate that those with ADHD are better drivers when they use manual transmission rather than automatic,[2] which is consistent with our strong impression that people with FAST MINDS traits do better when an activity is involving and engaging. Alternately, people find stimulation on the road in less safe ways, such as driving at high speeds, taking curves aggressively, crowding the car in front, driving with knees, or driving while talking, texting, or eating. What is keeping the driver engaged has little to do with safe driving—and often quite the opposite. Filling a car with stimulation is now even easier, with TVs, DVD systems, GPS, Bluetooth technology, and so forth, making it even more dangerous.

Developing routines and finding ways to make tasks and challenges more stimulating or interesting are keys not only for driving, but for building relationships, knowledge, and a career. People with fewer organizational habits often thrive by taking on stimulating activities in organized environments that hold them accountable. Where they need to, they keep routines and accountability in place to stay on a more organized path.

RECOGNIZING YOURSELF

- ☐ Is it hard to stick with resolutions and organizational strategies?
- ☐ Is it hard for you to delegate tasks to others?
- ☐ Does your work lack meaning?
- ☐ Do you spend time doing pleasurable things when you should be getting work done?
- ☐ Do you come up with new ideas, projects, and hobbies instead of developing skills or mastering old ones?
- ☐ Do you "go it alone" instead of asking for help?

Rewards and the ADHD Brain

Everyone's brain is primed to recognize rewards and to keep them in mind for a time. The further into the future the reward is expected, the harder it is to focus on that goal. Impulsivity happens when the brain prefers short-term rewards over larger, longer-term rewards.[3] Adults with ADHD have even more trouble hanging on to future rewards than those without ADHD, research suggests. One neurobiological explanation for this may involve a key part of the brain's engagement circuit, which we introduced in Chapter 2, as being important for forming habits—the basal ganglia. Brain scans of people with ADHD show less activity than expected during a task that offered a long-term financial reward, suggesting that differences in this region may explain FAST MINDS nearsightedness in decision-making.[4] This difference can have a profound effect over time. Making good choices about what to eat, for example, requires holding the long-term rewards of a good diet in mind—so trouble with farsightedness can mean eating too many unhealthy things. Or this nearsightedness may lead someone to hang out with their friends instead of working on assignments due later in the week. In one famous study of the implications of farsighted decision making, young children were given a marshmallow and told that they could eat it now or resist temptation for a few minutes and be given a second one. Later in life, those able to delay gratification were shown to have higher academic and social achievement.[5]

Many people keep rewards in mind when they have to do an odious task. Doing the dishes after a friend cooks a nice meal is a way to return the favor and encourage them to do it again. The long-term reward is a peaceful, mutually supportive relationship. Listening to a spouse or child talk about their day despite being tired has the same reward. Grades are an important motivator for most students; with creative teachers and interesting material, the sheer joy of knowledge can be a great reward. At work there are formal rewards such as pay increases and promotions but also the small daily rewards that are probably more important, such as a co-worker's compliment, the satisfaction of solving a tricky problem, or simply doing something well. These can all encourage people to do their best and also reinforce positive behavior.

If it's harder to keep the rewards for activities in mind, people are less likely to engage in them. Why bother working on a report due in a month when any reward is that far off? Why bother to try consistently on schoolwork if you don't have a clear picture of the career that school is leading you to? FAST MINDS symptoms also reduce how often efforts are rewarded. When the student with ADHD works hard but loses many points through careless mistakes on an exam, that gives them a negative experience, not a reward.

JOHN: FINDING THE RIGHT HABITAT

John got a job as a graphic designer after graduating from college and immediately found himself struggling. "I was just left to do my own thing there," he says. "It was such a change from college—working on my own, no meetings, no collaboration—just an e-mailed assignment and a cubicle to complete it in." His productivity and sense of accomplishment started to drift downward. He began showing up later in the morning, calling in sick more often, and feeling more anxious about deadlines he'd left to the last minute.

His girlfriend noticed John's slide and called him on it. She helped him think through his options—should he try to change his attitude, angle for a new job in the same firm, move on? After a few weeks of deliberating, he decided to look for another job, and he was lucky enough to find one quickly. Working at his new firm was immediately better. Projects were well defined, deadlines were clear, and there was enough teamwork and peer interaction that he never felt he was in it alone. His work was respected and his creativity frequently complimented. Because they were a team, John could volunteer for tasks he knew he could do well and lay low when chores he didn't find engaging were being assigned. John couldn't show up late or get sidetracked for long without feeling like he was letting down someone he respected—and he rose to the occasion. "Here, I am a part of the meetings. They ask my opinion," he says. "Sure, I still have to do some tough assignments with long hours, but we like working together, and I want to put in that extra effort."

John is now the lead designer of a small group at his firm, a rank he feels he would never have reached with his previous employer. The "right" fit wasn't just about finding a job that suited John's skill set but finding one that helped him stay engaged, rewarded, and motivated. "It took me a bit longer to grow up, and I know I have to keep my goals clear," he says. "I won't go back to coming across as not caring, not following through, because I owe more to myself, and to the people I love working with now."

RECOGNIZE THE IMPACT

- ☐ Would other people say that you get bored easily (hobbies, school, work, relationships, etc.)?
- ☐ Would other people say that you are inconsistent in your everyday life (school, habits, activities of daily living)?
- ☐ Would you want to rely on yourself as a key member of a team that worked on a tight timeline?
- ☐ Have other people noticed that you are attracted to stimulating, new experiences and avoid the tedious stuff?
- ☐ Do other people think that inconsistency and boredom has created stress in their relationship with you?

Create Your Own Structure

In previous chapters we have explored habits for adapting to FAST MINDS traits and the importance of identifying critical moments when taming impulses and making good choices lead to more productive paths. This chapter acknowledges that sticking with good habits at critical moments is much easier in the right environment—one that complements your strengths and addresses your challenges and gives you accountability. We call such organizing, supportive elements of the environment *structure*.

Adding structure can make a big difference in ADHD, but it can be a challenge to create or maintain it yourself. It's often easier to have someone else establish and reinforce the structure than to set one up on your own. Military service certainly offers a more structured experience than the average job, for example, and some people, once used to that kind of structure, can adopt it as their own and thrive. Other people with FAST MINDS don't do well in environments where they are micromanaged. For them, like John, working on a team may be a useful structure, making each member accountable to the others and allowing people to figure out their own way of getting their part done, focusing on areas where they excel and handing off assignments that aren't a good match.

There are obviously different kinds of structure. We think the kind that works best is whichever naturally motivates you, holds you accountable, and provides support for the things you don't do well. This support can help you have a clear path for progress and can even provide a source of meaning, inspiration, or energy when times get tough; it can help steer you toward success.

A good place to start is to remember what has helped you stick with difficult things in the past, whether that was graduating from high school, maintaining a relationship, pursuing a passion, or succeeding in a job. Those things were probably important to you because they had meaning. Maybe you stuck with high school because it meant so much to your mother; you stayed in a relationship because the two of you were happy together and brought out the best in each other; your enthusiasm for a hobby was contagious, rallying other people who then kept you motivated; you thrived in a work environment that respected what you had to offer and didn't mind your shortcomings, and so on.

It may seem to be the opposite of structure, but sometimes varying a habit, as long as it keeps accomplishing the same purpose, is the key to keeping it going. We know people who have expensive ways of doing this, such as buying new electronic gadgets every few months to keep repetitive tasks such as using a calendar and reminder system interesting. There are also less expensive ways, such as adding a new colleague to project meetings to encourage fresh ways of thinking.

Whatever structure helps you practice good habits and stay off less productive default paths is the best one. Just remember, structure should play to your strengths, support your challenges, and provide

If Someone You Care About Has a FAST MIND

You can be helpful to someone with ADHD by helping them develop structures that support their strengths and compensate for their challenges.

- Do they often lose sight of rewards at the end of a task?

- Can you help them identify where they have trouble practicing and sticking with useful strategies?

- Can you help them identify what helped them practice new skills in the past, and how that structure could apply?

- Do they have ideas about how you or other people could be involved in helping them monitor or be accountable in their practice of new strategies?

- Do you think they are in the right environment, have the right people to help them, or are even in the right career? If not, can you help them realize changes to create a better fit?

the accountability you need to keep you on track. And it's okay to vary the elements of structure over time—as long as they work for you.

What You Can Do

The rest of this chapter introduces principles for adding useful structure to your life. We're *not* suggesting that you try all of these at once; instead, think of these as options in a toolkit. When there's a lot at stake and you really need to motivate yourself, setting a deadline may be the best approach—but deadlines usually don't work as daily motivators.

Your goal should not be to live the military lifestyle, with every minute accounted for all day long. In fact, we think it's probably healthier for people to have some unstructured downtime every day. We suggest that you pick a few habits that foster constructive environments or patterns—such as having planning time with colleagues or family, using a calendar, keeping your wallet and keys in a set place, or making time to hear about your spouse's day. Whatever is high-yield for you is the best thing to do. We also explain some strategies for turning these goals into habits and then for holding yourself accountable for those changes so that this year's resolutions don't become next year's regrets.

REWARD YOURSELF OFTEN

Everyone needs to feel rewarded for a job well done or a task completed. With FAST MINDS, it is even more useful to provide rewards for effort. If you love video games, let that be your reward for an hour every evening—but only after you've done the dishes or listened to your family members talk about their day, or made significant progress in some project that needs to get done. If, in the middle of a task, you find yourself getting bored with it, remind yourself of the reward to come as soon as you're finished.

Daily rewards shouldn't be expensive, just little things that make you happier, such as listening to your favorite music, taking a bubble bath, or playing with your dog. For really difficult tasks—such as taxes—give yourself a bigger reward or outsource this task. It can be helpful to brainstorm a bunch of possible rewards at once, so you don't have to think one up every time you want to reward yourself. When they start to get stale, simply have another brainstorming session and add more.

Write down a few rewards now to get yourself started:

_____

_____

_____

_____

_____

FORMING NEW HABITS

When parents remind their children twice a day to brush their teeth, they are teaching the child a habit—they are the child's peripheral brain and accountability system, until tooth brushing becomes routine. When learning to drive, the instructor, plus fear of crashing, do the same thing. Some people don't need peripheral brains to establish habits—they just need to tell themselves to do something for a few days, and the habit is somehow seared into their brain. These are the people who remember to take all ten days' worth of antibiotics, or who never need a reminder about a weekly meeting. For everyone else, the best way to form a habit is through consistent **practice**, and here we discuss two allies of practice: **peripheral brains** and **accountability**.

Writing a scheduled meeting on your calendar is a good way to remember where you need to be, but even better is a calendar system on your computer or handheld electronic device that flashes a reminder or sounds an alarm ten minutes before the meeting. For some, the best reminder would be the colleague who swings by your desk en route to the meeting or who reminds you to prepare for it. As the reminders come, week after week, the more likely it is the meeting will become a habit. Then getting there won't take effort anymore, just as turning on your car's turn signal doesn't require conscious thought. Monday morning will simply equal "meeting" in your mind.

As we discussed in Chapter 5, a peripheral brain is something or someone outside yourself who can help you with everyday functioning, especially in areas that are most challenging. The peripheral brain augments and helps. Other people and gadgets can help you out, both with tasks that are extremely difficult for you and by measuring your progress as you work on a new habit. Set an alarm reminder, put a note on your calendar, create a meeting with a coworker or your loved one.

Maybe you and your partner could both decide to make the half hour after dinner cleanup time. You can put on some mutually agreeable music and both wash, mop, scrub, and vacuum, dividing the work according to preferences, skills, or this week's job chart. For a work meeting, make it a mutually useful process by setting an agenda, giving time for all of you to speak, and explaining progress toward important goals.

A number of people who participated in a CBT trial that Dr. Surman contributed to said the most important part of the study for them was having someone to work with—to hold them accountable. You don't need to be a research subject to find people who can be your peripheral brain, holding you responsible for things you've said are important to you.

Sometimes a peripheral brain, such as a life coach or an administrative assistant, can provide accountability. Make sure if you're hiring a coach that it's someone with whom you feel comfortable and someone who will focus on your strengths instead of always telling you all the things you did wrong.

Think back on the three areas you identified in Chapter 1 or similar situations that you want to flow better in your life. List three habits that would make that more likely to happen. For each, come up with a peripheral brain reminder—an interaction with a person or a physical reminder—that could help you develop that habit.

For example, you might note stopping work and leaving for a weekly meeting as a habit that would help you be on time and a fifteen-minute warning on your electronic calendar as a reminder.

HABIT   **REMINDER**

_____   _____

_____   _____

_____   _____

_____   _____

_____   _____

_____   _____

Think about the times you have been successful. There was probably something holding you accountable: a favorite teacher you wanted to please, a friend checking in on you to make sure you were on track, or maybe what the event or situation meant to you.

We have changed the old saying to "You can lead a horse to water, but you can't make him *think*." Even in the best environment, it still takes something inside to do mentally difficult tasks. If a task is onerous or boring, someone with ADHD can find it especially difficult to complete. *Wanting* to do it can help immensely. That is why we try to help people understand that clearly identifying the **meaning** of the activity they are trying to incorporate into their life. We encourage them to look at the bigger picture and keep their ultimate goal in mind, to hold themselves accountable to it.

Having a conscious notion of a larger goal can make a dramatic difference in your motivation, patience, and determination. Some things, in their mundane drudgery, may be harder to see as meaningful. But next time you have to do the laundry, try thinking about how hard you've worked to be able to afford these clothes, and how important it is for you to be seen as a capable, put-together person. Those clothes are not just dirty wads of fabric; they're a potent symbol of your success and the image you and your family members project to the world. When your attention starts to drift, reminding yourself of this larger aim can help keep you from going too far away.

Make your motivation explicit. If there's a habit you really want to stick with, note your motivation on your calendar or pin it over your computer monitor. Share your motive with someone you trust, to make it more real, and enlist their help with the mission.

Some people we know explicitly carve out times in their schedule for each important role they play or goal in their life. They may turn off all their electronic devices in the evenings, or between six P.M. Friday and nine A.M. Monday, for instance, to focus on family time.

They may set aside one lunchtime a week to handle household chores such as calling the electrician or scheduling an oil change. They may designate one evening a week for a poker game, a knitting circle, or a volunteer effort.

Think about what is most meaningful to you in each of your life's major roles. Are you hoping to live more healthily? Be a better friend or partner? As a parent, are you hoping to raise independent, self-sufficient, intelligent kids? Do you want a fulfilling job where everyone's work is well respected? Or will you put up with some craziness as long as the money and hours are good enough to allow you to pursue your true extracurricular passions? Articulate those deeper goals here—and maybe pin them on your office wall or desktop, so you'll have them easily accessible.

Again, note three habits you want to form and think about the deeper meaning or goal of this activity.

HABIT   **MEANING**

_____   _____

_____   _____

_____   _____

_____   _____

_____   _____

If you are having trouble finding meaning that is significant enough to motivate you, perhaps you need to create your own meaning by connecting a reward to each step of an activity. For instance, finishing the next step in a difficult assignment means you can then treat yourself to a fancy coffee from the coffee shop.

In many elementary classrooms, the day's schedule is posted every morning. Any time children start to get distracted, they can look up at the schedule and know instantly how long they have to wait until recess, math, or dismissal. The schedule makes the day's events more concrete and helps the child literally see the rewards that are coming. If there's something they are not enjoying, a glance at the schedule can help them have something to look forward to.

Some people look over their tasks for the upcoming day and schedule breaks, or other tasks that are more rewarding or at least more comfortable, after a chunk of harder work. It can also help to know that if work is done, you will allow yourself to do things such as checking favorite websites or e-mail. If impulses for pleasurable or lower-priority activities pop into mind, the strategy we described of writing down these "popcorn" thoughts can help defer them to a time when the reward is earned.

The rewards and breaks you give yourself will keep you on track if you use them when you have finished a meaningful step. Some people set up a mental rule that they will review whether their reward plan is "deserved"—a glance at your to-do list or calendar should help you see whether it's really time for a break or whether stopping now means you'll neglect an important task. It can also be worth asking yourself, "How will I feel at the end of the day if I reward myself now, or if I keep working?" A sense of accomplishment at the end of the day may be more important than a planned break or diversion.

NOTICE WHERE YOU NEED A NEW PATH

Everyone has habits, both for good and bad. Sleeping on a certain side of the bed is a habit, as is brushing your teeth before or after breakfast. Letting the mail pile up, plopping down on the couch before cleaning up the dinner table, and putting off working on a presentation until the last minute are all habits, too. You may think of these habits as the steps that carry you along the path through your day. We have noted that everyone has less desirable default paths that require effort to avoid. The right kind of structure can make forging new paths easier.

Here are three examples of how people found structure that allowed them to practice the habits they wanted to:

1. Tiffany is extraordinarily generous to others and the center of her family, but rarely takes the time to care for herself. She is naturally motivated to give, and give and give. What holds her accountable is fulfilling commitments to other people—she was able to run the Chicago Marathon, for instance, because doing so meant a lot to her trainer.

A few months ago, Tiffany tore a ligament and stopped getting exercise. She realized she was starting to drag and feel down, but she kept filling her schedule with things for other people instead of going to a gym. She got herself on a healthier path when a friend, who is a water aerobics instructor, invited Tiffany to join a class—and she saw this as a way to support her friend. So Tiffany was able to get off her default path of not exercising by using her natural motivation to help a friend—and helped herself at the same time.

2. For Herman, the default pathway is to accumulate more and more stuff—"junk," his wife calls it. To him, every item is fraught with meaning, and it takes forever for him to decide what to do with it. So the stuff just keeps adding up, aggravating his wife and making it

hard for him to find things. Herman joined Clutterers Anonymous to help him forge a new route around this default pathway. The other members of his group have become his accountability system. Every week, he has to go before them and explain what he's done to let go of things. Herman is slowly becoming more aware of the critical moments when he prioritizes objects in his life over the benefits of letting them go—more space in his house, fewer distractions in his environment, and less mental preoccupation.

3. For Josephine, a blazingly smart research scientist, her default pathway is to get excited about the big picture and not worry about the details. She is thoroughly convinced of the importance of a discovery she's made, and she thinks everyone else should be as well. She's having trouble "wasting" her time on replicating the experiment, justifying each assumption, and systematically describing her results—all the things she needs to do before she can publish her discovery and share it with the world. Her default path is to be distracted by the excitement and energy of the big idea but have an unclear path to manage all the details.

The big "aha" moment for Josephine came when she thought of taking her problem to her former thesis advisor, a man who is naturally methodical. He helped her to clarify the path she needed to take, to gain the clear vision we talked about in the prefrontal checklist in Chapter 4. Josephine talked with him at each step of the experiment to make sure she did the work carefully and that it supported her ideas. Her paper was recently accepted for publication in a prestigious scientific journal.

These three people learned to overcome their default paths: first by becoming aware of them, and then by using other people or situations to bring clarity and accountability to their practice of better habits.

Write down some examples of the steps that lead you down some of your default pathways:

_____

_____

_____

_____

_____

Now, using the models of Tiffany, Herman and Josephine, indicate healthier paths of action you would like to take rather than your default paths. Write down elements of structure—the kinds of rewards and reminders that can help you keep to a path of better habits such as natural motivators or accountability you can capitalize on.

BETTER PATH   **STRUCTURE**

_____   _____

_____   _____

_____   _____

_____   _____

_____   _____

FINDING THE RIGHT ENVIRONMENT FOR YOU

It's so much easier to stay on track if you're in a situation or environment that fosters your strengths and supports your challenges. If you love science and hate being in crowded places, then try to find work in a lab rather than at a busy hospital. This sounds obvious, but often disengagement is really a mismatch between skills and situations. Aptitude and vocational assessments that identify gifts and strengths can guide you to a new academic and vocational path. A good fit between your strengths and the choice of the kind of work you do is critical. Put yourself in as many situations as possible that match your skills and interests—and you will find a lot of your boredom melting away. Look for activities and jobs that foster what excites you; look for friends who share your passions. Having something you like to do, something to look forward to, will help you get through the boring bits.

But it's not enough to just be good at or care about what you do; you need support for the parts of life that don't come naturally to you. That's what a good environment is all about. Just as John realized that he needs to work somewhere that relies on teamwork rather than individual efforts, so you need to think about what the best environment will be for you. That doesn't mean you can always get this kind of environment, but if you don't know what it is, you won't know what to strive for. Sometimes you can also create it for yourself. Even in a company that values individual effort, you and a close colleague can have each other's back. The key aspects of an ideal environment can include the following:

- Availability of people to provide accountability. Consider working alone versus working in a group; taking a large class where you can get lost versus a smaller one where you can get to know your professor; working in a giant organization where you might see the boss once a year versus a small office where you know everyone; working for someone who is a visionary with infectious passion and sense of direction versus someone who just wants to get the job done.

- Regular rewards.

- The sense of purpose or meaning in the mission of the place.

- Your appreciation of the role that you are in.

- Availability of resources (including people) to do things you are not good at.

- How much (for how long, at what risk) you will be accountable only to yourself.

STEPS TO PRACTICING HABITS

Once you have identified critical moments when a new habit can keep you on a better path, use the following principles to add structure to your practice of the habit:

☐ Automate or outsource reminders to practice the habit, such as setting up a weekly meeting, a calendar note, or an alarm.
☐ Write down the long-term goal of the habit.
☐ Use natural motivators to ensure practice such as other people to whom you can be accountable or adding shorter-term rewards.
☐ Be on the lookout for distractions and barriers that make less productive "default" habits easier.

KEY POINTS

■ Self-improvement strategies take practice, and FAST MINDS traits can make routine practice harder.

■ Structure your environment to make it easier to practice better habits.

■ Setting clearly defined goals and short-term rewards will help you practice strategies.

■ Tracking progress, using reminders, and being accountable to others will help you learn better habits and patterns.

Feel Well, Function Well

For Rachel, ADHD isn't something she *has*. It's something she *is*. ADHD colors every minute of her life when she's awake and even possibly when she's asleep. Some people bound out of bed in the morning restored and full of energy. Not Rachel. She struggles to get to work by nine, despite three cups of coffee. The sinking feeling in her stomach that comes with realizing she slept through her second alarm clock—again—is all too frequent. The realization that she forgot to bring her lunch in with her is familiar also, as are the selections at the vending machine downstairs.

On a good day, Rachel gets home in time to watch a show at seven P.M. On a bad day, she doesn't eat her microwave dinner until nine. She eventually gravitates from the TV to the computer—and somehow, she ends up going to bed late again. The next morning, bleary-eyed, she has to drag herself through the first two hours of her day, until the coffee finally kicks in.

There is an unhealthy rhythm to the life of many people with FAST MINDS traits—a pattern in which their needs are neglected. We see so many people managing to hold together one domain of life—often work or school—but lacking dedicated time or energy for much else. Research from Dr. Surman and others demonstrates that people with ADHD are more likely than their peers to have trouble maintaining healthy personal habits such as getting enough sleep and exercise and eating a balanced, nutritious diet. For some, it is as if the healthier, balanced path in life is like a narrow uphill ridge where one misstep leads into unhealthy territory. When the person is physically drained from lack of sleep, exercise, and nutrients, FAST MINDS symptoms have freer rein, and a vicious circle spins.

Nearly everyone we know who has succeeded at managing their ADHD has done so, in part, by working on these healthy habits. They can't simply "decide" to sleep, eat, and exercise better. Instead, they often have to change critical moments in their daily patterns. For some, stocking up on healthy snacks, creating a "screens dark" time, or scheduling the gym into their calendar is enough to get on a healthier path. Others, who can't follow such habits naturally, impose them on themselves with planning and effort.

We're not suggesting that people turn into automatons, but rather understand themselves well enough to identify the minimum set of practices they need to function well. In this chapter we look again at what can help you form new habits and demonstrate that a great way to start forming them is to take care of yourself.

How the Brain Makes a New Habit

As we noted in earlier chapters, the brain's prefrontal cortex is crucial for consciously controlling behavior, and the basal ganglia helps manage behavior that involves goals and rewards. It turns out that these two regions communicate via different pathways when animals are learning a new behavior, versus when the behavior has become a reflexive, natural action. This means that when an animal is learning to press a lever for a reward the first time, it uses different brain circuits than when it presses it already having learned that the action produces a reward.[1] The cerebellum also contributes to physical learning.[2] These three regions—the prefrontal cortex, the basal ganglia, and the cerebellum, as we noted in Chapter 2—are among those that show differences in brain scan studies of individuals with ADHD. Thus differences in these brain regions could explain why it is harder for some people with ADHD to learn new habits.

It is important to understand that habits take time to become automatic, just as it takes people months or years to become experienced drivers. In a study that asked participants to add a daily activity—eating, drinking, or exercise—and practice it daily, it took them each an average of 66 days, and as long as 254 days, to make this new habit automatic.[3]

RECOGNIZING YOURSELF

Here are some signs that you may have a problem taking care of yourself:

☐ You are a "night owl" and regularly get to bed later than you should to get a full night's rest.

☐ You rarely manage to get a minimum of seven hours of sleep on work/school nights or are often tired.

☐ You figure out where, when, or what to eat at the last minute and don't have planned, quality meals.

☐ You don't eat regularly throughout the day.

☐ You eat more than you planned to.

☐ You don't plan ahead for healthy meals.

☐ You often consume sugar and/or caffeine to keep going through the day.

☐ You rarely exercise or are inconsistent with it.

☐ You spend more time than you think you should on pleasurable activities—for example, online communication, shopping, eating, sexual activity, gaming, and social websites.

The Basics

The body and brain's well-being depends on getting the energy and chemicals needed to function, and rest to recover from stress and strengthen learning. Ideally, people need seven to nine hours of sleep; reasonably sized, healthy meals several times a day; and regular aerobic exercise. Although many people fail to match this pattern, the daily lives of people with ADHD are often far more erratic and irregular than average. When we ask people why they stayed up late or missed a meal, we often hear that time "just got away" from them. When we ask why they exercise intermittently, they often mention time—saying they don't make the time for it. Some people explain that they spend the time when they should be taking care of their bodies trying to stay on top of daily demands or doing things for other people. Others seem to be pursuing a life they think they *should* be leading, trying to live up to standards, such as always agreeing to friends' requests, entertaining like Martha Stewart, or doing extra, unnecessary projects at work.

Compensating for FAST MINDS traits can be exhausting. Time lost during the day to distractions can mean work that stretches much later into the evening. The strain of having multiple thoughts at once, or of containing those multiple threads, can take a toll, as can the added stress of always working under crushing deadlines. So people with FAST MINDS probably have greater needs for the basics of sleep, exercise, and good nutrition than average. Once the body is short on nutrients, energy, or sleep, it can be even harder to compensate for FAST MINDS challenges. Thus it is no surprise that deprivation of sleep and nutrition leads to even worse FAST MINDS symptoms.

Young adults often push the limits of overindulgence in sleep deprivation, alcohol, and pleasure-seeking activities. Just as a candy bar that prevents hunger in the short term may be an unhealthy, unsatisfying memory later, so, too, caffeine can backfire by keeping people awake at night and decreasing sleep depth. Alcohol, too, may help people fall asleep but then disrupts sleep quality later in the night and interferes with sleep's restorative power.[4] While older adults don't tend to push these limits quite as dramatically, the negative cycle of youth often lingers, with unhealthy short-term responses leading to more problems later.

So What Do You Need and Why?

EXERCISE

U.S. government and other experts recommend at least thirty minutes a day—ideally sixty—of moderate to vigorous exercise, such as brisk walking.[5] Adults should also do muscle-strengthening activities twice a week or more. Exercise for staying in shape may not be the same thing as exercise that helps shed stress and clear the mind. Many people we work with get a lot out of exhausting themselves physically a few times a week. If this sounds unimaginable, it is okay to start slowly and build up. Activity can be broken down into shorter bursts throughout the day. And exercise doesn't have to do be done at a gym. Mopping the floor or scrubbing the tub can be an aerobic activity, as can horsing around with the kids. The key is to boost your heart rate.

Studies repeatedly demonstrate the health effects of exercise:

strengthening the heart, pumping up energy levels, improving people's moods—think of the "runner's high."[6] Exercise can help people sleep deeper and better. Research even suggests that a key element of the memory system used for keeping thoughts and tasks in mind, a brain area called the hippocampus, may grow new cells in people who exercise more than those who don't.[7]

SLEEP

The amount of sleep a person needs varies by individual and across the life span; infants, children, and teenagers need more sleep than their parents. For adults, the average need is between seven and nine hours. What's clear is that too little sleep is destructive. Short sleep, according to the National Sleep Foundation, can lead to the following:

- Increased risk of motor vehicle accidents

- Increase in body mass index—because of an increased appetite caused by sleep deprivation

- Increased risk of diabetes and heart problems

- Increased risk for psychiatric conditions, including depression and substance abuse

- Decreased ability to pay attention, react to signals, or remember new information

Research by Dr. Surman and others shows that many people with ADHD have trouble getting a good night's sleep. In one study that Dr. Surman and his colleagues conducted, adults with ADHD went to bed later than those without ADHD and had a wider range of bedtimes from night to night.[8] They were more likely to take an hour or longer to fall asleep and were more likely to have trouble sleeping well and getting up in the morning. Adults with ADHD were also likelier to be sleepy during the day. These sleep problems, the study found, were connected to the ADHD, not to any other accompanying mental health problems the person may have had.

Modern life, with electric lights, televisions, and electronic gear, is mismatched with human biology, which evolved to respond to the cues provided by the sun. The biological clock is designed to speed up certain bodily functions at times of the day when people need more energy—such as the morning—and slow down around bedtime, to allow for sleep. Two systems help this happen; scientists call them *the sleep drive* and *the alerting signal*.[9] The sleep drive, as it sounds, is the biological urge to sleep. The longer people are awake, the greater the drive to sleep; during sleep, the sleep drive fades, allowing them to wake up the next morning.

The alerting signal also drops off during sleep, but it picks up during the day to counteract the sleep drive and allow people to stay alert for sixteen to seventeen hours a day. This alerting signal tends to wane temporarily late in the afternoon, explaining why people often report feeling sleepy then, though they often bounce back soon after. The signal reaches its peak of alertness in the late evening and then starts to decline. The combination of the strong sleep drive and the falloff in the alerting signal makes the body naturally ready for sleep.

Staying awake past a normal bedtime throws this signal system out of whack. The increased drive to sleep and reduced alertness explains why it's dangerous to drive late at night or when sleep deprived. A short night means the sleep drive hasn't dropped down fully yet, so sleepiness is carried into the next day; meanwhile, the alerting signal is still in its overnight, reduced stage. This combination of high sleep drive and low alerting signal can make mornings particularly challenging.

The opposite happens when people sleep late—as when they are trying to catch up on sleep over the weekend. Then the sleep drive is reset by more sleep, but sleeping in means the alerting signal's peak is shifted later—so people can be at their peak of alertness just as they need to go to bed to get enough sleep for the next day.

The best way to get a good night's sleep is to work *with* rather than *against* these natural tendencies. Being awake for a long time means the urge to sleep will get stronger. The alerting signal tends to increase over the same time but then falls quickly. The best time to go to bed is just after the alerting signal begins its descent, when you start to get sleepy—not after you've already gotten your "second wind."

Other processes are involved in the sleep-wake cycle, too. Some people swear by taking doses of melatonin, which is naturally released in the brain at lower light levels after sunset and encourages the body to sleep. If it never gets dark, because lights, computers, and televisions are always on, the levels of this hormone won't rise to promote sleepiness. Although people usually tolerate melatonin well, we always advise watching for negative effects of any agent that impacts brain function. It is not clear whether taking melatonin supplements is any more helpful for falling or staying asleep than simply using light exposure to reset the body's clock.

Some people think they need less sleep than the seven to nine hours recommended—that they're just natural *short sleepers*. Researchers think this is uncommon. "There aren't nearly as many [short sleepers] as there are people who think they're short sleepers," Daniel J. Buysse, a past president of the American Academy of Sleep Medicine, told the *Wall Street Journal*.[10] Only 1 to 3 percent of the population actually needs less than seven hours of sleep a night, Buysse said. The rest are sleep deprived.[11]

RECOGNIZE THE IMPACT—WHAT WOULD OTHER PEOPLE SAY?

☐ Would other people say you are inconsistent with your daily routines?

☐ Would other people say you have crazy eating, sleeping, or exercise habits?

☐ Has your inconsistency with routine (sleeping, eating, etc.) created stress in your relationships with other people?

DIET

The human body is designed to send "feed me" signals when the body's nutrient supply is running low. In today's world, though, our desire for food is so easily sated—and triggered—that many people don't even know when they're hungry. Walking through the kitchen can lead to pangs, even within an hour of dinner; watching a burger commercial can prompt cravings, as can driving past stores or billboards. Almost wherever you are in an urban or suburban environment, your every eating whim can be met within minutes.

Much of this food, of course, is fattening, but it's also low on the nutrients needed for optimal health, energy, and brain power. A candy bar may give a quick buzz, but that spike in blood sugar leads to an equally quick bust. It's much more effective to derive energy from a mix of protein and carbohydrates, which provide a fast, but smaller burst that delivers steady power for longer. Power bars and energy drinks are often advertised as the answer to long-term energy needs, but many are little better than candy bars and soda.

There's also some suspicion that food colorings (the stuff that creates neon-orange drinks, blue lollipops, and shades not found in nature) may bring out ADHD-like symptoms in some people. The United Kingdom and European Union restricted the use of artificial food colorings, after a 2007 study showed that the colorings increased hyperactive behavior in toddlers and children[12] although to date there is no clear evidence that such additives cause people to have the disorder.

Some people who take ADHD medication report that the drug suppresses their hunger. Once the medication wears off, in the evenings, some of them have a rebound increase in hunger. For people like this, it may help to change the release pattern of the medication or the type of medication. It may be even more important in these situations to eat a few small, healthy meals throughout the day so blood sugar levels aren't low when the medication wears off.

As with sleep, there's no "right" amount of calories or balance of foods people should eat. Although 2,000 calories a day is a rough estimate, a person's activity level and biochemistry make all the difference. A professional athlete may need 5,000 calories to keep up her strength; a middle-aged office worker with a slow metabolism may need to eat just 1,200 a day to avoid weight gain. It is quite clear, though, that too many people in industrialized countries eat too much: too much overall, and too much of certain foods, such as red meat, dairy, French fries, white rice, and especially white bread. Red meat and dairy contain unhealthy fats and, over a lifetime, can damage the heart and blood vessels. White rice and white bread are stripped of vitamins and fiber; eating whole grains is better for the heart, reduces risk of diabetes, and is less likely to lead to constipation and cancer.[13] Potatoes are mostly starch, which the body digests like white bread. Pizza accounts for 4 percent of the American adult's daily diet, and French fries another 2 percent,[14] so clearly the message hasn't gotten out yet.

The Harvard School of Public Health has developed a "healthy eating plate" to help people do a better job of eating a balanced diet. Harvard recommends eating lots of fruits, vegetables, and whole grains; getting protein mainly from fish, nuts, and poultry; eating healthy oils such as olive oil and canola instead of butter; and drinking water with most meals.

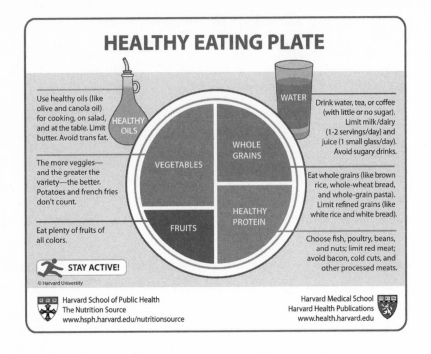

Psychological Well-Being and Healthy Patterns

People in mental distress have a harder time caring for themselves. Depression, anxiety disorders, eating disorders, and addictions—which we know are common among people with ADHD—are all frequently accompanied by worsening of sleep quality and poorer self-care. Often, treating these related conditions improves sleep patterns, motivation, and the ability to take care of oneself. It can also work the other way. Lack of self-care can be a sign that another condition, such as depression or anxiety, needs more support. Eating a healthy diet, exercising, and getting enough sleep can also improve mental health. Exercise triggers the brain to release endorphins, the chemicals responsible for the runner's high, and some studies have shown that exercise works as well as a placebo in treating depression.[15] One study also showed that getting exercise boosts the effectiveness of anti-depressant medications.[16]

Critical Moments for Self-Care

The critical moment to act in service of self-care is often predictable. With a morning job, most people need to be asleep by eleven P.M.—earlier if their work responsibilities start before eight A.M. A critical moment to act may come at 10 P.M. when instead of transitioning away from electronic devices, the person chooses to watch another show or begin an electronic game or two. It may come in the early evening when the person gives in to a nap, even though that means they won't be tired at bedtime. It may come even earlier in the day when the person decides to take a break from an urgent project and doesn't think of it again until nine P.M., or when they sleep in, continuing the cycle of a late-shifted schedule.

The critical moment for food may come in the cafeteria line—pizza or a salad, a bacon cheeseburger or salmon sushi. Or it may come earlier, at the grocery store, when extra effort to get protein-rich snacks to sustain blood sugar throughout the day could make a difference, and planning ahead for the rest of the week reduces the call of the vending machine and drive-through.

For exercise, the critical moment may come when one chooses to keep working instead of going to the gym or doesn't get up early enough to work out before work. It may come when the gym clothes never made it into the laundry, and now there is nothing clean to wear. Figuring out where to act at such critical moments makes it easier to actually get to exercising—which will hopefully soon become a habit, with a rise in endorphins for a reward.

If Someone You Care About Has a FAST MIND

The best possible thing you can do for someone with self-regulation problems is to help them identify unhealthy default patterns and figure out which critical moments need to change. As we discussed in the last chapter, you may be able to provide more accountability for their efforts to change and help them feel less alone in the process. Prearranging the role you will play with them is a good idea. But telling them what to do probably won't work. Decide together where information, feedback, or reminders from you would be helpful. If they've asked you to help them keep a regular bedtime and mealtimes, then they have given you the right to hold them accountable for those things.

They may value a simple, prearranged style of feedback—but not criticism. "You wanted me to let you know when you started burning the candle at both ends with work and sleep deprivation" will likely go better than "Why can't you work less and have a better sleep routine?" Just acknowledging that they live by a different rhythm—one that, like FAST MINDS traits themselves, is not completely under conscious control—can create a positive environment for change.

You might provide structure for critical moments by doing the following:

- Keeping healthier food in the house and/or making sure dinner is on the table at roughly the same time every night (if it's there, they're more likely to eat it).

- Modeling good sleep hygiene (see the next section) and getting a good night's sleep yourself. Maybe cut a deal to stay up late and do something fun together every Saturday to break up the routine.

- Accompanying your loved one to the gym and sharing workout goals.

WHAT YOU CAN DO

Taking good care of yourself is a crucial foundation for functioning at your best and getting what you want out of life. When a person has unhealthy patterns of eating, sleeping, or exercise habits, it will take conscious effort to break them. Treating ADHD with medication may make it easier to remember when to eat, sleep, or exercise and stick to the habits that make up the new routine. But often even on medication, individuals with ADHD have default paths that lead away from healthy activities and require conscious effort and mindfulness to avoid.

IMPROVING SELF-REGULATION

Now that you understand the importance of self-regulation, we'd like to offer you some suggestions for improving yours. Some of this may seem obvious and some impossible. Again, we're not suggesting that you transform yourself into a robot whose life is governed by the need to sleep, eat, and run. Our aim is to help you get a foothold on patterns that may be worth trying to establish or break. We're not going to tell you what time to go to bed, just suggest that you think about setting a bedtime for yourself so that you'll have the energy to function tomorrow; that you eat well-balanced, healthy meals for the same reason; and that you make a concerted effort to exercise and manage stress. All of those things will help your body function better, which will allow you to function better, with better internal resources to control your attention and your mood.

We find that establishing a new habit or pattern often comes down to identifying critical moments when effort and willpower can have the most effect. If you can identify highest-yield moments of action that make a new pattern of behavior more likely, it isolates what you need to remember, practice, and stay on top of. For some things, it may be eliminating an obvious pitfall, such as a cupboard full of junk food, when eating regularly and healthy is your challenge, or late-night shows that you could record and watch later, instead of getting keyed up when it's time to wind down. Other new habits may take protecting time in your calendar.

Although we focus on eating, sleeping, and exercise in this chapter, the principles for changing habits to enrich your life are the same no matter what the habit is. We could be talking about other high-priority habits for well-being, such as making more time for people in your life or activities you enjoy or regularly managing your finances.

The work of changing habits can be easier if it is not just for you. The motivation to help another person may be useful for keeping yourself accountable. Getting into better patterns of sleep, exercise, and nutrition with the people you spend time with can help those relationships as well as be a mutual gift of health. If you have a child or loved one with FAST MINDS challenges, addressing your patterns of self-care is doubly important for you. Modeling how to live a patterned life can save them a lot of anguish later.

As we have discussed, it takes time for new patterns to become habits. When establishing a new sleep schedule, the first few mornings are likely to be hard, but after that, your body clock should work in your favor, helping you feel better in the morning and reinforcing your new habit. For some patterns, though, it will take vigilant attention to the critical moments when less healthy habits can creep back.

Let's look at what some people we know have done to stick to habits:

Rachel uses exercise to improve her self-regulation. "I definitely feel very different after exercising," she says. Though sometimes she'll read something job-related while riding an exercycle, usually her exercise time helps her detach from the day. "After work, if I don't go right to the gym and work out, it's hard for me to make a transition to dinner or happy hour." Her time at the gym or on a run helps clear her head of the clutter of the day and focus on something new. On a recent vacation, when she was supposed to be just relaxing with her boyfriend, Rachel was starting to feel like a caged animal. Her boyfriend ended up grabbing her sneakers and begging her to take a run. She did, and the rest of the day went better.

Nate, the superorganized man from Chapter 5, says his heart palpitations helped persuade him to take better care of himself. The doctor he saw for his racing heart made him give up the coffee that had been his constant companion. "I realized I was self-medicating. I was a complete disaster without it." Caffeine-free, Nate again sought help for his ADHD. The first time he'd tried ADHD medications, they hadn't done anything for him. But after he gave up coffee, the pills prompted a big improvement. "Now I definitely think they are more effective than the caffeine. I don't miss coffee. I still love the flavor and smell, but I don't miss it at all." Giving up coffee also dramatically improved Nate's sleep. He can go to bed at a decent hour now, sleep through the night, and wake up feeling refreshed. "I was always a horrible sleeper. I'm sleeping better than I have in my whole life."

Michael, the less-organized man we introduced in Chapter 5, says he's in a committed relationship with ice cream—chocolate chip, to be exact, but he'll settle for cookie dough if he has to. When he and his wife have their self-regulation under control, they can help each other practice restraint. "During the good periods, we kind of support each other with, 'Maybe the entire pint is not a good idea,'" he says. Their sense of humor makes it easier to get back on track, where they might get mired in negativity instead.

All three of these people improved their self-regulation. Rachel knows that she can give more of herself to each day with her workout, and she defends time in her schedule for it. Nate realized that his caffeine habit was hurting his body and mind. Michael's relationship with ice cream exemplifies the regular struggle that many people have with habits—and the importance of having strategies for critical moments that keep healthier goals clearly in mind.

Your challenges will likely be different from theirs, but it's important to listen to and respond to the messages your body is sending you. If you are tired, stressed, or unfulfilled or have problematic cravings or urges, figuring out how to create and enforce habits that meet these needs in a healthy way should be your first priority.

Ask yourself these two questions:

1. Which of your everyday patterns is getting in the way of your health? Is it a chronically late bedtime? Not eating regularly? Not getting exercise?

2. What critical moments lead to those patterns? Think back in time to what might have made a better pattern more likely. Is it preparing ahead of time so you have what you need? Sticking with your plan so you don't do something else instead? Keeping pitfalls such as unhealthy snacks and video games out of reach?

THE FAST MINDS
TWENTY-FOUR-HOUR CYCLE REVIEW

We described the paths of activity that people are used to and take little active energy as default paths. These paths are made up of a series of habits, some of which interfere with self-care, such as watching TV at night or sleeping in instead of getting up to exercise. To become more aware of where you can act to get out of poor self-care or other activities, it helps to look at whether you are getting your daily needs met in every twenty-four-hour period. It will help you begin to decide what a better schedule would look like and what actions to take to keep to that schedule.

INSTRUCTIONS

Thinking of recent days, or starting with today, use this chart to record whether you are meeting self-care needs in a healthy way. Where you write No on this chart, consider prioritizing trying to change that to a Yes. You can copy a version of this chart from Appendix D and use it to track how your typical day changes over time. For example, you could take it to a meeting with a family physician or specialist to discuss healthy lifestyle plans or complete it intermittently to be mindful of your progress on self-care. Later in this chapter we describe how to come up with an action plan to better meet your needs.

BRAINSTORM HABIT CHANGES

Now that you have become more mindful of your lifestyle choices, how do you change them? For some people, just realizing that a pattern is causing problems is enough to initiate a plan for change. For others, a structured plan to initiate change may be the solution.

As we have emphasized in the chapter on being your own chief executive, protecting time for your priorities is critical. If your obligations fill every day, leaving little room for self-care, you will not bring your best to your obligations. Alternately, there may be "hollow" fulfillments in your life, such as video gaming, the Internet, or TV, that are distractions or pitfalls. You can take action to make time for activities that better fulfill your needs. Look carefully at what trade-offs you may need to make. Maybe you can combine activities—such as watching TV while you exercise.

SLEEP/WAKE CYCLE	Day 1	Day 2	Day 3	Day 4	Day 5	Day 6	Day 7
Did you wind down and relax before bed?							
Did you get 7–9 hours of sleep?							
Did you maintain a restful, dark sleep environment?							
Did you wake early enough to start your day on time?							
Did you avoid caffeine?							
Did you avoid napping today?							
Did you go to bed early enough to allow yourself 7–9 hours of sleep?							

NUTRITION	Day 1	Day 2	Day 3	Day 4	Day 5	Day 6	Day 7
Did you eat a healthy breakfast?							
Did you have healthy food in your house to eat?							
Did you eat small meals regularly across the day?							
Did you avoid fast or "junk" food?							
Did you use protein and carbohydrates for energy?							

EXERCISE/RELAXATION	Day 1	Day 2	Day 3	Day 4	Day 5	Day 6	Day 7
Did you exercise for at least 30 minutes?							
Did you have workout gear prepared ahead of time?							
Did you take time during the day to relax?							

Think of what self-care is missing for you in the pattern that you identified on the FAST MINDS Twenty-Four-Hour Review. Are you getting seven to nine hours of sleep? Do you have a pattern of healthy meals spread throughout the day? Do you get thirty to sixty minutes of daily exercise? What problematic default paths create these deficits, such as going to bed late, not planning meals, or socializing instead of exercise? To help think about alternative habits that actively avoid those paths, note your answers to the following questions:

1. Are external distractions involved?
   Are you getting sucked into late-night video gaming?
   Watching TV shows you could be recording?
   Doing work in bed?
   Eating too late at night?

2. Are there internal distractions leading you along default paths?
   Do you eat late at night because you're bored?
   Do you feel like you deserve a reward at night for struggling through long, demoralizing days?
   Do you feel like you have to spend all your time taking care of everyone else in the family, leaving yourself stretched too thin?

3. Would a pause button help you make a better choice in a critical moment?
   Can you make the choice a more thoughtful one, more deliberate?
   Are you staying up late because it hasn't occurred to you that being tired tomorrow will have consequences in your life?

4. What structures might help?
   Can you use a checklist or list of steps to plan and stay on track?
   For some people, having a note on the fridge helps them remember to pack their gym bag, do what they need to do to get ready for bed, or make healthy shopping trips.

Can you add purpose, such as a routine of planning for the next day before going to bed, or catching up on news while exercising?

Does a short-term reward or involving others hold you more accountable?

Does tracking progress help?

Helping Develop Healthy Habits

For people who struggle to adopt new habits, it is critical to choose one or two new habits at a time that are worth the effort. You want to also make the new habit **as interesting and meaningful as possible.** Here we list tips for some of the most important habits—for sleep, eating, and exercise—*not* expecting that you will use them all, but hoping that they spur your own creativity and help you develop strategies that enable you to fit new habits into your life:

Tips for Sleeping Better

Some well-established tricks are designed to help people get a good night's sleep. These are basically aimed at supporting biological day and night patterns and establishing a wind-down period with lower stimulation to allow the body's natural hormones and brain chemicals to trigger sleep.

If bedtime is a problem for you, ask a spouse to remind you gently that it's time for bed, or keep the same sleep-wake cycle as they do. If that doesn't work or you live alone, setting an alarm may help, or pairing with a friend who has a similar problem—or a different one—so you can help each other through your challenges. You could also give yourself a reward for getting to bed on time: say, allowing yourself to read for thirty minutes if you make it to bed by a certain time.

If you take a stimulant medication, take it early in the morning so that it has worn off by bedtime, allowing you to have an organized bedtime routine.

Here are some additional sleep tips from the Harvard Medical School's Division of Sleep Medicine:[17]

1. Avoid caffeine, alcohol, and nicotine for at least three to four hours before bedtime or eliminate them altogether. All of them can interfere with falling asleep. And don't forget that caffeine isn't only in coffee—it's also in tea, chocolate, and energy drinks.

2. Make your bedroom a sleep room. Your bedroom's primary purpose should be for sleeping and falling asleep (sex is okay, too). If you have trouble falling asleep, it may help to keep computers, TV, and other activities out of your bedroom. Make your bed as comfy as possible. A quiet, dark, and cool room can help you sleep better, so consider dark curtains or an eye mask, earplugs or a white-noise appliance such as a ceiling fan, and doing what you can to maintain a comfortable temperature. If your pet is waking you up during the night, it may be time to find another sleeping arrangement—for the pet, not you!

3. Establish a good bedtime routine to ease your transition from wake time to sleep time. The last hour before bed is not a good time to watch scary TV shows, play violent video games, or have emotional phone conversations with friends. The hormone the body secretes under stress—cortisol—will also keep you awake. If you're troubled by something, write it down briefly and then leave those thoughts on the paper.

4. Don't lie in bed awake for hours. If you've tried to fall asleep in vain for twenty minutes, get up, go to another room, and do something relaxing for a little while before trying again. Try the same strategy if you wake up in the middle of the night and have trouble falling back to sleep.

5. To get your body clock to perform at its best, go to sleep and wake up at the same time every day, and get lots of natural light in the mornings.

6. If you need a nap, keep it short and not too close to bedtime.

7. Finish dinner a few hours before bedtime to give your body time to digest. If you're hungry late at night, eat a small snack that you're sure won't give you indigestion. Don't drink too much in the evenings, so a full bladder won't disturb your sleep.

8. Exercise, but not too late in the day. If your body is pumping out endorphins, it may not be able to relax enough to sleep.

Tips for Eating Better

To keep your brain operating comfortably, and to avoid the poor eating choices that come with hunger, eat nutritious food throughout the day rather than skipping meals. Start your day with a good breakfast. Avoid the temptation of grabbing fast food. Try setting up weekly lunches with friends or regularly pack a healthy snack. It doesn't take long to put a small handful of almonds into a resealable bag, or grab baby carrots and hummus, or an apple and a small container with peanut butter (try the all-natural kind made from just peanuts and salt, instead of the processed brands you probably ate as a kid, which are filled with corn syrup and other sweeteners). Small baby food jars are a great way to control portions of fattening foods. Setting up a no-vending-machine or no-fast-food rule can also help you avoid impulsive temptations and encourage you to plan ahead better.

Next time you have the urge to overeat, try using the pause button and making a more mindful choice, going for a walk, or just drinking water. If you're eating for emotional reasons, the thought record exercises from earlier chapters may help.

If motivation is your problem, set up a challenge with a friend or colleague to see who can live healthiest—and then win it!

Stock your house with healthy foods and force yourself to go out for treats such as ice cream. Food writer Michael Pollan suggests that at the grocery store, people should shop mainly in the outer aisles, where the produce, dairy, and meat are usually kept, instead of the central aisles, which are filled with highly processed foods. Processed foods are usually oversalted and loaded with empty calories from fat and refined grains. Stock up instead on apples, bananas, and oranges, which are usually available year-round. "If you're not hungry enough to eat an apple, you're probably not hungry," Pollan says in his book *Food Rules*. He also recommends eating only items your grandmother would recognize as food; stuffed pockets don't count.

Some people like using their weekends to cook healthy food for the rest of the week. A batch of soup cooked on Sunday can last most of the week; tomato sauce leftovers can be reused on pasta, home-made pizza, and vegetable stew. It's easy to prepare a container of tuna or egg salad for lunches through the week.

Tips for Exercise

The good news is that exercise can be addictive. Once people see what regular exercise can do for them, self-motivation gets much easier. Many people we know with ADHD swear by their daily work-out to burn off extra energy. Without it, they are buzzing with distractions. Exercise can also reduce stress and anxiety, improve focus, and help people feel better about themselves. Working out (though probably not right before bedtime) can also lead to a better night's sleep.

Do what you enjoy. If you don't like running, don't worry about it. There are plenty of other physical activities. If there's nothing you really like right now, start experimenting. Try golf (carrying your own clubs, of course), tennis, squash, handball, volleyball, basketball, ballroom dancing, belly dancing, ballet, spinning, Pilates, hot yoga, biking, ice skating, ice hockey, field hockey, inline skating, downhill skiing, cross-country skiing, swimming, water polo, or walking the dog. There's almost an endless number of options. Using an exercise video is better than nothing, as long as it boosts your heart rate. But hunting for the remote doesn't count. Nor does stress that makes your heart race.

If you're getting sick of one form of exercise, mix it up. It's probably better to use different muscle groups, anyway.

Get a buddy to exercise with. You can help motivate each other and hold each other accountable. This may be particularly important as you start new habits. Once you're used to working out every day, it will be easier to maintain the habit alone.

Remember how much harder it is to get started than to maintain a pattern. Next time you're tempted to skip a workout, make sure it doesn't derail you and force you to start building the habit all over again. But it's also okay to cheat every once in a while. Breaking the rules occasionally can help keep your pattern more interesting.

MAKING EACH DAY HEALTHIER

Looking at the FAST MINDS Twenty-Four-Hour Cycle Review and the tips for improved sleep, eating, and exercise patterns, decide on an action plan for healthier habits you want to adopt. You will want to make these changes one at a time. Making new habits takes conscious effort and practice, so any structure you can create is critical until you have established a routine.

List the thoughtfully planned actions that can improve the chance of fulfilling a good self-care schedule:

For each self-care need, make a list of actions that will protect your self-care time (e.g., start winding down for bed early; pack your gym bag the night before; eat planned snacks).

SELF-CARE NEED   **NEW ACTION OR HABIT**

_____   _____

_____   _____

_____   _____

_____   _____

_____   _____

You can use the FAST MINDS Critical Moment planner below to indicate when you will do any of these actions or habits that need to happen at specific times.

Now, list the changes in structure that will make it easier to stick with your plans for new habits. Look at the list on pages 182–86 to come up with what will make it easier to practice the new habits, such as ways of reminding yourself to do them (e.g., set an alarm on your phone to remember to put clothes out for the next morning) or avoid pitfalls that will get in the way (e.g., reduce distraction by recording late-night TV shows).

NEW SELF-CARE ACTION OR HABIT   **STRUCTURE TO MAKE PRACTICING IT EASIER**

_____   _____

_____   _____

_____   _____

_____   _____

_____   _____

FAST MINDS CRITICAL MOMENT PLANNER

Need to Address	Action to take	What days should you act?	6 a.m.	7	8	9	10	11	Noon	1 p.m.	2	3	4	5	6	7	8	9	10	11
Sleep	Start preparing for bed 90 minutes ahead	Every day																*		
Healthy Eating	4 small meals	Every day		*				*				*				*				
Exercise	Prepare gym bag	Tuesday Thursday Saturday															*			

Instructions: This chart can help you plan the critical moments to act to better meet your daily needs. Consider particular moments where you can pre-empt the pitfall of a time-wasting or unhealthy activity by planning. 1. In the first column note what personal need (e.g., sleep, healthy eating, exercise) you are addressing. 2. In the second column, note which days you can take action (workdays, weekends). 3. In the third column, list out actions to take. 4. Use an * to mark when to act during those days. See first three rows for examples.

In the next chapter, we talk about the social challenges that often come along with FAST MINDS traits.

KEY POINTS

- Regular sleep, healthy food, and exercise are often the best "medicine."

- Matching your behavior to biological rhythms optimizes alertness and self-control.

- Identify critical moments that can derail your daily habits or set you up for success.

- Support new habits with elements of structure such as reminders, accountability, and goal tracking.

Help Other People "Get It"

In a conversation, Taz forces himself to pay attention to the other person for a second or two, then predicts where the conversation is going and tunes out. His prediction is often wrong, though, so he misses what the other person is saying. Or he blurts out a remark that he thinks is relevant, only to be met with a blank or quizzical stare. Sometimes, if he's particularly antsy, he'll drop a provocative comment on purpose to keep up his own interest in the discussion. This impatience and intensity often turns people off before they get to know him at all.

Taz's social isolation started early. He had only one close companion in grade school, a calm, patient girl two years his senior. Socially, he always seemed alone, even in groups of children. He was never invited to birthday parties or sleepovers. By age seven, Taz was aware of his isolation. By fourth grade, he told his parents he wished kids would give him another chance. But they didn't. He became a magnet for school bullies, who saw him as an easy target because he did weird things, overreacted to insults, and was often publicly scolded by teachers. Taz took their teasing to heart. By the time he reached adolescence, he was lonely and his self-image was battered.

In playgrounds and cafeterias, it almost seems as if other kids can recognize children with FAST MINDS, even without a diagnostic label. They often target these differences, particularly when a child is quick to get emotional. The non-ADHD children push the hot buttons, bullying the FAST MINDS kid. Being socially stigmatized in this way tears at the child's self-esteem and is heartbreaking for the parents. Often educators seem immune to these situations and offer little support to the family.

Social differences continue into adolescence, and making and keeping friends during the increased complexity of a teenager's life is a challenge. Finding a clique that fits is difficult; kids with FAST MINDS who struggle socially may associate with only one or two people who, like them, are different in their interests and on the social fringe. Continued academic underachievement compounds these problems, and the teen may become demoralized, feeling their future doesn't offer much.

By adulthood, many with FAST MINDS still struggle to understand why they haven't been accepted for who they are. They have felt different all their lives.

In this chapter, we highlight the impact of FAST MINDS on the social style of adults. As we've noted before, thriving with FAST MINDS challenges is much easier for people who can use others as a resource. This chapter also offers a guide to building reliable, lasting, mutually supportive relationships, by identifying the critical interpersonal moments that get in the way, and the skills that enable success.

RECOGNIZING YOURSELF:

- ☐ Do you forget details of what people say to you?
- ☐ Do you jump around as you tell a story, go on too long, or lose track of your thoughts?
- ☐ Do other people complain that you don't listen well?
- ☐ Do you feel impatient, wanting people to cut to the chase?
- ☐ Do you find yourself pretending you heard what other people are saying, or asking people to repeat themselves?
- ☐ Is it hard not to show your emotions?
- ☐ Have you always felt different socially?
- ☐ Do you find that most people don't "get you"?

Social Skills and ADHD

The social difficulties of ADHD begin in early childhood. Little boys with ADHD often act out and have trouble following rules, which draws negative attention from teachers and peers—though this often helps get them an early diagnosis. Little girls with ADHD may be chatty, quick in conversations, and easily bored.[1] Studies consistently show that children with ADHD have more trouble making and keeping friends.[2] Girls can be rejected both by their peer group and by adults, who find their chattiness irritating and inconsistent with societal norms.

Some people with ADHD seem to win social acceptance because they have traits that make them popular, such as athletic ability, good looks, or humor. These gifts can mask their challenges or make other people more willing to risk social capital to befriend them. Howie Mandel, who reports that he struggled with ADHD and other challenges in his book *Here's the Deal: Don't Touch Me*, makes it clear that he never felt like he fit in as a kid, despite—and often because of—his oddball sense of humor. But being funny sometimes gave him social cachet.

Without those extras, people like Taz may be left even more isolated. Classic studies in children demonstrate that peers are often unwilling to accept ADHD differences.[3] In adolescence, life generally gets harder for those with FAST MINDS, as social expectations and complexity increases, and "fitting in" becomes more important. Impulsivity, distractibility, and being overly giddy, silly, goofy, and "not cool" can be real social problems. One study of college students showed that different versions of ADHD can affect social acceptance differently.[4] Distractibility seemed to be more of a turnoff, while impulsivity and hyperactivity were perceived to be more "fun."

As we saw with Taz, the social challenges of FAST MINDS traits are often visible in simple conversations. Half-listening in conversations causes real problems in relationships. "You're not listening to what I'm saying to you" is a frequent refrain from significant others. Not listening plus cutting people off in conversation is a recipe for disaster. Being impatient or quick to react emotionally also leads to real difficulties in relationships.

Many people with ADHD tell us that in larger social groups, they find the Ping-Pong of conversations impossible to follow, making it hard to know when to speak. Some even turn down social invitations because they can't function comfortably in a group—leading to isolation.

From the perspective of the other person, a conversation with a person with a FAST MIND can be bewildering and annoying. People with FAST MINDS can miss cues that they have said enough and end up delivering a Shakespearean soliloquy to an audience that is not interested. FAST MINDS thinking can sometimes come across as scattered and nonlinear, leaving the person without ADHD with no idea of what's being said.

RECOGNIZE THE IMPACT—WHAT WOULD OTHER PEOPLE SAY?

Do other people:

☐ Ask if you are listening, or ask you to repeat what they just said?

☐ Ask you not to interrupt them?

☐ Get frustrated in conversations with you?

☐ Leave you out of things you want to be a part of?

☐ Frequently remind you of what you need to do?

MICHAEL: AIMING FOR ACCOUNTABILITY

Michael's second wife has learned how to hold him accountable for drifting off. She'll say: "You just went away, didn't you?" He's not really aware of when he wanders off, but her words help him tune back in. "They're typically nonjudgmental and not angry," he says, so he can hear them.

Michael has long had trouble sustaining relationships. He's not good at nonverbal cues, sometimes says inappropriate things, and has impulse control problems in conversation. He means well but often forgets to follow through on relationship-building activities, such as keeping up with his relatives.

OLIVIA: GETTING BACK ON TRACK

Olivia, a teacher, recently assessed for ADHD and depression, was getting poor performance appraisals and was worried about getting fired. She went to her principal, admitted she was struggling, and explained that she had a medical condition that contributed to her organizational challenges. She articulated what she felt would help her and asked for suggestions where she wasn't sure. The principal assigned Olivia a mentor whom he knew was systematic and organized. With her mentor, Olivia set up a board in her classroom to write down her teaching plans and assignments. The two decided to have a joint grading party twice a semester, to catch up on all the papers they hadn't yet returned. Olivia also asked her mentor for advice on managing out-of-class communications with parents and students. Olivia noticed that her mentor wasn't as quick to blame herself for problems as she was and that she could put more responsibility on parents and students by communicating in writing, which was more efficient for her than talking. With these supports in place, and medication to address her dual diagnoses, Olivia felt more in control and better about herself and her teaching skills. She began deriving genuine pleasure out of her work for the first time since beginning her teaching career.

Telling Others You Have ADHD

One of the biggest questions people with ADHD face is whether to tell others they have the condition. Some people are free with their personal information. Others are so ashamed of not being like everyone else that they can't bear to tell anyone, and so they keep their diagnosis to themselves to avoid any chance of being discovered.

In the United States, under the Americans with Disabilities Act, a person with a recognized disability impairing learning or ability to work (including ADHD) is entitled to some protection and support where the condition impacts their ability to be employed or to learn.[5] A school or workplace is expected under the law to make "reasonable accommodations" to allow fulfillment of the person's role as a student or worker. But the definition of *reasonable* varies—it does not typically include permission to change educational requirements or a job description, for instance. Schools and employers may require formal documentation of a disability before providing accommodations.

SCHOOL: Many colleges offer supports for struggling students. Classic accommodations include extra time on tests to reduce stress, allow for processing speed and graphomotor challenges, and catch errors; a special location for test taking in a distraction-free area; a complete set of class notes; audio versions of reading material; and tutoring. Schools often require formal neuropsychological testing to show that your brain performs differently than others' before they give accommodations. However, many people with ADHD test just fine, which can make it harder to convince schools of the need for help. Some schools only require documentation from a clinician that you have a medical reason for accommodations such as mentoring and extra time for assignments.

WORK: Workplaces traditionally offer far fewer supports, though the range varies tremendously. The law gives employees the right to "reasonable accommodations"—which means low-cost supports such as software to sync work and personal calendars or a cubicle in a quiet part of the office or adjacent to a naturally organized co-worker. Though prejudice is illegal, it may be extremely difficult and expensive to receive legal satisfaction, so people are generally careful in the workplace about admitting to a disability that is not physically obvious. For the most part, people with FAST MINDS traits must make their own way in the working world, developing their own systems for effective organization, communication, and performance.

When to Tell at Work

We suggest strongly that you delay talking about a diagnosis at work until you've thought through the possible consequences of doing so. Your boss may be extremely supportive, getting you what you need to do your best. Or maybe not. By maintaining your privacy, you retain control. Privacy rules in the United States protect workers from revealing their personal medical information—so if one chooses to formally request accommodations under the Americans with Disabilities Act, the medical reason can be worded simply as "a medical condition."

Instead of talking about a diagnosis with your boss or colleagues, we suggest instead you first devise solutions to organizational problems that plague multiple people in the office—not just those with diagnosed ADHD. Having clear inter-office communications benefits everyone. So does an agenda at every meeting and a summary of action points at the end. All workers need good organizational tools, such as calendaring systems and space for paperwork. You can ask for noise-canceling headphones or a desk in a quieter corner without talking about ADHD.

You may also be able to get more of what you need by offering help, rather than asking for it. If writing things down keeps you focused, you could offer to keep the minutes at meetings. If sitting down with your boss helps keep you on track, offer to do so more frequently and bring a clear agenda to help ensure that you are satisfying workplace priorities. If you are on a team, avoid tasks you know you won't do well by quickly offering to do what comes more naturally to you. Then you can use the team to provide accountability, with deadlines and protected time to work together. We've also seen people have great success by asking for an in-house mentor—ideally, an experienced, naturally organized, inspiring person—who can help them get and stay on track.

If you do decide to ask your employer for help with FAST MINDS challenges, know the right place to go by doing your homework first. Your human resources department may have clear policies or suggestions that your supervisor is not even aware of. Other co-workers with ADHD may have found solutions you can present to your supervisor. Again, note that you can talk about your "medical need" for assistance without specifying a particular problem or condition. But it's important to be explicit about the accommodations you think will help and what role you would like the company to play. This is more on point and less confusing to nonclinical people than using a label such as *ADHD* or *learning disability*.

Disclosing the condition can be constructive in some situations. Zoe Kessler, the ADHD blogger, ended up telling her bosses about her ADHD after she was called on the carpet for an out-of-character mistake. She asked the higher-ups to sit down with her and explained calmly and slowly that she has ADHD and had gone without her medications for three days before making the error. In the year since, Zoe says she feels that her reputation at work has only improved. "The people I work for are highly conservative and business-minded. I'm amazed at how well it went over and I have no idea why. They don't seem to care about my diagnosis. They probably appreciated my honesty."

When to Tell Family and Friends

Obviously, there is no formal requirement or guideline for when to talk about FAST MINDS traits with a family member, friend, colleague, or person you are dating. What can help any relationship is to be honest about the challenges you face. Many celebrities, sports stars, and business leaders have disclosed their ADHD. What's important is to find people in your sphere who will accept your traits and get your deal. When a young adult discloses a new diagnosis, parents often feel remiss that they didn't pick up on it earlier.

We also recommend keeping mutual goals in mind, not just your own goals. Use the pause button to think carefully before making promises or saying yes to new requests. It's better in the long run to tell someone that what they are asking for is not your strength than to agree to something you aren't likely to deliver. Instead, you could offer something that allows you to shine and that you're likely to follow through on.

TAZ: FINDING FRIENDS

Taz was adopted as an infant by a professional couple who later learned that his birth mother was a seventeen-year-old with ADHD.

Even in kindergarten, Taz needed accommodations to get through the day. He had extra time with the teacher to help him focus. On outings, he was always the child holding the teacher's hand to make sure he stayed with the group. He was closely supervised on the playground, where he usually chose solitary activities such as playing in the sand. By the time he was formally diagnosed with ADHD at age seven, he had a desk in the hall and was given permission to work out his restlessness by going to the gym when he needed to.

From grades three to five, Taz attended a special school for boys with ADHD and related learning issues. The school had small classes, individualized teaching plans, and special socialization groups where he was taught how to advocate for himself. He did well, and by grade six, he wanted to try public school again. Fortunately he was tall, so there was no bullying this time, but he still needed accommodations. He was allowed to produce all of his homework on a computer, because of a writing disorder. He got extra time for written work and was taught to keep a day planner of his assignments. Though encouraged to join clubs and sports, Taz usually chose solitary activities such as swimming, music, and computer games.

Taz's social life finally started to improve in high school. He had a bigger group of kids to choose from and was able to find some who shared his passion for computers and animation. Now twenty-three and a recent university graduate, Taz has a number of good friends. He still occasionally offends them, but he's quick to apologize and they are generally quick to forgive him. He is getting better at accepting their suggestions for how to be a good friend; he often checks with one of them or someone else he trusts for feedback on his behavior. He's learned how to recognize whether he is talking too much or monopolizing a conversation. Taz has an IQ of 140—borderline "genius." For a long time, he was confused as to why, with so much to offer, he wasn't more popular. Now, with a strong group of friends, that question doesn't matter to him anymore.

Best Friends Forever

Great friends or supportive spouses can make all the difference, keeping you on track and focused. A good friend at work can remind you when it's time to move on to the next project, help you stick with projects until they're done, and keep your spirits up. Starting and maintaining friendships takes effort for everyone—but for people with FAST MINDS and social skill challenges, it also takes some strategy.

Stephanie Sarkis, a psychotherapist and author, wrote on the website www.everydayhealth.com about how she and her best friend support each other through their ADHD: Each woman texts the other every time she marks off a to-do list item or when she feels the need for a quick pep talk.[6] "Just having that person there who knows that you have something due can be a huge help. And for both of us it's really helped our productivity," Sarkis wrote. "Texting is nice because it's really quick. Sometimes we'll text back, 'Way to go!' or 'Good job.' Just hearing that encouragement can really help you push through the next task."

Be careful not to go too far in your reliance on friends, though. If a friend is regularly cleaning your house and doing your laundry without getting paid for it, you have gone too far. If a spouse is doing 90 percent of the housework and childcare, you have gone too far. It is fine to get someone to help hold you accountable to your own standards and desires, but you have to respect their own needs and lives.

What should you look for in a friend? Zoe Kessler offered this advice in an online column: "I and many of my ADD/ADHD friends look for patience, support, and a good sense of humor in a friend. When I find myself in a situation in which someone is abusive, irrational, or acting inappropriately, I wonder if my social skills are to blame. A call to my dearest friend puts things in perspective. She knows what I feel in my gut—that it's not always me who's wrong."[7] It's truly a relief to have some people around whom you can drop your guard—people who will overlook the FAST MINDS habits of not filtering comments, going for the emotionally intense topic, or seeming restless.

Should you search for friends among others with ADHD? That's up to you. Some people find it hard to cope with a friend who is as disorganized as they are (or more so); others find it freeing to know that their friend has some of the same challenges they do. Probably a mix is best. It's great to have a few friends who can understand where you're coming from, accept you for who you are, and not get mad when you get lost in a conversation or forget about a planned lunch date. Working with their ADHD behaviors may also help you be more understanding about the people who work with yours.

Friends and particularly your spouse should be able to bring out the best in you and compensate for your weaknesses, as you do for them. Life may be more challenging if neither of you can fill out a tax return, remember to lock the door at night, or manage to get dinner on the table. That's when your class clown skills may come in handy; humor—and some extra spending money—may be the best weapons you have against such natural disorganization.

Being Your Own Best Friend

Everyone needs to learn how to advocate for themselves—getting what they need so they do and feel their best. If you have ADHD, it may be harder for you to self-advocate because of low self-esteem or because your difficult childhood was filled with more pressing needs than learning these skills. Now that you are an adult, you need to recognize that you are the only one who can truly look out for you—your parents can't do that anymore, and it's not a job for your boss, either. If you need something in your work environment to change, the burden is on you to figure out what that is and to seek a solution, whether it's moving your desk, getting a peripheral brain, or finding a different job.

If your relationships aren't fulfilling your needs, try to figure out what that's about. Are you expecting too much of your spouse? Do you depend on him or her to be your best friend, your house cleaner, your tax preparer, your moral support, your organizer, *and* your parent? Try writing down what you are looking for and see if there are healthy ways to get it elsewhere—hire a cleaner and an accountant; get more of your needed moral support from friends; learn to appreciate your spouse for the things he or she is naturally great at providing. It may help to fill out an inventory together, agreeing on who has what talent and which weakness. That doesn't mean the one who doesn't mind doing dishes needs to do them *every* night, but that you both are aware of where you need support and where you excel.

Having clear roles at home, the way you do at work, may be useful to help divide the labor and hold family members accountable for their share of the chores.

CHARLOTTE: ACCEPTING DIFFERENCES

Charlotte never wanted to be part of the "ADHD club." All the other girls she knew with ADHD "wore their diagnosis on their sleeves," she says. She felt some used ADHD as an excuse when they couldn't get their homework done, talked about their medication, and bragged about getting extra time to finish standardized tests. "That never felt like a cool club to me. I'd much rather be in the club of people who don't need to work this hard," she says. So she hasn't told many people about her diagnosis. In college, only her two best friends knew.

But she also realized when she got to college that she wasn't the only one who had reasons to struggle—nearly everyone had some challenges, whether it was coming from another culture or having difficult family issues. Charlotte says her ADHD stopped feeling like a "problem" to her and started feeling more like just who she is. Facing a huge workload in graduate school, she went to the disability support office and is glad she asked for help.

If Someone You Care About Has a FAST MIND

Having a relationship with someone with ADHD—as with anyone—has its joys and frustrations. They can be loads of fun to hang out with but accidentally blurt out family secrets. They may appear insensitive with personal comments. They may be warm and loving yet so limited in their other friendships that their need for you feels suffocating. They may be deep and thoughtful yet unable to handle the small talk at parties. They may seem committed to you one minute and out the door the next. They may be intense when you want peace; talkative when you crave silence. They can be impassioned and also quite irritable.

Your friendship and love is particularly important for the person with ADHD, who may have a hard time making other friends. You can continue to support them by encouraging and praising their success, helping them set priorities, and then holding them accountable for the things they say they want to do. The key to a healthy life in close relationship with someone with ADHD is *balance* and *accommodation*. Balance means distributing tasks between yourself and them based on strengths and challenges, and accommodation means doing things a different way as long as it fulfills the same goals. A team does its best work when the best person is assigned to each job.

You should not be put in a position of taking over their life or completely neglecting your own. Their diagnosis helps explain their challenges, but it doesn't let them off the hook—they still have to do the job for which they are paid as well as their share of the parenting and housework. That doesn't mean that you need to alternate months for balancing the checkbook. If your ADHD spouse is terrible at household finances, then keep this task for yourself or delegate it to someone else. But any relationship in which one person carries 90 percent of the responsibility, doing or paying for housework, upkeep, and parenting, isn't healthy and won't last.

You may be the one who needs to set boundaries on their demands. You may also have to make it clear how they can act to meet your needs, such as showing up at dinner to eat food you've lovingly prepared or not tuning out in conversations.

When you can, try to focus on their intentions—what they want to do—not what they actually do. Having read this far, you understand that those two are often not the same. They may become easily bored, begin to half-listen to what you have to say, and drift off—but this doesn't mean they don't care about you as much as you care about them.

Here are a few suggestions for helping someone with a FAST MIND bring their intentions more in line with their actions:

■ Decide together on critical moments that need improvement in your relationship.

■ Set boundaries on how you expect to be treated; having FAST MINDS traits is not an excuse for hurtful behavior.

■ Help them plan and practice the message they want to communicate before big meetings or other critical moments.

■ If emotion is getting in the way of conversations, agree ahead of time that either of you can call a timeout to calm down or take time to refocus on the purpose or goals of the conversation before continuing.

If you and your child both have FAST MINDS, that can add extra stress in the family. But it also offers opportunities for accountability and to be a great role model.

WHAT YOU CAN DO

A big part of taking care of yourself is getting what you need from other people. If you're easily distracted at work, what you need may be an office with a door you can close or walls that aren't glass. In a relationship, you may need someone who understands that you'd rather pay for a cook or housecleaner than be relied on to do the domestic chores yourself. But getting that help can be a challenge if FAST MINDS features make it harder to communicate your needs.

So when does it make sense to ask for help? And what should you ask for?

Unfortunately, in most situations if you tell someone you need help because you are disorganized, can't focus, or have ADHD, they will have little idea of what may be helpful. Be clear about what you need, and other people will have an easier time helping you meet that need.

PRACTICING PRODUCTIVE COMMUNICATION

In your next meeting or conversation, try some of these strategies for effective communications:

- Imagine you are in a CNN interview. Speak in sound bites: two to three sentences and stop.

- Try listening more than talking—make a game out of it, if that helps.

- Before speaking, check whether what you are about to say is truly a reply to their last comment or to a tangential idea.

- Write down what you want to say to make it more concrete.

- Match their level of emotional and personal content.

- Set a mutual agenda for the conversation from the outset.

MANAGING EMOTIONAL COMMUNICATION

We talked in previous chapters about the importance of knowing when you are operating in an emotional frame of mind—and how emotional impulsivity can sabotage interpersonal health. Plenty of conversations are emotionally fraught: a talk with your estranged mother or soon-to-be-ex-spouse, an annual review at work, a request for an extension so you'll have more time to work on your final paper. We've already walked you through approaches that should help you better manage such loaded social interactions, but here's a quick summary to help you translate those ideas into a social setting:

Be aware of your own reactions and hot buttons. Actively anticipate common situations in which you are likely to overreact— keep them on your radar screen.

Don't miss critical moments. Catch a critical moment early in the conversation and try to defuse the tension then, before it can build up. If you notice that you always get into conflict with your boss when you've forgotten to eat lunch, make sure to grab a bite before your next afternoon meeting.

Hit the pause button. If you're tempted to react in anger or frustration—at yourself or the person across from you—hit the pause button, acknowledge that you have a right to feel that way, and then try to defuse it constructively, perhaps by cracking a joke.

Use a peripheral brain. Can you avoid a difficult conversation entirely by delegating it to someone else? If a client really pushes your buttons, can a colleague handle that account instead? If your sister is much better at managing your mother's emotional outbursts than you are, can you both agree to let her take the lead on these issues and let you pick up a different task?

BEING EFFECTIVE INTERPERSONALLY

Here are some suggestions for specific challenges we've seen in people with FAST MINDS:

Do you have trouble making friends? Analyze how you behave in social situations and try to become aware of things you may do to push people away. Ask people close to you for tips or help.

When someone is talking, do you quickly assume you know what they're going to say and either tune out or steer the conversation to a topic you're more interested in? Do you see why this might annoy someone? Once you become aware of this instinct in yourself, you can try to do something about it. If your boss comes to you with a long request and you feel you may lose interest, take notes to help you look and feel engaged in the conversation. If she is asking something of you, ask her to be clear and summarize the request back to her to make sure you are on the same page.

Can you see a pattern in your disengagement from communication? Having a conversation with your supervisor after sitting through a long meeting may be a recipe for disaster if you are feeling restless and not present mentally. Try scheduling critical interactions on mornings when you can be at your best, such as after being well rested and exercising.

Do you tend to monopolize a conversation? Sometimes people with ADHD get so involved in the topics that interest them that they forget others may not share their passions. If this is a problem for you, find a way to give yourself regular reminders to take a break and ask the other person for their opinion or what interests them. Some close friends will be able to tell you when you're taking too much control of the conversation. You can also start looking for the social cues people use to demonstrate boredom: flat or blank facial expressions, fidgeting, or frequent glances at a watch or nearby activity. If you see these, you might ask your conversation partner what they think or give them an opportunity to steer the discussion in a different direction.

Do you frequently forget meetings or other things that are important to people you care about? This is another chance for us to say again how important your schedule calendar is. If you're concerned people will make fun of you for writing so much down, consider that missing a meeting is more likely to cost you an important relationship.

Do you keep people in your schedule? Friendships are two-way streets. If you want someone to pay attention to you, make sure you protect time in your schedule to catch up on what is happening in their life.

You are not alone in this world, but other people can't read your mind and predict what you need. You need to learn how to ask for what you need and give something in return. If you are careful to maximize the quality of your relationships, you will also build a valuable resource for support as you face FAST MINDS challenges—other people.

KEY POINTS

Here are some suggestions for getting better at everyday conversations. If these are a challenge for you, don't try to start doing them all at once. Try one at a time and use strategies discussed in previous chapters such as reminders and rewards to practice these habits.

■ Keep the other person's purposes in mind. By definition, a conversation is between two people. The other person wants to participate as much as you do. Try talking half as much as they do and see what happens.

■ Show interest by making eye contact and asking questions.

■ Don't "multitask" while talking—put the cell phone out of reach!

■ Express confidence and positivity—use humor and smile.

■ Gather evidence for what you think is the other person's opinion—rather than assuming that your impression is correct.

■ Ask rather than tell.

■ Choose the right place, time, and style—discussing complex issues may not work in casual situations or over Twitter.

■ Press the pause button if you're feeling rash, impulsive, or emotional. Ask to continue the conversation later, when you're more in control and have done a thought record to ground your perspective.

■ Be clear about any follow-up items. If either of you is expected to take action as a result of the conversation, make that clear before the end, summarize key points, and plan for a way to follow up. If you agreed to do something, write it immediately in your calendar and protect time to get it done.

PART III

Building the Life You Want

10

Make the Most out of Medication

During his fourth day on ADHD medication, Marshall noticed a change for the better. He realized he wasn't worrying about whether he had forgotten an important meeting or task. He just *knew* what to do next. He described it as the feeling you get as a kid just after mastering a bike without training wheels—riding for the first time with confidence, speed, and freedom.

A day later, Marshall had to sit through three hourlong meetings and was able to tune into what everyone said. The burgeoning mess on his desk was not a pile of things to do, he realized, but a result of his improved productivity. A day later, as he felt his usual irritation rising at a co-worker, he was able to channel that annoyance into doodling on his notes. Instead of being totally distracted by the co-worker, Marshall was able to follow what was being said in the meeting.

Over the next few months, Marshall negotiated gradual increases in his medication with his doctor, using his baseline symptoms as a way of monitoring functional improvement with each increase. He'd feel woozy for a few days and put up with a couple of additional side effects but nothing uncomfortable. Though still carrying a lot of baggage from forty years of undiagnosed ADHD, Marshall was slowing starting to feel more in control of his life.

———————

So far, this book has explored various ways that FAST MINDS traits can impact someone's life, and principles and habits to help address those traits. In this chapter we talk about using medications to manage clinically diagnosed ADHD. We discuss who may benefit from medications, which features medicines are likely to change—and which they won't, what risks to consider, and some specifics to discuss with clinicians who may or may not know much about ADHD.

Medication prescribed correctly and given at the right dose helps people stay engaged, focused, and on track. This can translate into better listening and reading, as well as improvements in getting around to, sticking with, and finishing tasks. These improvements can have a broad impact on the FAST MINDS challenges of ADHD:

- People **F**orget less if they are tuned in more.

- They find **A**chievements easier if they're not wasting their time spinning their wheels.

- They don't get **S**tuck as often if they can focus and figure out a new path to take, and they aren't as **T**ime-challenged if they can tune into what's going on around them, or as **M**otivationally challenged if they know they will be productive when they start work.

- They aren't as **I**mpulsive if they can pause longer and clearly focus on the consequences of their actions.

■ They aren't as **N**ovelty seeking if they are more engaged in what they've already begun.

■ And they aren't as **D**istracted or **S**cattered if they can tune out distractions and follow through on putting things in their place.

Virtually everyone we've talked about in this book who was diagnosed with ADHD has told us that medication has been transformative for them. They consider it an essential part of their self-care—but not the answer to all of their problems. In particular, many people struggle with organizational problems despite being on medication—they may find themselves better engaged in tasks, but still have trouble doing the right task at the right time. This is where the personalized skills we have explored in this book come in. As is commonly said, "Pills don't teach skills." All of these successful people also work on themselves in the ways we have suggested thus far, and most of them use the nonmedical approaches that we discuss in the next chapter as well.

Many of the stories we have told have been about people diagnosed with ADHD at a time when they were struggling in their home, work, school, or personal lives. Many other adults have milder or fewer FAST MINDS traits or find supportive environments and never suffer as much. For them, nonmedical approaches may be sufficient, and medication may not be warranted.

Response to medical treatment, like ADHD itself, varies by individual. Some people need higher doses to benefit; others respond to low doses. It's impossible to predict who will do best on which ADHD medication or at what dose. A carefully planned trial-and-error process is the only way to figure it out. Many clinicians who are unfamiliar with ADHD don't understand this process and think that if the first dose doesn't work, the patient won't benefit from medication or must not have ADHD at all. The same doctors wouldn't "give up" or say their patient must be perfectly healthy if the first dose of a cholesterol-lowering medication wasn't immediately effective.

Medications such as stimulants increase vigilance and focus in people without ADHD as well—which is probably what contributes to the high rates of stimulant misuse by students and athletes. We advise strongly against using these agents to augment function, because the risks have not been studied for people without clinical reasons for treatment. We also strongly believe that it is unhealthy and also unethical to try to create new capabilities through medications, while it is perfectly appropriate to compensate for a well-understood, impairing condition.

The proper medication at the proper dose should "feel" right and provide substantial improvement. We know people who think they have to tolerate uncomfortable side effects, not realizing that there are other medications without these consequences, or who think they are getting all they could from medicine when a different agent might help more.

Making an Informed Choice

Some people choose not to take medication because they don't like the idea of it. Other people may have conditions that mean they won't tolerate ADHD medication. The next chapter is devoted to nonmedical therapies and approaches that can help with some aspects of ADHD. But in our experience, where they are tolerated, nothing is as effective at addressing ADHD as quickly as prescription medications.

Some people think that taking medication for ADHD is a sign of weakness, that they're not trying hard enough to battle ADHD on their own. But no one would tell an asthmatic that they should skip their inhaler and just "try harder" to breathe. We think that if a safe treatment is available for a challenging condition, it's rational to use it.

Usually, we recommend that people consider medication after determining that changes to their environment are not enough to address ADHD challenges. By adulthood, many people have already figured this out through trial and error. Whereas parents make medication decisions for their children, adults with ADHD must decide for themselves how to deal with their brain's differences. The choices are to do nothing and continue to cope with the challenges, make lifestyle changes, or add medication to those lifestyle changes. We suggest viewing new treatment as an experiment, with a set time period and explicitly stated goals. It helps doctors to know those goals, and goal setting allows people to decide whether the medication is addressing their target symptoms.

Successful medication treatment improves the brain's ability to control what is engaging—what it pays attention to. Strategies that didn't work before may work on medication. If you had trouble sitting down to plan your week or could never follow through on putting your keys on the hook by the door, try again once you've initiated treatment. You may find it easier to plan, keep those plans in mind, and follow through on the little habits that make or break critical moments in your day.

Reading may also be a new experience for you once you start medication. Many people with FAST MINDS find it hard to read because their minds wander too much. But medication allows them to focus for long enough to get absorbed by a story or derive useful information from what they're reading—some for the first time ever.

People occasionally tell us they want to take medication "as needed" for ADHD—to cover key time periods or meetings with clients. An artist we know takes medication on days she has to meet with clients or manage sales, but not on studio days, when she doesn't have to be as self-disciplined. Technically, the diagnosis of ADHD requires impairment in two major life roles, such as school, work, or home function. If someone is fine with remaining untreated in many roles and parts of their life, it raises the question of whether they meet the full diagnosis and whether medication treatment is necessary, or whether changing the demands and tasks in those challenging parts of a person's life would be a better approach.

Biological Action for ADHD

Most ADHD medications affect the availability of dopamine and norepinephrine in the brain. In a typical brain, a neuron (nerve cell) pumps these chemical messengers into the gap between itself and an adjacent cell and also reabsorbs these chemicals. Medications generally block this reabsorption, so more of the chemicals are available in the gap, or synapse, to "talk" to other neurons. This changes the patterns of communication among neurons.

Unlike medicines for conditions such as depression, the effects of ADHD medication are usually noticeable within a few days if the dose is appropriate. One man we know was on the verge of flunking out of medical school, and his girlfriend was ready to walk out. Within a day or two of starting medication, he noticed he had stopped cutting her off midsentence, and within ten days, he had passed enough of his medical exams for the school to give him another chance.

Drug Safety

ADHD medications have been used for more than sixty years—for ADHD or other conditions—and are considered safe when prescribed accurately.[1] But there are certain holes in the research. Because we know the treatments are largely effective, it would be unethical to do a long-term study in which some people were given medications and others were not. Most studies comparing medication to a placebo last for just six weeks; a smaller number of studies have followed people on treatment over a year or two. As is true of most medications, we simply don't have systematic research to tell what health risks are involved in taking ADHD medications for years or decades or how effectiveness changes over time.

Safety studies have shown that ADHD medications can increase heartbeat and blood pressure but do not pose major heart risks for those who are otherwise healthy. One recent study looked at more than 1 million children and young adults taking ADHD medication and showed that they had no higher risk of serious heart problems than the general population.[2] Similarly, a recent study of more than 150,000 adults who received stimulant medication for an average of 1.3 years found no increase in cardiovascular problems when compared to adults who did not receive stimulants.[3]

A special consultation with a heart specialist may be warranted for people with a family history of or prior experience with heart rhythm problems, differences in heart structure, fainting or losing consciousness, chest pain, reduced ability to exert themselves, or family history of sudden death, particularly at a young age.

Treatment may be less straightforward for people with other kinds of mental health challenges, such as mood disorders, anxiety distress, or a history of substance use. Sometimes, these other conditions need to be improved before ADHD can be managed or before ADHD medication can be tolerated.

Studies of ADHD medications focus on treating ADHD, so they often intentionally exclude people who have other mental health conditions, such as bipolar disorder or depression—which, as Dr. Surman has shown, accounts for more than half of people with ADHD.[4] Therefore, we can't assume that people with these other conditions will benefit as much from or tolerate medications as well as people with just ADHD. Everyone who takes medication responds differently, because of genetics, drug sensitivities, or environmental context.

One of the largest and longest of the ADHD treatment studies followed 133 clinic patients taking medication. Half of them continued with the treatment for at least two years, and most saw improvements in their ADHD.[5] About 45 percent were also treated for anxiety or depression at the same time. Although most of the participants avoided significant side effects, one person had hallucinations, another became aggressive, and a third became paranoid. Other mental health conditions probably contributed to these reactions, but the fact that they can occur is a reminder that it's important to have good follow-up clinical care. Most ADHD medications should be avoided

Research Spotlight

In 2008, Dr. Surman contributed to a study led by Dr. George Bush (not either of the former presidents!) to see which brain regions were affected by ADHD medications.[6] They asked twenty-one adults with ADHD either on placebo or treated with methylphenidate, a stimulant, to play a simple game while their brains were scanned in a special MRI machine. They were asked to do a task that involved paying attention under changing conditions and suppressing the impulse to type the number they saw rather than its position on the screen. The brains of participants on medication showed greater activity in the cingulate gyrus and dorsolateral portions of the prefrontal cortex, as well as the parietal cortex—all regions we have discussed as critical to engagement. Such increases in activity indicate that ADHD medication may either correct an underactivity that leads to ADHD or compensate for that underactivity by activating the engagement network.

by people who have experienced impairing agitation, mania or hallucinations.

Our advice is that the need for treatment, the "best" treatment, and the safety of treatment should not be taken for granted. People and their doctors should closely evaluate their needs over time, including what their life would be like without medication or at a lower dose, as well as how treatment should be changed to manage other conditions such as depression or anxiety that may come and go. The long-term theoretical risks of being on a medicine, however unclear, are still risks—and should be weighed against the benefit the agents clearly provide.

Types of Medications

There are two basic types of medications—**stimulants** and **nonstimulants**. Stimulants are based on two essential molecules: methylphenidate and amphetamine, which have both been used to treat ADHD and other conditions for more than sixty years. The name *stimulant* is confusing because rather than increasing activity levels, stimulants can decrease overactivity in people with ADHD. Stimulants are thought to have their effects by increasing levels of dopamine and norepinephrine in parts of the brain that are important for control of behavior.

Nonstimulants make up the other class of ADHD medications. The nonstimulant most commonly prescribed for ADHD in adults is atomoxetine, which also increases norepinephrine in parts of the brain. Nonstimulants often take longer to work—weeks rather than days when starting a new prescription. The side effects of nonstimulants are often similar to those of stimulants, including mild physical discomforts. Each dose of a nonstimulant often lasts longer and tends not to keep people awake as stimulants do. They also are not typically abused, making them appropriate for people at risk for substance use or in early recovery.

Stimulants are considered better than nonstimulants at reducing ADHD symptoms. A recent review of nineteen studies using thirteen different medications found that stimulants had more effect than non-stimulants on ADHD symptoms.[7] However, we know many people for whom a nonstimulant is more effective for their particular version of ADHD than a stimulant. People respond differently to different medications, so it is important to work with a clinician to find the right one.

Technological advances in the past decade have produced longer-acting drugs, allowing people to take just one dose a day. Where available, we strongly recommend these long-acting stimulants over short-acting ones because they're more convenient and effective throughout the day. Ongoing research by several research groups, including by Dr. Surman and his colleagues, is exploring whether other drugs and even special nutritional agents can improve ADHD and organizational challenges as well as or better than existing medications.

MARSHALL: FINDING THE RIGHT DRUG AT THE RIGHT DOSE

After starting on a small dose of one medication, Marshall and his doctor decided that there was room for improvement in his ADHD symptoms, and they increased his dose several times over the course of his visits (this is called titrating up *medication). He felt that the drug had helped calm down his thinking and reduced his urges to interrupt conversations and make inappropriate jokes. But he was still spacing out, procrastinating, and having trouble sticking to important tasks, and he was also bothered by dry mouth and the overstimulation that left him not feeling like him-*

self for parts of the day. Each time he went back, he felt that his doctor increased his dose without much discussion about what the medication was helping or what he could do about the side effects. Overall, though, he was happy with the benefits. His giant to-do list slowly began to shrink. "With each item crossed off, I get a little bit stronger and gain a little bit more pride in myself," he wrote on his blog. "I suppose you could say my self-esteem is improving."

About ten months into his treatment, he decided he couldn't stand the side effects anymore. He decided to take charge and got a second opinion. That doctor switched him to a different stimulant medication. After the dose was boosted a few times, Marshall said he's finally found the sweet spot. "It's been remarkably side effect free for me," he says. "Now I have a sense of mission, a sense of ability and confidence that I have never experienced before."

Marshall's physical health has also changed dramatically since beginning medication. He has lost fifty pounds, mainly by ending his "self-medication" with Coca-Cola (he was drinking at least

Pills, Pumps, and Patches

Today, ADHD medication comes in tablets, capsules with different release mechanisms, and even a patch.

Although physicians are often more comfortable with one form than another, the different types are useful because each releases medication in different patterns—and people sometimes tolerate one better than another. For example, if someone has a headache a couple of hours into a dose or feels tired as the medication wears off, changing to a different release pattern of the same active ingredient may avoid these symptoms. The switch changes how the medication levels rise and fall in the system.

eight cans a day) and alcohol. He simply decided when he started
medication that he wanted to see the effect of the drugs—not of the
caffeine and alcohol—and he quit them both cold turkey.

"I was drinking to avoid the pain of what I saw coming up,
which was a nonstop conveyor belt of failure, and to forget about
the past and all the things I had not accomplished." Now he says
he doesn't need to drown his sorrows.

Managing Side Effects

Like any drug, all ADHD medications may have side effects. Luckily,
most of them are minor, but some may be uncomfortable or discon-
certing. We recommend that anyone who "doesn't feel right" on
ADHD medication discuss a change to a different medicine with their
doctor. The effects are different enough between active ingredients
and release patterns that often another agent will feel better.

The most common side effects from stimulants include decreased
appetite, dry mouth, jitteriness, and mild increases in heart rate or
blood pressure. Nonstimulants have similar side effects, but they vary
by medication. Atomoxetine, for example, can produce nausea and
fatigue and, rarely, can affect liver function. Concerning effects are
uncommon, though, when medication is carefully prescribed. On
Marshall's first day of stimulant medication, for instance, he had trouble urinating. That went away quickly, but if it hadn't, he might have
wanted to switch medications much faster than he did. Infrequent,
serious side effects are always possible, so reporting anything uncomfortable is a good idea. Generally, if a physical side effect is going to go
away, it will within several days. Anything lasting more than a week
is likely to persist.

People on medications should have their heart rate and blood pressure measured regularly, since the drugs can trigger increases. It's im-

Caffeine and ADHD

Some people with ADHD find that caffeine—the most common central nervous system stimulant consumed worldwide—helps them function more productively. They may self-medicate with caffeine. Marshall's eight Coca-Colas a day certainly fit that pattern.

Caffeine is a weak stimulant, and it rarely makes a substantial difference in focus. Nicotine is a far more powerful stimulant.

Caffeine plus stimulant medication may be too much for some people, compounding sleep problems, jitteriness, muscle tension, and headaches. Once ADHD treatment is started, people often notice that they want or need less caffeine.

Again, caffeine is a good example of how variable individual reactions can be to agents that are active in the brain. Some people are sensitive to caffeine or find that it lasts a long time in their system. Others are hardly touched by it.

portant to know that all stimulant and many nonstimulant ADHD medications can impact heart rate or blood pressure. Different drugs can have different effects, so it may be worth trying another prescription.

With any medication, it's advisable to increase and decrease doses gradually. Some people report fatigue or low energy when they go off stimulants. This gradual tapering may alleviate unnecessary discomfort.

OTHER COMMON SIDE EFFECTS:

Sleep problems: Stimulant ADHD medications can interfere with sleep—but they may also improve the ability to sleep. In a review of sleep effects in two large stimulant trials, Dr. Surman found little difference between those taking medications versus placebos.[8] Medications can also help with organization in the evenings, including sticking with pre-bedtime routines, so it's worth experimenting with long-acting drugs to ensure adequate coverage across the day. It is important to figure out how long a stimulant acts in your system and to make sure it wears off one to two hours before bedtime.

Loss of appetite: Stimulants are not great weight loss aids, but they do decrease appetite—and this can mean poorer nutrition or too low a weight. Some people get rebound hunger as the medication wears off. Discuss changing medication or dose if you feel strong effects on your appetite or eating pattern; remember to get optimal brain nutrition.

Nausea: Taking medication with food can help reduce nausea.

Jitteriness/agitation/too much energy: Stimulants are motivating agents, but produce unsettling drive or jitteriness in some people. Changing dose, release pattern, or the agent can help.

Irritability and mood or "personality" changes: Some people feel withdrawn, moody, edgy, or obsessive on a stimulant. These effects do not tend go away, and a change in the release pattern or to another medication may be needed.

Headaches: Taking medication with food, drinking more water, switching the dosing schedule, reducing head and neck tension through relaxation or massage, and changing to a different release pattern or medication may help reduce medication-related headaches.

Dry mouth: Drinking more water, chewing gum, or sucking on hard candies can reduce dry mouth.

MARSHALL:

No one could accuse Marshall of being lazy, but like many people with ADHD, he's prone to jumping from one activity to the next. One day, a few months after starting medication, he noted an interesting pattern:

"*Yesterday I went up onto the roof to caulk the brick in the chimney. Then I noticed the gutters were full of leaves, so I emptied them. Then I cleaned out the garage. Then I used my new blower (it was my birthday present!) and blew out the garage, and the yard, and the driveway. And then I broke down some large cardboard boxes and put them in the recycling bin. Then I organized my tools in the garage. Then I sat and looked at the lawn. Then I sprayed weed killer on my driveway. Then I cleaned up the garage a bit. Then I cleaned out my car. Then I went back inside, having accomplished my initial task, which was caulking the roof. But at least it was the weekend, and I didn't have hugely pressing items to do. And at least I was actually productive. The problem, as you might imagine, is that . . . there are higher-priority items I could have been doing with my time.*"

Marshall was able to focus on a number of tasks and complete each one, but he says he was being productive without following priorities—getting things done, but not necessarily the things he really should be doing. "*I need to remember to be productive with priorities—not without.*" So, although medication may get people going, it may not get them going in the right direction. That requires having the right approach to critical moments.

Now, with the help of medication that addresses his ADHD symptoms more, and after a year of learning how to set priorities, Marshall is much better at being productive in constructive ways. His thinking is more focused, too. Instead of having multiple channels of thought running through his head simultaneously—which he compares to watching several channels of TV at once—he can stick to one channel at a time. Marshall says he doesn't feel like he's given up anything by experiencing only one thought channel at once. "*I can still go there if I wish, but I'm no longer at the mercy of it.*"

If Someone You Care About Has a FAST MIND

Remember that you are not the one taking the medication—it's up to the person with ADHD to make the decision. If you personally disapprove of medications for ADHD, consider the cost that continued struggles will have on the person's long-term well-being. For some, starting medication helps people live a productive, engaged life and limits other kinds of distress, such as anxiety, depression, drug abuse, alcohol abuse, or other mental health problems. We think medications, prescribed under a doctor's supervision, are a healthy answer to serious challenges.

If you want to help someone who is starting ADHD medication, you can provide important perspective on improvements and side effects. Giving them your supportive perspective on how their experiment is going will be invaluable.

WHAT YOU CAN DO

BEING YOUR OWN SCIENTIST

When you start ADHD medications or switch to a different drug, it is important to keep track of improvements, side effects, and other issues. Think of it as being a scientist, with yourself as your own research project.

When starting a new medication or changing dose, it is important to track and log your response and any side effects. Come up with some system for recording your starting point and any changes. You don't need the perfect system, just someplace where you'll be able to look back and compare how you're feeling at some later point with how you felt before you began medication. If you like charts, make a spreadsheet, noting FAST MINDS symptoms and possible side effects on one axis and drug schedules and responses on the other. Or use the one we've provided here and in Appendix C. You can photocopy it and fill it out every week or two as you start a new drug regimen.

Before starting a medication, consider FAST MINDS traits, noting which ones take effort or are a problem for you. Rate the magnitude of the problem. If you feel that your forgetfulness is ruining your life, give that a 10; if being time-challenged isn't your issue, then give it a 1 or leave it off entirely. It may help to show this chart to someone who knows you well to make sure you have recorded all your significant issues and to help you track changes. Tracking how you respond will help you notice improvements and find the right treatment. Bringing the tracking chart we provide here and in Appendix C to your doctor's appointments will help you remember what to discuss and help your clinician provide better care.

Your clinician should start you at a low dose of a particular drug and then increase it if FAST MINDS symptoms have not improved and you do not have uncomfortable side effects. The medical adage is, "Start low, go slow." Gradual increases allow you to evaluate the effectiveness of your medicine. Your body will probably adjust to a new dose within several days, if it is going to, so sometimes it is worth waiting that long to see if a physical side effect such as dry mouth becomes more tolerable. But if you're hoping to change your behavior with your mother, whom you see only every three months, you may have to wait a while to figure out whether the medication is helping you enough. If side effects become too disruptive, you should talk to your doctor about returning to the next lowest dose.

As you may remember from high school science class, when conducting an experiment, you want to change only one variable at a time. The week you start medication for ADHD is not the time to go

FAST MINDS TRAIT TRACKER

FAST MINDS TRAITS	Before treatment (Rate how challenging [1–10])	Fill in dose, week, and new rating during treatment (1–10)		
Forgetful		Dose ___ Week ___	Dose ___ Week ___	Dose ___ Week ___
Achieving below potential		Dose ___ Week ___	Dose ___ Week ___	Dose ___ Week ___
Stuck in a rut		Dose ___ Week ___	Dose ___ Week ___	Dose ___ Week ___
Time-challenged		Dose ___ Week ___	Dose ___ Week ___	Dose ___ Week ___
Motivationally challenged		Dose ___ Week ___	Dose ___ Week ___	Dose ___ Week ___
Impulsive		Dose ___ Week ___	Dose ___ Week ___	Dose ___ Week ___
Novelty seeking		Dose ___ Week ___	Dose ___ Week ___	Dose ___ Week ___
Distractible		Dose ___ Week ___	Dose ___ Week ___	Dose ___ Week ___
Scattered		Dose ___ Week ___	Dose ___ Week ___	Dose ___ Week ___
Other Challenges (patience, mood stability, etc.)				
Other positive impact of medication; note duration of effect				
SIDE EFFECTS				
(Physical discomfort, mood or personality change, sleep pattern change)				
When do side effects occur during the day?				
Other negative impact of medication:				

on a crash diet, quit smoking, or move across the country. If you make dramatic shifts in more than one area of your life, you won't be able to tell whether side effects or improvements were from the ADHD medication or from something else.

When you start medication, it's a good idea to be well rested and to have already cut back on things that are counterproductive or that may reduce potential benefits, such as excessive use of alcohol, marijuana, and other addictive substances. If this is a problem for you, we strongly suggest discussing with your clinician whether to address addiction issues before ADHD. In our experience, people who drink only in moderation and avoid marijuana and other illegal substances enjoy much better outcomes than those who don't abstain.

Following your drug regimen as a science experiment will help you keep better track of changes and ensure that you are getting the most out of your medication.

RECOGNIZE THE IMPACT—DO OTHER PEOPLE SAY:

Now that you're on medication, how do you know if it is worth taking or doing a good enough job? The goal should be a real impact in your function, changes that really matter. If you can pay better attention on a medication but you're still forgetting about key meetings, maybe a change in medications or dose would help more. Ask yourself and someone you trust whether the improvements you've made in the first few weeks and months of medication are significant advances: Have they really improved how you function in the world? Have they addressed challenges that really matter to you?

Specific behaviors may get better sooner than larger patterns; for example, you may quickly notice that you are reading more easily, but it may take a while for that to translate into better grades. One month and two months after beginning treatment are useful times to measure effectiveness. Reflect on the three roles or situations you noted at the beginning of the book that you wanted to improve in your life—would other people notice that your being on medicine has helped them?

TAKING A MEDICATION VACATION

ADHD is a dynamic neurological condition, meaning it isn't the same all the time. Frontal regions of the brain develop substantially into the early third decade of life, and thus some people may mature out of ADHD. We know people who go off medicine after long periods, noting less need for it. In some cases, changes in the demands of life (type of work, amount of help from others) may reduce the need for medicine. Some people tell us that new organizational habits they learned while on medication persist while on lower doses or off medication. We suggest that people, in consultation with their prescribing doctor, take time off medication at least once a year or try a lower dose to make sure they still need what they are taking.

Because some people have mild withdrawal symptoms when they stop medication, we recommend tapering down the dose, usually over a few days. Several days without medication provides valuable information about whether the treatment is still necessary and effective. Carefully choose times when the risk will be lowest to take a medication vacation, say during a slow period at work or after a long spurt of success.

As you lower the dose or take a medication vacation, revisit the trait tracker, filling it out both before your break and at least several days later.

Key Things to Know: Working with a Prescribing Clinician

- Stimulants and nonstimulants can have many of the same effects and side effects. The main difference is that stimulants may have more impact on ADHD but are less appropriate for people with substance abuse problems.

- Different release patterns of the same active ingredient have different effects.

- Physical side effects usually decrease over a period of several days if they are going to, so gradually increasing dosage generally makes them more tolerable.

- Long-acting medication is more convenient and offers better coverage.

- Any medical assessment should involve looking for other conditions that may come along with ADHD, such as anxiety and mood issues. These conditions may also determine other treatments that could be appropriate.

What to Bring to Your Initial Visit

- A summary of the FAST MINDS traits you identified and situations or tasks they impact most, as identified in Chapters 1 and 2.

- Information on childhood FAST MINDS symptoms. Notes from old teachers and from family can help.

- Notes on when/whether these symptoms started and stopped over time.

- A list of ALL PRIOR MEDICATIONS and their doses (your pharmacy may have this for you), and notes on which ones helped and which ones caused side effects.

■ Specific examples in any of your life roles (e.g., student, worker, homemaker, spouse) of where it is hard for you to engage as you feel you should and what you do to try to engage.

■ Examples of what would make taking a medicine worthwhile for you in each of your major daily roles (parent, employee, colleague, volunteer, etc).

■ Someone who knows you well. If that's not possible, consider having someone fill out a FAST MINDS trait tracker in this chapter (or Appendix C) about you. This person can add perspective on your challenges, and two voices will give the clinician a better picture of your situation.

Follow-Up Visits

Let's imagine how the first visits with a diagnosing and treating clinician should go. If your clinician gives you too quick a diagnosis, holds only a brief meeting, and offers a one-size-fits-all treatment strategy ("You should be on medication, here's the one"), we think it's a good idea to seek out a second opinion. Your clinician should not be threatened by your wanting to discuss the patterns you have noticed in your function. Also, it is appropriate to ask for a second opinion, particularly if your clinician is unsure about how to proceed in terms of managing side effects or lack of response to treatment.

If you meet criteria for ADHD, the next step is to identify the targets of treatment—this may be the FAST MINDS symptoms that are most burdensome to you. Another good goal for medication treatment: Make the personalized organizational solutions you have explored in this book easier to try or stick with.

The choice of a treatment should be a team effort in which you share with the physician what you have learned about the options from this book and other sources, and hear what they suggest. Working together, you can explore which options, both medical and non-medical, target your pattern of challenges, as well as risks and benefits. If your doctor doesn't specialize in ADHD, it is particularly important that you review the options in this and the next chapter to help your clinician become aware of them, too.

For detailed information on ADHD medications, check out the websites of the National Institute of Mental Health (search for "ADHD"), the National Resource Center on ADHD (produced by Children and Adults with Attention Deficit/Hyperactivity Disorder [CHADD]) and the Centre for ADHD Awareness Canada (CADDAC). Be careful about the quality of online resources, however. People may be more likely to contribute online if they have had an extreme experience, and some sources of information are more reliable than others.

As part of the treatment process, you can review FAST MINDS symptoms using the trait tracker at every doctor's visit to identify which behaviors are improving and which are not.

Be Sure to Tell Your Prescriber Quickly If:

- Your personality is different on medication.

- You experience new feelings or problematic behavior from the medicine—feeling "high," "buzzed," "too good," "racy," agitated, suspicious, or "edgy."

- You notice your heart racing (particularly over 100 beats per minute at rest) or your resting heart rate increases by more than ten beats per minute.

- Your blood pressure rises above 135/85.

- You lose sleep.

- You are physically uncomfortable.

These side effects suggest that either the medication is not right for you or you are on the wrong dose.

In the next chapter we discuss nonmedical approaches that are helpful for many people with FAST MINDS.

KEY POINTS

- Medication is an important cornerstone in the treatment of ADHD.

- Be prepared for your visit with a prescribing clinician by anticipating what they need to know and being aware of treatment options. Don't assume they will be aware of them.

- Establish which FAST MINDS traits you want to target with treatment and track changes in these traits.

- Significant side effects should go away within a few days. If any persist, discuss them with your clinician.

- You have many treatment options, so if one medicine doesn't work, switching to an alternative could help.

11

What Else Works

Kathleen finds it's not *one* thing that makes a difference in her ADHD, but a lifestyle of healthy choices and supports—including a boyfriend who understands her challenges. When Kathleen was diagnosed with ADHD at the tail end of a divorce, her self-esteem was battered. She needed help learning to view herself in a better light. Seeing a psychotherapist over the last few years has been "incredibly powerful" in helping her realize she's not a bad person. Learning cognitive behavioral techniques in therapy helped her become better at replacing her negative, emotional thoughts with more rational, productive perspectives. She also found unexpected help in an online class in positive psychology—the scientific study of what allows people to thrive. The class reminded her of her own resilience and strength in coping during the end of her marriage and the trials of ADHD. It helped her focus on the things she does well, such as handling special projects at work. And it gave her permission to make mistakes and learn from them. "I don't think of mistakes as tragedies and horrible things any more," she says. "So I didn't get to somewhere on time today . . . What was that about? What can I do differently?" she asks now. Not, "What the hell is wrong with me?" This kind of supportive self-talk is as constructive as her negative self-talk was damaging. Every success breeds more success, she often reminds herself.

She also carefully chose organizational strategies that she wanted to practice. It helped to make a plan with her therapist and review her progress. She has developed basic skills, such as writing appointments in her calendar as she makes them and setting deadlines for herself. Now that these have become habits, they're easier to do consistently, she says. Instead of feeling overwhelmed and panicky when faced with paperwork, she knows she can get it done—which makes it easier to focus on the work. She farms out as many repetitive, boring tasks as she can to a man on her staff who excels at following rules. She uses her cell phone to set reminders—getting things out of her head and into her phone so they don't distract her. Sometimes she'll turn on a timer for ten or twenty minutes and challenge herself to see how much work she can get done before it goes off. Other times, she'll catch herself resetting the alarm for a third time and realize she needs to change her focus.

To manage her personal finances, she's enrolled in a class at a nearby night school. The discipline of studying for her midterm on taxes and setting up a personal income statement is taking away the fear and mystery that always surrounded money for her. Taxes and bills now seem like a challenge instead of an insurmountable hurdle.

Her boyfriend has also been a huge help. He has ADHD, too, so he's understanding and supportive of her struggles. Diagnosed as a child, he has had more years to develop his own self-awareness and knowledge of ADHD, so he can provide Kathleen with perspective and constructive feedback. His discipline for exercise also helps get her out of bed and onto the elliptical trainer or into her beloved dance studio. She even remembers to practice mindfulness sometimes.

Kathleen has also learned how to recognize the signs that she's headed for trouble. She recently found herself playing game after game of solitaire on her phone. She noticed the pattern, realized it happened most when her medication was wearing off, and turned the game into a reward for accomplishing harder work.

All this takes constant vigilance, Kathleen says, and her struggles aren't over. But now she accepts who she is, believes in herself, and sees those problems as challenges she can rise to, not evidence of her inadequacies. "I know there's nothing 'wrong' with me," she says.

Many resources besides medication can help people thrive with ADHD, whether they have the diagnosed condition or some FAST MINDS challenges. The three-legged stool of supports we have emphasized throughout this book—cognitive behavioral techniques, mindfulness practice, and organizational habits—are all taught and emphasized by many different types of organizations and specialists. This chapter is designed to guide readers to professional and community resources that best suit their skills and needs.

We also describe nonmedication treatments for ADHD that show promise and merit more research. Unfortunately, there are large gaps in our knowledge about the impact that diets, nutritional supplements, and physical or mental practices may have on ADHD. We review current research and make some suggestions about what's worth experimenting with and what we think still needs more evidence before trying.

Cognitive and Behavioral Therapies

Formal treatment with therapists trained in CBT can be a powerful resource for addressing personal challenges with feelings, thoughts, and behaviors. As we've shown in Chapters 3 and 5, using thought records and identifying thinking errors can be useful for breaking up patterns of negative thoughts, leaving more mental energy to set up and stick to priorities and goals. Capturing thoughts by writing them down and deliberately creating a distraction-free space to work may also be helpful for quieting internal and external distractions. A research group led by Dr. Stephen Safren, which included Dr. Surman, showed that the kinds of CBT techniques embedded in this book, when combined with medication, improved ADHD symptoms substantially more than medication alone.[1] Other researchers have come to similar conclusions studying group sessions of CBT rather than one-on-one training.[2] We strongly recommend working with a therapist trained in CBT where possible—but any professional with a psychological or rehabilitation interest may be able to use this or other books to assign and monitor self-change. There are also several good self-help books based on CBT for mental health challenges— particularly depression and anxiety (see Appendix F for examples).

Organizational Coaching

Just as an athletic coach helps an athlete practice certain skills needed to excel on the field, professional ADHD and organizational coaches train people to adapt to their daily challenges. A good coach helps different kinds of people with organizational issues and can help you reduce external distractions and create systems and habits that make sense for you. A good coach can also hold you accountable, meeting with you regularly to suggest specific organizational strategies and ways of increasing structure, support your morale, and help you measure progress toward your goals. Any organizational skill that is hard can be supported through coaching. For example, a coach might help you break down a project into steps, remind you of a timeline for completing college applications, or plan a daily schedule that reminds you to eat well, clean up, and exercise. A coach might come to your home or workplace and help reorganize the environment, setting up a spot for you to put your house keys or go through the mail for example. Or a coach might check in by phone weekly to make sure you are practicing a habit, such as using a planner. Sometimes, all you might need is an initial push in the right direction. In other cases, checking in with a coach on a regular basis may help you tame clutter or keep your life from getting disorganized. Everyone's requirements are different, and professional coaches are trained to individualize interventions.

Organizations such as the Institute for the Advancement of ADHD Coaching set ethical and treatment standards for coaches, so you may want to look for a coach who is certified by such a group. Formal training programs for coaches exist, but the training of individuals varies widely. Although some researchers have looked at coaching, its effectiveness has not been well studied.[3]

Developing Mindfulness

As you can probably tell from what you've read so far, we believe that being aware of your mind state is important for adapting to FAST MINDS traits. We included a mindfulness exercise in Chapter 4 to improve internal distraction by focusing on the breath and letting thoughts pass. When practiced regularly, this kind of exercise is promising for several areas of mental health.

Whether mindfulness training can improve the ability to tune out distractions and improve control of attention is still unclear.[4] Findings are also mixed thus far on the effectiveness of mindfulness practices on depression.[5] Further study is necessary to determine whether mindfulness can be seen as a treatment—but there is strong anecdotal evidence for its value as a tool for self-awareness. And its role in stress and pain reduction has been well established.

Some studies suggest that consistently practicing mindfulness may help adolescents and adults with ADHD better control their attention and reduce impulsivity, stress, and anxiety.[6] It is attractive to imagine that people can "flex the muscle" of focus, through mindfulness practice, in ways that make it stronger—but, though logical, we don't know if that is true. Some people describe mindfulness and other meditative practices as helping them more quickly identify the moment they are disengaging, so they can pause and reengage.

ZOE: TOO HYPERACTIVE TO MEDITATE?

Zoe Kessler says she'd rather jump off a cliff than sit still for five minutes, but she's become a devotee of a kind of active Mahayana Buddhist meditation. It allows her to use several of her senses at once—chanting, rubbing prayer beads, smelling incense, and looking intently at an object. "I've got a whole bunch of stuff going on," she says, which lets her stick with the meditation and enjoy a kind of peace from it. "In my early thirties, my dad said to me, 'You're a much nicer person when you chant.' It's a very objective way of addressing my irritability. It definitely helps me to chill."

Zoe also loves yoga, which allows her to achieve a kind of tuned-in peacefulness. She does a twenty-minute routine most mornings and finds that it calms and centers her for the day. Many variations of practices ground and calm the mind. Some people prefer more active yoga or walking meditation or find their physical workouts meditative.

Seeking Professional Help and Support Groups

If there is a skill that is not your forte and you can afford to seek professional advice for it, it usually pays dividends to do so. A number of different specialists can address different types of FAST MINDS traits, including the following:

- Psychologically trained therapists can provide emotional support, assist with self-esteem issues, and help patients work through grief. Consider couples or family therapy for relationship issues. Dialectical behavior therapy (DBT) can be helpful for people who are emotional, are easily irritated, and have difficulty getting along with others. DBT, which combines CBT and mindfulness, has been shown in one moderately sized study to help reduce ADHD symptoms.[7]

- Career counselors can do aptitude testing and help people find career paths that best suit their skills and challenges.

- Neuropsychologists can assess learning profiles to help figure out appropriate learning styles and situations.

- A good financial planner can help with organization and follow-through, making sure taxes are paid on time and plans are laid for college and retirement.

- Vocational rehabilitation or counselors can help people who are badly matched to their job and want to find a better fit.

- Experts in behavioral parent training can be extremely helpful where there is conflict in families and parenting skills need attention.

- An organizational consultant may be able to help address some of the giant stacks and piles in the office, house, car, or garage.

But be sure to set up a better system for the flow of things into those spaces; note critical moments when new habits and accountability can keep the junk from piling up again.

Some people find social encouragement and validation from support groups, such as Children and Adults with Attention Deficit Hyperactivity Disorder (CHADD, www.chadd.org), which has many chapters across North America. These like-minded comrades in arms "get it," which can be a relief for people who are used to feeling alone. The Attention Deficit Disorder Association (www.add.org) also offers support groups and factual information about ADHD.

There are also twelve-step programs for addictions such as alcoholism (Alcoholics Anonymous, www.aa.org), drug addiction (Narcotics Anonymous, www.na.org), and hoarding (Clutterers Anonymous, http://sites.google.com/site/clutterersanonymous/). These are all easy to find online. Other online tools (see Appendix F) are a source for social accountability.

Other Learning Opportunities

Building a life that is engaging can be easier for lifetime learners. Once FAST MINDS symptoms are managed better, many people seek new career options, study skill supports (learning centers, assistance programs at school), communication skills (speakers' groups such as Toastmasters), or workplace training (outside consultants or coaches). Regularly trying new kinds of supports is a great way to stay engaged in an organized life.

Kathleen says she's totally motivated by learning new things, so when she's struggling with something, taking a class on the subject can make a big difference. A psychology course may offer you new insights into yourself and a new way of thinking about your challenges. A personal finance course can help take the mystery (and terror) out of checkbooks and tax returns. A course in popular culture may help you in social situations when everyone else is talking about a TV show you wouldn't otherwise have seen. Local community colleges and continuing-education programs provide a great range of options to help you adapt and engage in our changing world.

Books and Seminars on Organizational Systems

Many books, seminars, and courses are designed to help people get organized. Finding a system that works is individual, though—what works for someone who is naturally organized may not work for you. Other organizational resources may not account for the struggle to form habits that can be part of FAST MINDS, but you can adapt their message using the principles we emphasize. One of the most important principles is to adopt strategies that involve the highest yield for the least effort, which often takes trial and error. We also explored ways of embedding systems of structure and accountability to help form and stick with any organizational system you choose.

How to Evaluate Claims You See About ADHD Treatments

New treatments are being studied for ADHD, and it is useful to understand how to evaluate claims made about treatments, so you can decide whether to pursue them. The gold standard for scientific evidence is a demonstration that a treatment works statistically better than placebo or fake intervention. This means that some test subjects get the real treatment and others get the sham treatment—but neither they nor the people delivering the treatment know who's getting the real thing until the end of the study. A treatment is also considered valuable if its success is repeated in a second or third study, the treatment had a large effect on symptoms, and the individuals participating in the study have similar challenges and circumstances as those who will receive it in the real world.

Although studies of groups demonstrate *average* effects, the question for an individual is how it will impact *that person*. The variation in results between participants suggest how likely it is that any individual will experience the average result. For example, in a study of 100 people that shows a 20 percent improvement in symptoms, nearly all the subjects may have improved by 20 percent, or some participants may have improved by 80 percent and others not at all. If you hear about a treatment that seems promising, look at what kind of research is being cited to support that promise. Being an informed consumer may start with a simple Google search, but again consider the sources of information you find online. Is it a single, small study with small effects that was done without a sham treatment to account for placebo effect? Up to a third of subjects may benefit during an ADHD clinical trial while on placebo. Or have multiple large studies comparing to placebo shown large effects? Brief descriptions of some of the most important research studies are available at sites such as www.pubmed.org, from the National Library of Medicine. Ask your doctor for help understanding how any research you find relates to you—or review it with a friend with medical or research expertise.

Some nonmedication treatments are difficult to study to a high level of certainty because it's tough to devise a perfect fake treatment, or because it is difficult (and expensive) to conduct a large study. Other factors, such as the cost, the likelihood of risks, and whether there are better-understood treatments, should also be considered in choosing a particular treatment.

What You Put in Your Mouth

The body doesn't function as well if given things it does not agree with. Early studies of ADHD considered whether sugar was a cause of ADHD, and although there is no clear evidence that this is true, there is recent interest in how ADHD may impact dietary choices and obesity.[8] Some recent evidence suggests that food colorings and preservatives may increase ADHD-like behaviors in children.[9] Elimination diets, in which foods that include such additives are removed, appear to reduce ADHD symptoms in some children with ADHD.[10] Limited research has shown that changing to a gluten-free diet—forgoing most bread, pasta, and other foods containing wheat protein—may reduce ADHD symptoms in some individuals.[11]

But there is no conclusion as yet that foods, colorings, or additives *cause* ADHD that persists into adulthood. Elimination diets are a good way to evaluate whether sugar, additives, or gluten are a problem for you. For example, for a month, cut out all foods with colors not found in nature—think neon-blue Big Gulps—and flavorings such as the MSG used in many Asian restaurants and some packaged foods. Ask someone to monitor your behavior as you eliminate these things, and see if you feel or act any differently without them. Eliminating gluten is tougher, because of the difficultly of eliminating all but specially labeled bread products—most sandwiches, pizza, breakfast cereals, and pasta have to go—and because gluten sneaks its way into all kinds of nonbread items such as some soy sauce and ketchup. Also, there's some indication that gluten may have to be eliminated for weeks, if not months, to see any real difference.

Our culture is highly caffeinated, and the use of "energy drinks" has skyrocketed. Many people feel that caffeine or energy drinks help them function better if they have ADHD or FAST MINDS traits. Studies have found that caffeine helps address ADHD symptoms, though not as well as medication.[12] Research also suggests that energy drinks can improve performance, but lower amounts may actually be more helpful than higher amounts, and they can be dangerous in combination with alcohol because they eliminate the sedation associated with getting drunk.[13]

Being alert and awake is different from having your attention under your control, but alertness is important for optimal function. Some people notice the distinction when they start a stimulant after self-medicating with coffee, noting the additional benefit on focus. Drinking too much caffeine or drinking it too late in the day can hurt some people's ability to sleep and/or function. The combination with medication may bring out side effects of medication and make sleep even tougher. Caffeine, like other stimulants, can heighten physical symptoms of anxiety, and people with anxiety issues often benefit from cutting back on their caffeine.

We often hear of people taking sleeping pills or other medications to help them sleep at night—but some agents actually impact the quality of your sleep and may linger into a slower and groggier morning. There may be better ways to manage sleep issues without adding an agent that dampens your mental acuity (see the sleep tips in Chapter 8).

Emerging Research on Natural Agents

More than two hundred studies have been conducted using natural agents to treat ADHD or related symptoms. Unfortunately, it is challenging to make recommendations based on these studies, because few have been done as randomized clinical trials—the standard for evaluating treatments. A review in May 2011 of studies in children and adults found only sixteen studies that met this high standard and was unable to conclude whether the treatments should be recommended for ADHD treatment.[14] These studies included positive findings in some but not all trials of zinc, iron, *Pinus marinus* (French maritime pine bark), and ningdong granule (a traditional Chinese herbal formula). Recently, Dr. Surman and other researchers have begun to study whether "medical foods"—forms of nutrition that the Food and Drug Administration certifies as medically useful—can be developed for ADHD. Here is a summary of nutritional supports that have received the most study so far.

Omega-3 fatty acids—These are a major component of cell membranes and are particularly rich in the connections between brain regions. Studies in children suggest that omega-3 fatty acids may help ADHD symptoms. In ten studies with placebo, researchers saw small improvements in ADHD traits when taking fatty acids.[15] Omega-3 fatty acids come in two forms—either DHA or EPA—and are found in fish, dairy, meat, algae, and some plant oils. EPA may have more effect for ADHD and for mood stability. Other studies have looked at whether lack of omega-3 is to blame for ADHD. In a review of eight studies, two found no differences between people with ADHD and controls, but six found ADHD to be associated with low omega-3 fatty acid levels and/or higher omega-6 to omega-3 ratios.[16] The fatty acid differences between ADHD and non-ADHD youth do not appear to be due to dietary differences and may reflect genetic differences in how the body processes these fatty acids.[17]

Zinc and iron—Although there's limited evidence that zinc and iron supplementation improve ADHD symptoms, deficiencies of these nutrients may be associated with ADHD.[18] One study suggests that taking zinc supplements may allow people to lower the effective dose of ADHD medication.[19] A study of iron supplements found that they made sense only for children with measured iron deficiencies.[20] Physical restlessness that prevents sleep can be caused by low levels of iron.

Magnesium—Low levels of magnesium can cause symptoms similar to ADHD, as well as twitching, tingling, and numbness. You may want to consider asking your doctor to test your magnesium levels if you have these symptoms, particularly if you don't eat a lot of magnesium-rich foods such as leafy vegetables, fruits, nuts, soy products, and whole grains. Research suggests that correcting a magnesium deficiency also improves related ADHD symptoms.[21]

Vitamin B12—Studies show that about 3 percent of adults over age fifty may have a vitamin B12 deficiency, and the risk increases with age. Low levels are associated with tingling or loss of sensation in the extremities, loss of balance, and memory changes. It can be readily treated with B12 supplements.

Exercises for the Brain

In neurofeedback, people practice exercises that increase certain brain wave patterns, monitored through electrodes on the scalp. There have been studies of such techniques since the late 1970s, and some studies in children with ADHD that compare such techniques to fake procedures note more improvement with the technique.[22] However, in many of those studies, participants and researchers were aware of who received the treatment and who received the comparison intervention. There is ongoing work to evaluate neurofeedback using "blind" research designs, and larger trials with such methods could clarify the benefits of neurofeedback.[23]

In one study of adults with ADHD, researchers concluded that evidence for the effectiveness of neurofeedback is promising but weak.[24] The researchers suggest that there may be more effective treatments that cost less. According to the study: "As patients and families have only so much time, energy, and money, they should be encouraged to evaluate whether to direct these limited resources to a promising but yet unproven, expensive, and time-consuming treatment, to other treatments with stronger evidence, or to other more pressing family needs." If you choose neurofeedback, we recommend using a center certified by an association such as the Biofeedback Certification Institute of America (www.bcia.org), which also offers tips for consumers.

Rehabilitation specialists have long given stroke or brain injury patients exercises that are thought to help them to regain their capacities to speak, write, and do other activities such as schoolwork. When certain parts of the brain are damaged, other regions can sometimes be trained to take over. In ADHD, there has been interest in whether similar brain practice could strengthen capacities such as working memory, which holds information while the brain actively manipulates it. Some people with ADHD have impairments in working memory, and researchers have begun to explore whether it helps to have them practice extensively via specially designed computer programs or other therapies. Some studies are promising, and hopefully large, well-controlled studies will clarify for whom these techniques are most helpful.[25]

Physical Well-Being

Some medical conditions can produce FAST MINDS–type traits, including direct brain damage and chronic physical conditions such as diabetes, metabolic disorders including thyroid problems, and sleep disorders such as restless leg syndrome and sleep apnea. Screening for conditions that impact the health of the brain should be part of a consultation with a physician before being diagnosed with ADHD.

Mind-body techniques, which focus on relaxing the mind by relaxing the body, have been shown to improve control over the parasympathetic nervous system, which can counter the stress-related fight-or-flight response.[26] Though these have not been well studied in people with ADHD, yoga, meditation, acupuncture, and massage may help some people achieve states of feeling more comfortable and re-

Questions to Ask of a Specialist

- What is their training and background?

- Do they frequently work with people with ADHD? Do they have one generic approach or tailor their efforts to each individual?

- Do they assign homework or offer in-session practice of skills?

- Can they give examples of helping people in similar situations?

- Are there other resources they find complementary to their work?

laxed. Remember the upside-down-U-shaped stress-performance curve from Chapter 4? Having a way to reduce stress may help you function in a more grounded, engaged mental zone.

Putting These Resources to Work

Think back on the personal strategies you have identified to work on in the exercises in the book. Hopefully, they highlight ways to effectively invest your time and effort. This chapter has offered some ideas of where to look for help, but even if you work with a specialist, it will help you to have a clear idea of what to prioritize. Whether through professional resources or resources at home, school, work or in your community, we want you to have the chance to practice skills and work with a team that offers the best possible support. Reviewing the principles from this book will help you personalize and get the most out of therapy, coaching, mind-body work, or trying a new organizational strategy.

Some medical interactions can be frustrating if clinicians are not comfortable with ADHD and related issues. Some services are not set up well for people with ADHD—no reminder calls before appointments, for example. We suggest you work through the self-help parts of this book, to maximize the chances of getting what you need from the resources you approach.

Community organizations for people with ADHD can be a great way to identify resources in your area. Local colleges that have a disability support office may have a list of professionals in the area that they call on for their students—and who might see you. Some professionals who treat more severe neurologic impairments, such as rehabilitation specialists who help people recover from stroke or brain injury, can be a good resource as well. The Internet also offers interactive options to make your efforts more interesting and part of something larger—online groups, interactive self-monitoring tools, and endless suggestions for strategies.

Many people find it useful to have one person with whom they touch base regularly, and others they use for consultations as needed. For example, one woman we know goes to a senior member of her church every couple of weeks to talk about her plans and make sure she is staying on track. They review whether she is sticking to the key things that have helped her grow and stay on top of her responsibilities—having a clear plan for the coming weeks, letting go of negative self-talk, making her self-care a priority. This constant source of support helps her remember to use the techniques she learned through CBT and helps her provide good information to her psychiatrist about how her medication is or is not helping.

Use this checklist to identify strategies—new habits, new resources, new elements of structure—that can help you the most. Put a check next to what you think would be the top three to five things you would want extra help on.

✓	Areas for Extra Help	Resources to Assist You
	Your understanding of how FAST MINDS or ADHD impacts your life	Psychiatrist; psychotherapist; coach who specializes in ADHD; group for ADHD or organization
	Building mindfulness skills to be less governed by internal distractions	Mind-body work (meditation, yoga, etc.)
	Practice decreasing negative self-talk, attitudes that get in the way of clear, engaged function	Mental health clinicians; CBT, dialectical behavioral therapy; self-help mental health workbooks
	Breaking tasks down into steps you can vividly hold in your mind	Organizational, job, or ADHD-specific coach; mentor, well-organized friend/family member; CBT
	Creating a low-distraction (actual and virtual) workspace at home, work, and school	Organizational or ADHD-specific coach; well-organized friend; employee assistance/human resources department; university/college student services department
	Making use of to-do lists and planners a routine	Self-help organizational books; organizational coach; well-organized friend/family member; rehabilitation specialist; phone apps
	Getting ideas for high-yield behavior patterns, systems, and habits	ADHD coach; support group; mentor, close friend/family member; student services department; rehabilitation specialist
	Training in using peripheral devices such as phones, computers, tablets	Classes by device companies; online tutorials; workplace; community college classes
	Eliminating things in your life that you don't do well or engage in naturally	Career counselor; ADHD coach; close friend/family member; aptitude and vocational counseling; financial advisor
	Chances to see other people apply useful habits	Mentor, close friend/family member; support groups
	Practice habits and systems with people	Close friend/family member; work colleagues; rehabilitation specialist; tutor
	Determining critical moments when you can make better choices	Close friend/family member; ADHD coach; support group; psychotherapist
	Adapting and choosing work, home, and social environments that match you best	Career counselor; ADHD coach; support group; aptitude and vocational assessment; close friend/family member
	Keeping healthy daily rhythms	Personal trainer; support group; close friend/family member; mindfulness
	Practicing social skills	Coach; Toastmasters group; close friend/family member; mindfulness
	Creating accommodations at work or school	Human resources department; school disability office; ADHD coach; close friend/family member

✓	Areas for Extra Help	Resources to Assist You
	Measuring progress by tracking challenges and being held accountable	Close friend/family member; ADHD coach; online tools
	Choosing educational, career, social, or other opportunities that can make up a more fulfilling life	Career counselor; aptitude and vocational assessment; mentor; shadow close friends and family
	Managing finances	Accountant/bookkeeper; credit/debt counseling

KEY POINTS

- Many community, professional, and self-guided resources can help you continue the organizational work you have started in this book.

- Seek supports that match your needs—such as accountability, skill practice, or treatment for ADHD or mental health conditions.

- ADHD treatments that have been shown to work in multiple studies under double-blind conditions are more highly recommended.

- Add accountability, rewards, progress tracking, reminders, and other forms of structure to make resources easier to engage.

- Measure treatment success by your ability to practice new methods for learning and coping.

Thriving on the Journey

Carlo, whom we wrote about in Chapter 4, thinks his ADHD slowed his advancement at work and nearly ruined him in school. But over the last few years, a new understanding of his challenges and a happy marriage have opened up new possibilities. In Antonella, he has found someone who accepts him as he has learned to accept himself. She values his strengths far more than she's bothered by his challenges. Whatever it takes to keep that relationship strong, he will do—even if it means dragging himself from his basement workshop in time for dinner or trying to watch the romantic movies she adores.

Antonella says it's obvious to her that their relationship is hugely important to him. And she loves him for it. "He's a wonderful husband. Very loyal. He'll do anything for me," she says. He writes her poems and love songs. He's Mr. Fix-It around the house. "He's so ambitious and driven and generous. I'm really proud of him and I think he's just great."

Of course, his foibles get annoying sometimes, and she worries about his inability to relax, but he has always been this way. "We all have our issues. The only thing he ever does that really annoys me is he works too hard," she says.

Carlo, like many people who have put in the time to understand and adapt to their FAST MINDS, is "making it." Notice we don't say that he has "made it." We believe that life is about constant adaptation—to the traits you were born with, to challenges expected and unexpected. Carlo will continue to have challenges. But he has changed what he can about himself and found a vision of the future he is accountable to: the family life he is building with Antonella.

———————

Throughout this book we have talked about the brain's capacities for engagement and the importance of both clear steps and accountability. It helps to know what you want on your horizon—and map out the steps toward it. This longer-range vision should be something that resonates with your values, what you really care about, whether it is financial independence, a loving relationship, or a more connected role in your community.

In this chapter, we want to pull together everything we've offered so far and help you see how to build an easier, more functional life for yourself, day to day, week to week, and year to year. People like Carlo, Kathleen, Marshall, Zoe, and others we've described in this book have learned to thrive in situations that once tested them and to build lives for themselves that play to their strengths, talents, and interests. Carlo and Antonella are ready to take the next big step: They're expecting their first child. Kathleen is feeling great about herself and her relationship. Marshall just started a new job. Zoe is writing a book because she's passionate about helping others with ADHD.

> "I finally feel there is a chance at feeling better. I am excited about the prospect of living and working to my maximum potential."*

They all began with awareness: acknowledging and celebrating their strengths, noticing when they started straying from the path they had chosen. They all crafted their own personal solutions, not following a prescribed path, but—like Carlo—tinkering in their basements until they invented something engaging and effective.

As they gained self-confidence, they were able to attempt and achieve more, building relationships and careers and shaping order out of chaos. Zoe, like many others, is coping with the grief of having been misunderstood for so long and is realizing that her challenges don't make her a "bad" person.

They all helped themselves by learning new habits and tools and bringing people into their lives who could support them on their journey. Kathleen, supported by her boyfriend, is taking that personal finance class so she can finally get hold of her bank account and get rid of the stress of bounced checks and outstanding taxes.

> "Focusing on my strengths and emphasizing the positive aspects of ADHD has been life-altering."

They also have all learned to surf the waves of life's challenges, adapting and adjusting to change rather than being sunk under its breakers. When Marshall's last job wasn't working out, he decided

---

* Throughout this chapter are quotes from real people about their experience of FAST MINDS self-discovery. We put these here as voices of hope, cheering you on, whether you are reading this for yourself or for someone you care about.

that he'd be better off as a consultant—despite his fear of change. In the third week of his new position, he was functioning better with treatment and a job more suited to his strengths but still stressed out. He sought the help of a therapist at his company's employee assistance program and dealt constructively with his anxiety. "I was able to put my fears in words—specifically my fear of looking incompetent, expecting I should appear one hundred percent all right, right off the bat." He worked on adjusting how he evaluates himself—and his workdays became far more comfortable. "I couldn't imagine I would be able to be in a job and not be overwhelmed and terrified. I'm very hopeful about it. It's very exciting for me."

Managing Your FAST MIND

OVER THE SHORT TERM

The best way of learning *how* to do something is to *do* it. Now that you've read this far in the book, you're ready to do the work of optimizing how you function. We suggest you look back over the self-help exercises that apply most to you and spend some time exploring actions you can take. Appendix A should help you review the options for new skills, structure, and treatment that you have explored in this book and create a wish list of habits to work on, changes to make in your environment, and resources to explore. Maybe some of the habits won't come unless you take medicine. Maybe you can do others with help from friends, community resources, or professionals. Prioritize what you want to work on now and make a stepwise plan to get there.

The first step for most people is a schedule. If you don't have one yet, do yourself a favor and make one. The schedule isn't meant to turn you into a robot, but to make it clear what your top priorities should be and what you need to accomplish each day, including essential activities, such as eating, exercising, and sleeping. Your daily and weekly schedule should also leave time to plan out your days and weeks. We suggest that you *transfer reminders of crucial habits—particularly ones that need to happen at a certain time—to your planner,* so you can clearly protect time for them and remember their importance. Set reminders for yourself using an alarm if applicable.

Remember: Forging a new habit is difficult, particularly for people with ADHD. As with learning how to drive or playing an instrument, you have to practice a habit many times before it becomes instinctive. Use whatever it takes to put the new habit on your radar for the first few weeks, and make sure to include time on your schedule to practice!

> "I have hope now that I can adjust my life to moderate this deficit and manage things better than I have in the past."

OVER THE MEDIUM TERM

Keep practicing in the medium term to ensure that you stay on top of your new habit.

Acknowledge that whatever system, structure, accountability, or habit you come up with, you are likely to get bored with it eventually (boredom often comes faster for people with FAST MINDS). You may need to reevaluate your approach every few months to keep it fresh. Periodically making time in your schedule to assess these strategies can help ensure that you don't lose your momentum. Just as setting a reminder will help you stick to your day-to-day plans, setting up an external prompt can help you over the course of weeks and months. Check in periodically with a coach, create a monthly alert on an electronic calendar, or meet an organized friend regularly to review your organizational approach.

Keep coming back to the key principles we've outlined in this book (we review them in detail in Appendix A):

- Edit emotional, negative thoughts.

- Use the prefrontal checklist: Make a clear path and manage your mental state and distractions.

- Plan to use the pause button where you need it.

- Use peripheral brains to help you achieve your goals.

- Identify the critical moment habits that will allow you to stay on track with systems that keep you well organized.

- Establish structures for keeping yourself accountable to your own goals and aspirations.

"The diagnosis gave me a tremendous relief of anxiety, a boost of confidence and morale and greater sense of independence and control."

CARLO: PUTTING IT ALL TOGETHER EVERY DAY

Carlo works with his ADHD on a variety of levels all the time. Many of the strategies that guide his daily life are ones we've focused on already. Here are some of them:

WORKING OUT: Though Carlo exercises every day—and it shows in his six-pack abs—he says he always had poor coordination. "I couldn't hit a baseball with a bat to save my life. In school, I was the last guy picked for every team." Now he uses a daily workout at the gym to blow off steam and boost his focus.

Meditation? "Oh, God, that's too peaceful. Jumping off a bridge with a bungee cord—to me, that's meditative."

TAKING MEDICATION: *Carlo says being on medication has helped him do things that used to be too boring for him to manage: reading, paperwork, a little bit of small talk.* "I could not sit down and read a page of text before—it was damn near impossible. Now, when I renewed my auto insurance, I read the insurance policy. Do you know anybody who's done that?"

Carlo says he still gets bored sometimes, but he can generally power through it. "In the real world, we've got to do our taxes. Is it really important? Yes, but it's hard to kick-start yourself, so that's what the medication does: It allows you to do the things that don't come naturally to you."

USING PERIPHERAL BRAINS: *Carlo forgets things from one minute to the next. If someone asks to meet him on the other side of the room in three minutes, Carlo writes himself a note on his BlackBerry and sets up an alarm.* "I would be dead without my BlackBerry," *he says.* He'd like to be able to remember something for three lousy minutes, but he's come to accept the fact that he can't. And he'd rather be teased for his note taking and make it to meetings on time than forget to show up.

Carlo has also accepted the fact that he stinks at house cleaning. Instead of getting into fights with Antonella over it, he does his part by paying for someone to tidy up. "If my old-world immigrant mother found out I had a housecleaner, man, I'd be in trouble. But I want a clean house and a clean car. In that time that I'm not cleaning, I'm down in my workshop building a new wind turbine."

Antonella steps in to set some boundaries, too. Carlo would naturally say yes to anything anyone asks him to do. She acts as his gatekeeper whenever she can, so he doesn't keep promising their weekends away.

HAVING THE RIGHT JOB: *Photography was the first career* *that ever interested Carlo, but he spent years listening to other people tell him it was the wrong choice because so few people succeeded in it. In high school, he worked in a factory assembly line, using an air wrench to screw in nuts. "That didn't last more than a few days. It was hell," he says. He worked for marketing firms for a few years, then software companies. "Things were constantly not getting done, and I didn't care. I didn't like a lot of what we were doing. It was like that school scenario all over again."*

A few years ago, he switched to television cameraman, which suits him to a T. He's good at it. He has an artful eye. And it fits his "thrill junkie" persona. When he gets to work, he never knows what he'll be doing or shooting that day—which is fine by him. "It's hard to make a dentist appointment, but it keeps life interesting. It allows me to function."

BEING SELF-AWARE: *Carlo doesn't waste much time reading fiction or watching chick flicks, unless his wife insists. But he's realized that he loves documentaries and nonfiction books. When he's learning something, he feels like he's being productive. "For a guy who flunked out of school, I'm consumed by learning. I love to learn," he says.*

He sets up rules to cope with his natural impulsivity. He won't allow himself to buy anything valuable without pausing—which he does by requiring himself to sleep on it first. And he researches every major purchase so much that other people rely on his opinion. Four friends bought the same TV after Carlo did, because they trusted he'd made the right choice.

PUTTING CHALLENGES IN CONTEXT: *Carlo went through his whole childhood and early adulthood wondering why he was such an oddball. He seemed wired faster than everyone else, talked with his hands, couldn't sit still, showed all his emotions. Like his father, he worked from the minute he woke up in the morning until his head hit the pillow at night.*

Then, a few years ago, Carlo decided to visit the tiny Italian village—"population: negative three"—where his father had been born and raised. The first day was a revelation. Instead of being an oddball in this town, he found that everyone he met was just like him.

"I realized there are thousands of me. It was wild. It was unbelievable," he says.

The trip made him realize how much his "weirdness" was just about context. In straitlaced North America, he is unusual, labeled with a disorder. But if he lived in his ancestral home in Sicily, he'd be an oddball if he weren't the way he is.

The trip has made him think differently about his ADHD: "A disorder? Sure. A defect? No."

"It felt comforting to be in a place where I am the norm and not have to explain how I act or think."

OVER THE LONG TERM

Treating FAST MINDS traits that interfere with life can open up a new horizon for deferred growth, such as going back to school, deepening career expertise, or developing relationships. If you are going to add on to your life, we suggest prioritizing what nurtures you, what will allow you to reach your potential in an environment where you can thrive.

Setting a three-to-five-year plan will help you think through what your priorities are and make you stick your head up and look around to see where you are going. Don't beat yourself up if you end up somewhere unexpected at the end of five years—everyone's life is subject to chance. But having that plan will help you match your daily actions with your long-term personal priorities and what you value.

Coping with FAST MINDS can be challenging and exhausting. Remember that the default paths you take through the day—the ones that comes most easily—include paths that can get you in trouble. We understand that it isn't easy to establish and stick to new habits if it means fighting your own biology. It's okay to give yourself permission to stray from the path a bit, to let down your guard every once in a while. But if you do it for too long—if you let these new habits slip away—you will have more practice to do to start again.

Sticking to these new patterns instead will be self-reinforcing. Each time you succeed, each time you catch yourself at a critical moment and chose a deliberate route rather than a default path, you will get closer to where you want to be. You will also start rebuilding self-esteem that has been battered by years (or decades) of negative self-talk and feeling out of place. Your brain may be making your life more challenging now, but you have the power to rewire it, to reroute at least some of its connections as you practice new patterns.

Managing Change

Life doesn't stand still. You may find the perfect boss—and she may leave the company for another post. You may finally have the children you've dreamed of, and learn that they have some of the same challenges you do. The changing contexts of life mean an ebb and flow of old or new tasks. You will be able to anticipate some of what you need from past experience, but sometimes things will throw you for a loop or pose unexpected hurdles. Those are good times to sit down with this book again, to revisit a coach, therapist, or other resource, and focus again on the habits you want, the strategies that help and the critical moments you may be missing.

As roles and responsibilities change—you become a parent or an empty-nester, you get promoted or switch companies—you may need to change your approach to FAST MINDS traits, too. The executive-function burden in your life will increase the more people you take care of and the fewer who are taking care of you. You may become a manager, have a child, decide to work alone, lose your administrative assistant. Shifting organizational demands are a common reason for needing to adjust strategies or even medication approaches.

There are some life changes that you can anticipate will take time to adjust to. We know many people who need to take life transitions slowly. But whether it's going to college, moving in with someone, starting a family, or balancing career and childcare—each will be an experiment in which you learn more about yourself.

We have emphasized the danger of blaming yourself for challenges you were born with, suggesting that you blame FAST MINDS instead where appropriate. But many times it will be even healthier to say that the problem isn't you at all, but the environment or the situation. Final exams, a new job, a move, a health crisis, and babies who cry all night are a stress to everyone. With an eye on the other side—a vision of where you are going—these life hurdles seem less overwhelming.

"It's a relief and a victory to finally have some answers and a plan to get better."

If you find your way to roles you care about and maximize how much of your day you look forward to, it will take less work to manage FAST MINDS traits. We talked about how accountability—often provided by a sense of responsibility to someone else—can help you adopt better patterns to meet your physical needs, such as sleeping, eating, and exercising. We recommend actively looking ahead to what will hold you accountable in the roles you take on. Some kinds of accountability, such as to your newborn, may not take much conscious effort to create. You are likely, for example, to get better at leaving work on time if it means seeing your baby again sooner. Others will take more active effort. The boring parts of your job may be hard to make scintillating, but would scheduling meetings with colleagues hold you accountable to the project?

When you're going through a major life transition, set aside time to consider whether your need for support is changing, too, and whether your structures are appropriate. If you aren't yet part of a community group, a time of transition might be a good moment to join, to share experiences and grow with others.

Whether you remain alone or are surrounded by understanding friends and family, it's a good idea to regularly remind yourself that you have been flying at a different altitude than other people. Adjusting to FAST MINDS takes hard—and sometimes secret—work. Just as athletes train in higher altitudes to improve their oxygen-carrying capacity and therefore their endurance, living with FAST MINDS has given you a capacity for adaptation—both to the inevitable challenges we all face in life and, often, to understanding the diverse and personal challenges of other people. Be fair to yourself by accepting your strengths, admiring your efforts to adjust and grow, and striving to fulfill who you are—not who you think you should be.

The Quest for . . .

In writing this book, we often thought about the famous quests of classic children's literature: the journey to Mordor in J.R.R. Tolkien's *The Lord of the Rings*, the pursuit of true love in *The Princess Bride*, even Harry Potter hunting for the pieces of Voldemort's split soul in *Harry Potter and the Deathly Hallows*. The main characters all reach their destinations eventually, but they travel through dark territory, face many tribulations, and learn much about themselves. Living with FAST MINDS is a similar journey: through distress, challenge, and insight (though without magic, as far as we know). Everyone's path will be different—determined in part by the secret shortcuts you stumble across and the mistakes you make. Sometimes you'll get singed in a fire swamp, surrounded by the enemy or lost from the trail. You will find terrain on your path that we haven't mentioned in this book, where it will be up to you to find your own way.

You also have some choices about how you're going to take this journey: Are you going to acknowledge your strengths and weaknesses and try to steer clear of areas that are likely to be most dangerous for you, or will you set off without even a water bottle and take whatever comes your way? We think your quest will be smoother if you have a map, some solid equipment, and a traveling companion or two—particularly if they believe in your powers. It will help to have a clear goal for today, this week, short term, and long term, and to break obstacles down into clear steps. Your trip is likely to be more interesting than the journey most people embark on. If you have FAST MINDS traits, you will probably notice things that others miss and devise creative solutions for fording streams and skirting roadblocks.

What is the object of your quest? We think the goal is less about the destination and more about how you take the journey. What we hope you will gain from the quest, however, is self-actualization: fulfilling your potential to be you. We encourage you to enjoy being you and contribute what you find meaningful. Understanding, accepting, and adapting to FAST MINDS is the secret to succeeding in the quest.

We, and the thousands of people whose experiences we've drawn on, wish you well on your journey and hope this book serves as a good companion along the way.

"I have been waiting for this day so I can finally proceed and enhance my quality of life."

FAST MINDS Pyramid for

Success with Adult ADHD

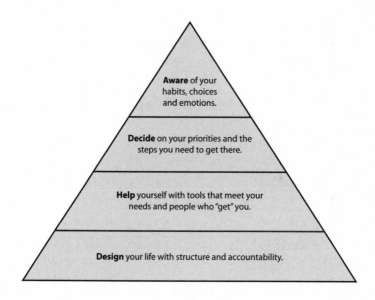

Aware: Be aware of your emotions, behavior, and habits as the first step in changing them.

Decide: Choose your own priorities and figure out the steps you need to get there.

Help: Provide yourself with tools that meet your needs and people who "get" you.

Design: Build a life with structure and accountability that will help you thrive.

Appendices

APPENDIX A

Summary and Workbook

We've chosen to repeat select exercises from the book here, to give you a place to collect the product of the work you've done. It will take working through the chapters to come up with your personalized solutions, but this is a place to remind yourself of the themes we've covered and to record the solutions you find. It may also be helpful as a review or to pick chapters to which you want to return.

The following is a chapter-by-chapter review of the book in workbook form, starting with the **FAST MINDS traits** from **Chapter 1**. Mark the ones that particularly resonate with you:

☐ Forgetful

☐ Achieving below potential

☐ Stuck in a rut

☐ Time challenged

☐ Motivationally challenged

☐ Impulsive

☐ Novelty seeking

☐ Distractible

☐ Scattered

Note at least three tasks or situations that FAST MINDS impacts in your life and are a priority to improve.

1. _____

2. _____

3. _____

In **Chapter 2**, we look at different **versions** of FAST MINDS and how they impact each person differently based on their strengths, challenges, and obligations. We give examples of "The Struggling Student," "Married with Children," and "The Distractible Daydreamer," as well as people who form habits easily and those who don't. We also note the presence of other mental health, learning, or social challenges.

Write a description of your version:

_____

_____

_____

_____

_____

When you are functioning at your best, you are probably engaged and in a state of **flow**. Write down three examples of when or where you are able to be engaged, or in flow.

1. _____

2. _____

3. _____

In **Chapter 3** we emphasize that **attitude matters**. Although you may have real disappointment, even grief, blaming FAST MINDS is healthier than blaming yourself. We introduce the power of **cognitive behavioral therapy** to transform how people feel and function by exchanging automatic negative thoughts for more rational ones.

Note some of your typical negative thoughts, and across from these, write non-emotional, balanced thoughts such as those a coach might remind you of. Try to turn them into a phrase you can tell yourself as needed to **defuse strong emotions**. For example, if a negative thought is "I am no good," your response to yourself might be "This is a challenge, but I am good at many things."

NEGATIVE THOUGHTS	BALANCED THOUGHTS
1. _____	_____
2. _____	_____
3. _____	_____

In **Chapter 4**, we emphasize that your ability to engage depends on the operating conditions of your **prefrontal cortex**. Where you have trouble functioning as you want to, it is important to consider whether you lack a clear plan or your brain is occupied or distracted.

Here is the **prefrontal checklist**:

PREFRONTAL CHECKLIST

■ Is the next step vivid and clear in your mind?

■ Are you internally distracted? (Are thoughts, feelings, or your mental or physical state preoccupying?)

■ Is your environment distracting? (Note sensory and virtual distractions and reminders of other tasks.)

A **planner**, a **thought-capture method**, and **to-do lists** are major tools for keeping clear plans in mind that your prefrontal cortex can work with. Making a time to plan—to prioritize and reallocate effort for periods ahead—helps create a clear path to accomplishment. We introduce the essential principle of capturing action items in your planner's time slots and the benefits of using role-specific to-do lists, building in flexibility where you need it.

If you haven't yet bought a planner or started using one on your phone or computer, do it now.

To help clear distractions so your prefrontal cortex can work better, be aware of where distractibility plays a role in your life. We discussed **internal** distractions (stress, thoughts, and feelings), and **external** distractions (honking cars, crying babies, messy desks). Through a **mindfulness** exercise, we encouraged you to note how busy and aware your mind is and your capacity to control that awareness.

Record some examples of how you are internally and externally distracted; across from these, note what can change your mental state or environment.

INTERNAL/EXTERNAL DISTRACTIONS	STEPS TO REDUCE DISTRACTIONS (e.g., thought record, mindfulness, exercise, using headphones, cleaning workspace, turning off Internet access)
1. _____	_____
2. _____	_____
3. _____	_____
4. _____	_____
5. _____	_____

In **Chapter 5**, we highlight the importance of being your own executive assistant to manage executive-function challenges with a sense of time, prioritization, and planning. **Peripheral brains**—planners, devices, computers, even other people—can allow you to outsource the faculties you don't do well.

Listed below are some common **executive-function challenges**. Across from these challenges, note **peripheral brains** that you could use to outsource (a coach, a secretary, a partner, a counselor, an electronic device or software application)—the more specific, the better. It is important to get systems or habits that work for you and then mindfully work them every day.

EXECUTIVE-FUNCTION CHALLENGE	PERIPHERAL BRAINS
Holding thoughts/plans in mind	_____
Remembering	_____
Sense of time	_____
Planning for the future	_____
Managing paperwork	_____
Setting priorities	_____
Other challenges you face:	_____

There are **critical moments** when a more careful choice or adaptive habit can have a big impact. Carefully select a few executive management skills that will be most meaningful to you. It might be when you don't write down a meeting time and then forget to attend, when you double-book your schedule without realizing it, when you decide to do one more thing that makes you late. Other critical moments involve not seeing next steps clearly, such as what you will need tomorrow or the sequence of activities that will transition you out the door. The critical moment could be that split second when you say yes without checking your planner and then feel overwhelmed the next day because you have taken on too much.

List routines and habits you'd like to have—such as doing the dishes right after dinner or organizing your desk every night before you leave the office—that would be beneficial. Then across from these, note what action you need to take at critical moments to ensure success. Consider using the Critical Moments Planner in Appendix E to map out when to take action.

ROUTINE OR HABIT	CRITICAL MOMENT ACTIONS
1. _____	_____
2. _____	_____
3. _____	_____
4. _____	_____

In **Chapter 6**, we discussed impulsive choices—poor choices—that derail people from a more fulfilling life. Some kinds of impulses are hard to control without medication. Others can benefit from a "pause button" approach. Anticipate critical moments in the "movie" of your life, scenes where you will be at risk, where with some pause you can plan for a different choice. Are you making impulsive choices about eating, spending, drinking, speaking, or something else?

Note examples of impulsivity (overspending, unhealthy impulse eating, risk-taking, impulsive communication). Also note which kind of impulsivity applies (emotional decision making, nearsighted thinking, or novelty seeking):

EXAMPLE OF IMPULSIVITY	KIND OF IMPULSIVITY (emotional, novelty seeking, nearsighted?)
1. _____	_____
2. _____	_____
3. _____	_____
4. _____	_____

5. _____ _____

6. _____ _____

Monitoring the thoughts and feelings that fuel impulsive choices using a **thought record** (see Appendix B) can give you a chance to develop more rational reactions.

In **Chapter 7**, we discuss how "structure" in your environment—usually consisting of **rewards** and **accountability**—can help you remain engaged with good habits at critical organizational and impulsive moments. Setting up short-term rewards you "earn" can help create and maintain new behaviors. For example, you can consciously delay checking a favorite website until you complete your priorities for the day. Accountability can come from "peripheral brains" such as an organized supervisor, coach, or child, or from being part of a team. These peripheral brains can help you "keep your eyes on the prize," so your actions have meaning. They can also help you form habits for getting through your everyday life.

Think about what motivated you to do effortful work in the past, such as helping others, working collaboratively, handling paperwork, or filling roles you care about (career, family, etc.). Seek out environments that offer the rewards and accountability that work for you—such as a job that you can do well, that you feel motivated to do, and that makes you feel responsible to others.

Note what holds you accountable or what you find rewarding. Across from these motivators, note any critical moments or habits, such as those you identified in the Chapter 5 exercise, that you could link to rewards or add accountability.

CRITICAL MOMENTS	WHAT HOLDS YOU ACCOUNTABLE OR IS REWARDING?
1. _____	_____
2. _____	_____
3. _____	_____
4. _____	_____

In **Chapter 8**, we explore how habits can be changed, using im-provement in self-care as an example. We explore how people with FAST MINDS traits often have trouble sticking to **healthy habits**. We review the science of how to change habits and what helps people achieve better sleep, eating, and exercise patterns. See Appendix D for the FAST MINDS Twenty-Four-Hour Cycle Review which you can use to monitor if you are meeting self-care needs.

Note any personal needs you are not meeting, such as adequate sleep, regular and brain-healthy nutrition, regular exercise, downtime for you, and so on. Across from these, note the critical organizational or impulsive moments that lead to less healthy habits. Think of what you say to yourself just before you don't choose a healthy path. And now across from those moments, note which of the tools we have dis-cussed could help in those moments: e.g., attending to the prefrontal checklist (clearer plan, less internal or external distraction); involving a peripheral brain; using a pause button; increasing structure (ac-countability, rewards).

UNMET PERSONAL NEEDS	WHICH TOOLS MIGHT HELP?
1. _____	_____
2. _____	_____

3. _____   _____

4. _____   _____

Use the FAST MINDS Cricial Moments Planner in Appendix E to clearly note any predictable times of day that you need to act to meet these needs.

In **Chapter 9**, we look at the combined impact of social skill challenges and FAST MINDS traits and how to get accommodation and help from others. Just being aware of how FAST MINDS traits impact others can be a powerful step. **Good communication** is two-way and of mutual interest. Improve conversation with a clear vision of what you want to say, plan the use of your pause button to limit your impulsive reactions, and practice reducing negative, emotional thoughts.

Note social situations (e.g., meetings with your boss, groups) or particular people (e.g., spouse, colleagues) with whom you become impatient or easily frustrated. Across from them, note solutions—can you consciously plan how, when, where, or about what you communicate? Can you reduce emotional communication? Can you use the "pause button"?

CHALLENGING SOCIAL SITUATIONS	POSSIBLE SOLUTIONS
1. _____	_____
2. _____	_____
3. _____	_____
4. _____	_____

Approaching work, school, or loved ones with possible **accommodations** can be more useful than revealing how you are different.

Schools offer extensive accommodation for learning styles, but jobs are not as likely to be flexible. Legal protections can help you get accommodations. In some cases, it's better to be specific about your needs and ask for support without discussing ADHD.

Note tasks or environments that are challenging (such as working in noisy spaces), and next to that write what accommodations you might request (e.g., using a conference room for work when it is not in use):

**PARTICULARLY
CHALLENGING TASKS**

**POSSIBLE
ACCOMMODATIONS**

1. _____   _____

2. _____   _____

3. _____   _____

4. _____   _____

In **Chapter 10**, we reviewed the risks and benefits of taking medication if you have ADHD, and how you can help a prescribing clinician optimize treatment. Medication can help improve the ability to engage in your daily activities, but many organizational challenges require a combination of medication and the approaches outlined in other chapters in this book. Bring your FAST MINDS checklist (see the Chapter 1 summary) to a clinician and track these symptoms using the FAST MINDS Trait Tracker (Appendix C) or the Adult ADHD Self-Report Scale (Appendix F) during treatment.

Note traits you'd like to target with medication (forgetfulness, distractibility, scattered thinking, etc.):

1. _____

2. _____

3. _____

4. _____

You may have to try several medicines to find the right one. Start low and go slow, and don't hesitate to inform your clinician about what you learn about medication choices (particularly noting that there are several types of ADHD medications, and many possible doses).

In **Chapter 11**, we review **other approaches** that are under development as treatments for ADHD, as well as personal practices, community resources, and professional resources that can enhance your work on FAST MINDS challenges. If a professional coach or other ADHD specialist is not available, individuals and groups can provide structure and a chance to practice new organizational habits.

Note challenges that you think might be addressed in nonmedical ways, and interventions from the resources you read about in the chapter that you feel may be helpful for you.

CHALLENGES TO ADDRESS   **NONMEDICAL RESOURCES**

1. _____   _____

2. _____   _____

3. _____   _____

4. _____   _____

In **Chapter 12**, we encourage you to **dream big** and then break down that vision into concrete steps you can achieve along the way.

Note several short-term, medium-term, and long-term goals you think would lead you to a more fulfilling life:

SHORT-TERM:

1. _____

2. _____

3. _____

MEDIUM-TERM:

1. _____

2. _____

3. _____

LONG-TERM:

1. _____

2. _____

3. _____

Make it a goal to revisit the most useful chapters and excercises in this book at regular intervals or when life brings new circumstances or challenges.

APPENDIX B

Thought Record

Here is a version of the thought record that you can use to practice training yourself away from negative thoughts that drain mental energy from the work it takes to manage FAST MINDS stumbling blocks such as impulsivity. We guide you through this in more detail in Chapters 3 and 6.

1. Brief description of the situation:

_____

_____

2. Context: When, where, how did it happen? What were the triggers?

_____

_____

3. How intense are your thoughts and feelings about the situation as you recall it (1 to 10)?

_____

_____

4. Did you make any of the following thinking errors? In what way?

_____

_____

All-or-nothing thinking

_____

_____

Overgeneralizing

_____

_____

Disqualifying the positive

_____

_____

Jumping to conclusions or mind reading

_____

_____

Magnifying or minimizing

_____

_____

Catastrophizing

_____

_____

Emotional reasoning

_____

_____

Personalization

_____

_____

5. Describe a more rational thought and response to the situation. Is there a phrase you could practice saying the next time a similar situation occurs?

_____

_____

6. Did you drain out some of the emotion? Think now of how you rate your reaction from 1 to 10 as you think of the situation again.

_____

_____

APPENDIX C

FAST MINDS Trait Tracker

Use this chart to record FAST MINDS symptoms and how these symptoms respond to medication. You may want to show them to a professional and track them over time. You also may want someone close to you to review the list to ensure that you rate these challenges accurately.

FAST MINDS TRAIT TRACKER

FAST MINDS TRAITS	Before treatment (Rate how challenging [1–10])	Fill in dose, week, and new rating during treatment (1-10)		
Forgetful		Dose _____ Week _____	Dose _____ Week _____	Dose _____ Week _____
Achieving below potential		Dose _____ Week _____	Dose _____ Week _____	Dose _____ Week _____
Stuck in a rut		Dose _____ Week _____	Dose _____ Week _____	Dose _____ Week _____
Time-challenged		Dose _____ Week _____	Dose _____ Week _____	Dose _____ Week _____
Motivationally challenged		Dose _____ Week _____	Dose _____ Week _____	Dose _____ Week _____
Impulsive		Dose _____ Week _____	Dose _____ Week _____	Dose _____ Week _____
Novelty seeking		Dose _____ Week _____	Dose _____ Week _____	Dose _____ Week _____
Distractible		Dose _____ Week _____	Dose _____ Week _____	Dose _____ Week _____
Scattered		Dose _____ Week _____	Dose _____ Week _____	Dose _____ Week _____
Other concerns . . . (patience, mood stability, etc.)				
Other positive impact of medication; note duration of effect				
SIDE EFFECTS				
(Physical discomfort, mood or personality change, sleep pattern change)				
When do side effects occur during the day?				
Other negative impact of medication:				

APPENDIX D

FAST MINDS Twenty-Four-Hour Cycle Review

Use the chart that follows to help you track if you are meeting the needs of each day, such as healthy sleep, exercise, and eating patterns.

FAST MINDS TWENTY-FOUR-HOUR CYCLE REVIEW

SLEEP/WAKE CYCLE	Day 1	Day 2	Day 3	Day 4	Day 5	Day 6	Day 7
Did you wind down and relax before bed?							
Did you get 7–9 hours of sleep?							
Did you maintain a restful, dark sleep environment?							
Did you wake early enough to start your day on time?							
Did you avoid caffeine?							
Did you avoid napping today?							
Did you go to bed early enough to allow yourself 7–9 hours of sleep?							

NUTRITION	Day 1	Day 2	Day 3	Day 4	Day 5	Day 6	Day 7
Did you eat a healthy breakfast?							
Did you have healthy food in your house to eat?							
Did you eat small meals regulalry across the day?							
Did you avoid fast or "junk" food?							
Did you use protein and carbohydrates for energy?							

EXERCISE/RELAXATION	Day 1	Day 2	Day 3	Day 4	Day 5	Day 6	Day 7
Did you exercise for at least 30 minutes?							
Did you have workout clothes or equipment prepared ahead of time?							
Did you take time during the day to relax?							

APPENDIX E

FAST MINDS Critical Moments Planner

FAST MINDS CRITICAL MOMENT PLANNER

Need to Address	Action to take	What days should you act?	6 a.m.	7	8	9	10	11	Noon	1 p.m.	2	3	4	5	6	7	8	9	10	11
Sleep	Start preparing for bed 90 minutes ahead	Every day																*		
Healthy Eating	4 small meals	Every day		*				*				*				*				
Exercise	Prepare gym bag	Tuesday Thursday Saturday															*			

Instructions: This chart can help you plan the critical moments to act to better meet your daily needs. Consider particular moments where you can pre-empt the pitfall of a time-wasting or unhealthy activity by planning. 1. In the first column note what personal need (e.g., sleep, healthy eating, exercise) you are addressing. 2. In the second column, note which days you can take action (workdays, weekends). 3. In the third column, list out actions to take. 4. Use an * to mark when to act during those days. See first three rows for examples.

APPENDIX F

Adult ADHD Self-Report Scale

ADULT ADHD SELF-REPORT SCALE (ASRS-V1.1) SYMPTOM CHECKLIST

Today's Date: _____

Please answer the questions below, rating yourself on each of the criteria shown using the scale on the right side of the page. As you answer each question, place an X in the box that best describes how you have felt and conducted yourself over the past 6 months. Please give this completed checklist to your healthcare professional to discuss.

PART A	Never	Rarely	Sometimes	Often	Very Often
1. How often do you have trouble wrapping up the final details of a project, once the challenging parts have been done?					
2. How often do you have difficulty getting things in order when you have to do a task that requires organization?					
3. How often do you have problems remembering appointments or obligations?					
4. When you have a task that requires a lot of thought, how often do you avoid or delay getting started?					
5. How often do you fidget or squirm with your hands or feet when you have to sit down for a long time?					
6. How often do you feel overly active and compelled to do things, like you were driven by a motor?					

This scale was adopted by the World Health Organization to identify symptoms of ADHD. Part A of this scale is used as a quick screen to see whether ADHD may be present. Many adults who have four or more symptoms at the level of frequency in the shaded area have ADHD. However, a clinical evaluation is required to confirm a diagnosis of ADHD. Part A and B together can be used to record ADHD symptom challenges over time.

	Never	Rarely	Sometimes	Often	Very Often
PART B					
7. How often do you make careless mistakes when you have to work on a boring or difficult project?					
8. How often do you have difficulty keeping your attention focused when you are doing boring or repetitive work?					
9. How often do you have difficulty concentrating on what people say to you, even when they are speaking to you directly?					
10. How often do you misplace or have difficulty finding things at home or at work?					
11. How often are you distracted by activity or noise around you?					
12. How often do you leave your seat in meetings or other situations in which you are expected to remain seated?					
13. How often do you feel restless or fidgety?					
14. How often do you have difficulty unwinding and relaxing when you have time to yourself?					
15. How often do you find yourself talking too much when you are in social situations?					
16. When you're in a conversation, how often do you find yourself finishing the sentences of the people you are talking to, before they can finish them themselves?					
17. How often do you have difficulty waiting your turn in situations when turn taking is required?					
18. How often do you interrupt others when they are busy?					

APPENDIX G

For Further Exploration

Here we list a selection of books and videos that may help you address your FAST MINDS challenges:

ADD-Friendly Ways to Organize Your Life, Kathleen Nadeau and Judith Kolberg, Brunner-Routledge, 2002.

The ADHD Effect on Marriage: Understand and Rebuild Your Relationship in Six Steps, Specialty Press, 2010.

The Art of Possibility, Rosamund Stone Zander and Benjamin Zander, Penguin Books, 2002.

Cognitive-Behavioral Therapy for Adult ADHD: Targeting Executive Dysfunction, Mary Solanto, Guilford Press, 2011.

The Disorganized Mind: Coaching Your ADHD Brain to Take Control of Your Time, Tasks and Talents, Nancy A. Ratey, Ed. D., St. Martin's Press, 2008.

Driven to Distraction, Edward M. Hallowell, M.D., and John J. Ratey, M.D., Simon and Schuster, 1987.

Eat, Drink & Weigh Less, Mollie Katzen and Walter Willett, Hyperion, 2006.

Find Your Focus Zone: An Effective New Plan to Defeat Distraction and Overload, Lucy Jo Palladino, Free Press, 2007.

Her Fast Mind: An In-Depth Look at ADHD as It Affects Women, video produced by Dr. Timothy Bilkey, 2012.

Is It You, Me, or Adult A.D.D.?, Gina Pera, 1201 Alarm Press, 2008.

Mastering Your Adult ADHD, A Cognitive-Behavioral Treatment Program (Therapist Guide and Client Workbook), Steven A. Safren, Susan Sprich, Carol A. Perlman, and Michael W. Otto, Oxford University Press, 2005.

Mastery of Your Anxiety and Worry: Client Workbook, M. Craske, D. H. Barlow, and T. A. O'Leary, Psychological Corporation, 1992.

More Attention, Less Deficit, Ari Tuckman, Specialty Press, 2009.

Out of the Fog: Treatment Options and Coping Strategies for Adult Attention Deficit Disorder, K. R. Murphy and S. Levert, Hyperion, 1995.

The Power of Resilience: Achieving Balance, Confidence, and Personal Strength in Your Life, Robert Brooks and Sam Goldstein, Contemporary Books, 2004.

The Relaxation Response, H. Benson and M. Z. Klipper, Harper Torch, 1976.

Scattered Minds: Hope and Help for Adults with Attention Deficit Hyperactivity Disorder, Lenard Adler with Mari Florence, Perigee Trade, 2007.

SPARK: The Revolutionary New Science of Exercise and the Brain, John R. Ratey, with Eric Hagerman, Little, Brown, 2008.

Survival Guide for College Students with ADHD or LD (revised ed.), Kathleen Nadeau, Magination Press, 2006.

Taking Charge of Adult ADHD, Russell A. Barkley with Christine Benton, The Guilford Press, 2010.

Ten Simple Solutions to Adult ADD, Stephanie Sarkis, New Harbinger Publications, 2011.

Wherever You Go, There You Are, John Kabat-Zinn, Hyperion, 1994.

You Mean I'm Not Lazy, Stupid or Crazy?! A Self-Help Book for Adults with Attention Deficit Disorder, Kate Kelly and Peggy Ramundo, Scribner, 2006.

Electronic Peripheral Brains to Consider

Here are examples of some digital resources that may be helpful. These sites are all current, accurate, and safe as of press time. The Web changes quickly, so we can't guarantee that all of these resources will be the best available when you are reading.

Tracking Health and Medication

- Medication-dosing diaries and reminder apps: http://itunes.apple.com/us/app/drug-diary/id399537600?mt=8
- Sleep pattern diaries: http://yoursleep.aasmnet.org/pdf/sleepdiary.pdf or http://science.education.nih.gov/supplements/nih3/sleep/guide/nih_sleep_masters.pdf
- Activity monitors: Products such as Fitbit (http://www.fitbit.com) and UP by Jawbone (http://jawbone.com/up) track activity levels and various health measures. These can be costly, so make sure you really need—and will use—what they're offering.
- Online health improvement social games: http://healthmonth.com/

Work Productivity Tools

- Website blockers:
  http://www.focalfilter.com
  https://chrome.google.com/webstore/detail/laankejkbhbdhmipfmgcngdelahlfoji
  http://visitsteve.com/made/selfcontrol/
  https://addons.mozilla.org/en-US/firefox/addon/leechblock/
- Organizational programs:
  https://workflowy.com

Reminders

- Programmable alarms (most cell phones have them; you can also use an online version such as http://onlineclock.net; some watches have vibrating alarms for discreet reminders)
- Timers (most large hardware stores sell kitchen timers, some in fun shapes)

Organizational Tools

- Online calendars: https://www.google.com/calendar
- Meeting scheduling programs: http://doodle.com
- E-mail filters (most e-mail services such as Gmail and Hotmail offer filtering)

Accountability

- Home organization and cleaning: http://flylady.net
- Online support groups, such as twelve-step groups: Alcoholics Anonymous, http://www.aa.org; Narcotics Anonymous, http://www.na.org; Overeaters Anonymous, http://www.oa.org; and Clutterers Anonymous, https://sites.google.com/site/clutterersanonymous
- Online reminder accountability: http://Habitforge.com; http://lift.do/
- Anti-procrastination websites: http://antiprocrastinator.com

ENDNOTES

CHAPTER 1

1. "Deficient emotional self-regulation and adult attention deficit hyperactivity disorder: a family risk analysis," Surman CB, Biederman J, Spencer T, Yorks D, Miller CA, Petty CR, Faraone SV. *Am J Psychiatry.* 2011 Jun;168(6):617–23.

2. "The prevalence and correlates of adult ADHD in the United States: results from the National Comorbidity Survey Replication," Kessler RC, Adler L, Barkley R, Biederman J, Conners CK, Demler O, Faraone SV, Greenhill LL, Howes MJ, Secnik K, Spencer T, Ustun TB, Walters EE, Zaslavsky AM. *Am J Psychiatry.* 2006 Apr;163(4):716–23.

3. "The worldwide prevalence of ADHD: a systematic review and metaregression analysis," Polanczyk G, de Lima MS, Horta BL, Biederman J, Rohde LA. *Am J Psychiatry.* 2007 Jun;164(6):942–8.

4. "Molecular genetics of attention-deficit hyperactivity disorder," Faraone SV, Perlis RH, Doyle AE, et al. *Biol Psychiatry.* 2005;57:1313–23.

5. "High risk for attention deficit hyperactivity disorder among children of parents with childhood onset of the disorder: a pilot study," Biederman J, Faraone SV, Mick E, Spencer T, Wilens T, Kiely K, et al. *Am J Psychiatry.* 1995;152:431–5.

6. "Causal heterogeneity in attention-deficit/hyperactivity disorder: Do we need neuropsychologically impaired subtypes?" Nigg JT, Wilcutt EG, Doyle AE,

Sonuga-Barke JS. *Biol Psychiatry.* 2005;57:1224–30; "Impact of psychometrically defined deficits of executive functioning in adults with attention deficit hyperactivity disorder," Biederman J, Petty C, Fried R, Fontanella J, Doyle AE, Seidman LJ, et al. *Am J Psychiatry.* 2006;163:1730–8.

7. Levine is a spokesperson for the ad campaign "Own Your ADHD," sponsored by Shire Pharmaceuticals. A video of the ad is available here: http://www.you tube.com/watch?v=7f_3OQxMfLU.

8. Here is one of hundreds of references to Phelps's ADHD: "A New Face for A.D.H.D., and a Debate," by Tara Parker-Pope, November 24, 2008, http://www .nytimes.com/2008/11/25/health/25well.html.

9. "Cammi Granato & ADHD: Female Role Model," Jeff Hamilton, *Psychology Today* online, September 1, 2011, http://www.psychologytoday.com/blog/pills -dont-teach-skills/201109/cammi-granato-adhd-female-role-model

10. His ADHD is mentioned in the promotional material for his autobiography, *Keep it Simple* (Pocket Books, August 26, 2003) on Amazon: http://www .amazon.com/Keep-Simple-Terry-Bradshaw/dp/0743417313.

11. "Behind the JetBlue founder's new startup," Patricia Sellers, *Fortune Magazine* online, July 13, 2010, http://postcards.blogs.fortune.cnn.com/tag/david -neeleman/.

12. "Career Advice from Powerful ADHD and LD Executives," Lois Gilman, ADDitude Magazine, Dec/Jan 2005, http://www.additudemag.com/adhd/article/ 754.html.

CHAPTER 2

1. "Sex and age differences in attention-deficit/hyperactivity disorder symptoms and diagnoses: implications for DSM-V and ICD-11," Ramtekkar UP, Reiersen AM, Todorov AA, Todd RD. *J Am Acad Child Adolesc Psychiatry.* 2010 Mar;49(3):217–28.

2. "Attention-deficit/hyperactivity disorder and its comorbidities in women and girls: an evolving picture," Quinn PO. *Curr Psychiatry Rep.* 2008 Oct;10(5): 419–23.

3. "Association between attention-deficit/hyperactivity disorder and bulimia nervosa: analysis of 4 case-control studies," Surman CB, Randall ET, Biederman J. *J Clin Psychiatry.* 2006 Mar;67(3):351–4.

4. *ADHD in Adults: What the Science Says*, Barkley RA, Murphy KR, Fischer M. New York: Guilford Press, 2008:378.

5. "Symptoms of attention-deficit/hyperactivity disorder in first-time expectant women: relations with parenting cognitions and behaviors," Ninowski JE, Mash EJ, Menzie KM. *Infant Ment Health J.* 2007;28(1):54–75.

6. "Maternal ratings of attention problems in ADHD: evidence for the existence of a continuum," Lubke GH. *J Am Acad Child Adolesc Psychiatry.* 2009 Nov;48(11):1085–93.

7. "Attention deficit hyperactivity disorder: an evolutionary perspective," Shelley-Tremblay JF, Rosén LA. *J Genet Psychol.* 1996 Dec;157(4):443–53.

8. "Cortical thinning of the attention and executive function networks in adults with attention-deficit/hyperactivity disorder," Makris N, Biederman J, Valera EM, Bush G, Kaiser J, Kennedy DN, Caviness VS, Faraone SV, Seidman LJ. *Cereb Cortex.* 2007 Jun;17(6):1364–75.

9. "Anterior cingulate volumetric alterations in treatment-naïve adults with ADHD: a pilot study," Makris N, Seidman LJ, Valera EM, Biederman J, Monuteaux MC, Kennedy DN, Caviness Jr VS, Bush G, Crum K, Brown AB, Faraone SV. *J Atten Disord.* 2010;13:407. DOI: 10.1177/1087054709351671, http://jad.sagepub.com/content/13/4/407; "Gray matter alterations in adults with attention-deficit/hyperactivity disorder identified by voxel based morphometry," Seidman LJ, Biederman J, Liang L, Valera EM, Monuteaux MC, Brown A, Kaiser J, Spencer T, Faraone SV, Makris N. *Biol Psychiatry.* 2010. DOI: 10.1016/j.biopsych.2010.09.053

10. "Functional magnetic resonance imaging of methylphenidate and placebo in attention-deficit/hyperactivity disorder during the multi-source interference task," Bush G, Spencer TJ, Holmes J, Shin LM, Valera EM, Seidman LJ, Makris N, Surman C, Aleardi M, Mick E, Biederman J. *Arch Gen Psychiatry.* 2008 Jan;65(1):102–14.

11. "Attention deficit/hyperactivity disorder in adults with bipolar disorder and major depressive disorder: results from the International Mood Disorders Collaborative Project," McIntyre R, Kennedy S, Nguyen H, Bilkey T, et al. *Prim Care Companion J Clin Psychiatry.* 2012; 12(3).

12. "Bipolar disorder and attention deficit/hyperactivity disorder in adults: differential diagnosis or comorbidity," Baud P, Perround N, Aubry JM. Rev Med Suisse. 2011 Jun 1;7(297):1219–22.

13. "Howie Mandel on OCD and ADD: I've been afraid of being labeled 'crazy,'" Hamilton J. *Psychology Today*, April 27, 2011.

CHAPTER 3

1. "When two isn't better than one: predictors of early sexual activity in adolescence using a cumulative risk model," Price MN, Hyde JS. *J Youth Adolesc.* 2009;38:1059–71. DOI: 10.1007/s10964-008-9351-2

2. "Modeling the pathways linking childhood hyperactivity and substance use disorder in young adulthood," Tarter RE, Kirisci L, Feske U, Vanyukov M. *Psychol Addict Behav.* 2007 Jun;21(2):266–71. DOI 10.1037/0893-164X.21.2.266

3. "Attributional styles and psychosocial functioning of adults with ADHD: practice issues and gender differences," Rucklidge J, Brown D, Crawford S, Kaplan B. *J Atten Disord.* 2007;10:288. DOI: 10.1177/1087054706289942, http://jad.sagepub.com/content/10/3/288

4. "Cognitive behavioral therapy vs. relaxation with educational support for

medication-treated adults with ADHD and persistent symptoms: a randomized controlled trial," Safren SA, Sprich S, Mimiaga MJ, Surman C, Knouse L, Groves M, Otto MW. *JAMA*. 2010 Aug 25;304(8):875–80.

5. "A combined treatment approach for adults with ADHD—results of an open study of 43 patients," Rostain AL, Ramsay JR. *J Atten Disord*. 2006 Nov;10(2):150–9. DOI: 10.1177/1087054706288110; "Efficacy of meta-cognitive therapy for adult ADHD," Solanto MV, Marks DJ, Wasserstein J, Mitchell K, Abikoff H, Alvir JM, Kofman MD. *Am J Psychiatry*. 2010 Aug;167(8):958–68. DOI: 10.1176/appi.ajp.2009.09081123

6. "Cognitive therapy: current status and future directions," Beck AT, Dozois DJA. *Annu Rev Med*. 2011 Feb;62. DOI: 10.1146/annurev-med-052209-100032, http://www.annualreviews.org/doi/abs/10.1146/annurev-med-052209-100032?journalCode=med

7. "Evaluation of group cognitive behavioral therapy for adults with ADHD," Bramham J, Young S, Bickerdike A, Spain D, McCartan D, Xenitidis K. *J Atten Disord*. 2009 Mar;12(5):434–41. DOI: 10.1177/1087054708314596

8. "Emotion processing influences working memory circuits in pediatric bipolar disorder and attention-deficit/hyperactivity disorder," Passarotti AM, Sweeney JA, Pavuluri MN. *J Am Acad Child Adolesc Psychiatry*. 2010 Oct;49(10):1064–80.

CHAPTER 4

1. "Cerebral glucose metabolism in adults with hyperactivity of childhood onset," Zametkin AJ, Nordahl TE, Gross M, King AC, Semple WE, Rumsey J, Hamburger S, Cohen RM. *N Engl J Med*. 1990 Nov 15;323(20):1361–6; "Task-specific hypoactivation in prefrontal and temporoparietal brain regions during motor inhibition and task switching in medication-naive children and adolescents with attention deficit hyperactivity disorder," Smith AB, Taylor E, Brammer M, Toone B, Rubia K. *Am J Psychiatry*. 2006 Jun;163(6):1044–51.

2. "Attention-deficit/hyperactivity disorder is characterized by a delay in cortical maturation," Shaw P, Eckstrand K, Sharp W, Blumenthal J, Lerch JP, Greenstein D, Clasen L, Evans A, Giedd J, Rapoport JL. *Proc Natl Acad Sci U S A*. 2007 Dec 4;104(49):19649–54.

3. "The unique contribution of emotional impulsiveness to impairment in major life activities in hyperactive children as adults," Barkley RA, Fischer M. *J Am Acad Child Adolesc Psychiatry*. 2010 May;49(5):503–13.

4. "Deficient emotional self-regulation and adult attention deficit hyperactivity disorder: a family risk analysis," Surman CB, Biederman J, Spencer T, Yorks D, Miller CA, Petty CR, Faraone SV. *Am J Psychiatry*. 2011 Jun;168(6):617–23.

5. "Abnormal amygdalar activation and connectivity in adolescents with attention-deficit/hyperactivity disorder," Posner J, Nagel BJ, Maia TV, Mechling A, Oh M, Wang Z, Peterson BS. *J Am Acad Child Adolesc Psychiatry*. 2011 Aug;50(8):828–37.

6. "Molecular mechanisms of stress-induced prefrontal cortical impairment: implications for mental illness," Hains AB, Arnsten AF. *Learn Mem.* 2008 Aug 6;15(8):551–64; "The stressed prefrontal cortex and goal-directed behaviour: acute psychosocial stress impairs the flexible implementation of task goals," Plessow F, Kiesel A, Kirschbaum C. *Exp Brain Res.* 2011 Nov 19 [E-pub ahead of print].

7. "Molecular mechanisms of stress-induced prefrontal cortical impairment: implications for mental illness," Hains AB, Arnsten AF. *Learn Mem.* 2008 Aug 6;15(8):551–64; "The stressed prefrontal cortex and goal-directed behaviour: acute psychosocial stress impairs the flexible implementation of task goals," Plessow F, Kiesel A, Kirschbaum C. *Exp Brain Res.* 2011 Nov 19 [E-pub ahead of print].

8. *ADHD in Adults: What the Science Says*, Barkley RA, Murphy KR, Fischer M. New York: Guilford Press, 2008:113–4.

9. "What does distractibility in ADHD reveal about mechanisms for top-down attentional control?" Friedman-Hill SR, Wagman MR, Gex SE, Pine DS, Leibenluft E, Ungerleider LG. *Cognition.* 2010 Apr;115(1):93–103.

10. "Neural correlates of dispositional mindfulness during affect labeling," Creswell JD, Way BM, Eisenberger NI, Lieberman MD. *Psychosom Med.* 2007;69(6):560–5; "Enhanced response inhibition during intensive meditation training predicts improvements in self-reported adaptive socioemotional functioning," Sahdra BK, Maclean KA, Ferrer E, Shaver PR, Saron CD. *Emotion.* 2011;11(2):299–312. PMID: 21500899.

11. "Mindfulness in medicine," Ludwig DS, Kabat-Zinn J. *JAMA.* 2008;300(11):1350–2. PMID: 18799450.

CHAPTER 5

1. "Dorsal anterior cingulate cortex: a role in reward-based decision making," Bush G, Vogt BA, Holmes J, Dale AM, Greve D, Jenike MA, et al. *Proc Natl Acad Sci USA.* 2002;99:523–8; "Human anterior cingulate neurons and the integration of monetary reward with motor responses," Williams ZM, Bush G, Rauch SL, Cosgrove GR, Eskandar EN. *Nat Neurosci.* 2004; 7(12):1370–5.

2. "Stability of executive function deficits in girls with ADHD: a prospective longitudinal followup study into adolescence," Biederman J, Petty CR, Doyle AE, Spencer T, Henderson CS, Marion B, Fried R, Faraone SV. *Dev Neuropsychol.* 2008;33(1):44–61. http://www.ncbi.nlm.nih.gov/pubmed/18443969

3. "Improving adherence and compliance in adults and adolescents with ADHD," Dodson WW. *Medscape Psychiatry Ment Health.* 2006;11(1).

4. "Dynamical origin of the effective storage capacity in the brain's working memory," Christian Bick C, Mikhail I, Rabinovich MI. *Phys Rev Lett.* 2009;103(21):218101. (2009) PMID: 20366069; "The magic number seven plus or minus two: some limits on our capacity to process information," Miller, GA

(1956). *Psychological Rev*.iew 1956;63(2):81–97. doiDOI: 10.1037/h0043158, PMID: 13310704.

5. "Neural suppression of irrelevant information underlies optimal working memory performance," Zanto TP, Gazzaley A, J Neurosci. 2009 Mar 11;29(10):3059–66. PMID: 19279242.

CHAPTER 6

1. "Behavioral inhibition, sustained attention, and executive functions: constructing a unifying theory of ADHD," Barkley RA. *Psychol Bull.* 1997;121(1):65–94. PMID: 9000892; "Common inhibitory mechanism in human inferior prefrontal cortex revealed by event-related functional MRI," Konishi S, Nakajima K, Uchida I, Kikyo H, Kameyama M, Miyashita Y. *Brain.* 1999;122:981–91; "The basal ganglia: focused selection and inhibition of competing motor programs," Mink JW. *Prog Neurobiol.* 1996;50:381–425; "Hold your horses: a dynamic computational role for the subthalamic nucleus in decision making," Frank MJ. *Neural Netw.* 2006;19:1120–36; "Functional significance of the cortico-subthalamo-pallidal 'hyperdirect' pathway," Nambu A, Tokuno H, Takada M. *Neurosci Res.* 2002;43:111–7; "Prefrontal cortex and impulsive decision making," Kim S, Lee D. *Biol Psychiatry.* 2011 Jun 15;69(12):1140–6. DOI: 10.1016/j.biopsych.2010.07.005

2. "The valence strength of unpleasant emotion modulates brain processing of behavioral inhibitory control: neural correlates," Yuana J, Menga X, Yanga J, Yaoc G, Hua L, Yuana H. *Biol Psychiatry.* 2012 Jan:89(1),240–51.

3. "Deficient emotional self-regulation and adult attention deficit hyperactivity disorder: a family risk analysis," Surman CBH, Biederman J, Spencer T, Yorks D, Miller CA, Petty CR, Faraone SV. *Am J Psychiatry.* 2011;168:617–23. DOI: 10.1176/appi.ajp.2010.10081172

4. "Bulimia nervosa symptoms in the Multimodal Treatment Study of Children with ADHD," Mikami AY, Hinshaw SP, Arnold LE, Hoza B, Hechtman L, Newcorn JH, Abikoff HB. *Int J Eat Disord.* 2009. PMID: 19378318.

5. "Impulsivity and long-term prognosis of psychiatric patients with anorexia nervosa/bulimia nervosa," Sohlberg S, Norring C, Holmgren S, et al. *J Nerv Ment Dis.* 1989;177:249–58.

6. "Are some individuals diagnosed with ADHD prone to alcohol abuse? Consideration of two possible mediating factors for this susceptibility," Maxwell A. *J Atten Disord.* 2011. DOI: 10.1177/1087054711427400, PMID: 22100688.

7. "Impulsivity as a mediating mechanism between early-life adversity and addiction: theoretical comment on Lovic et al.," Hosking J, Winstanley CA. *Behav Neurosci.* 2011;125(4):681–6; "Neurobehavioral disinhibition in childhood predicts early age at onset of substance use disorder," Tarter RE, Kirisci L, Mez-

zich A, Cornelius JR, Pajer K, Vanyukov M, Clark D. *Am J Psychiatry.* 2003;160: 1078–85; "Does childhood treatment of ADHD with stimulant medication affect substance abuse in adulthood?" Volkow ND, Swanson JM. *Am J Psychiatry.* 2008 May;165(5):553–5. DOI: 10.1176/appi.ajp.2008.08020237

8. *Mastering Your Adult ADHD: A Cognitive-Behavioral Treatment Program,* Safren SA, Sprich S, Perlman CA, Otto MW. Oxford, UK: Oxford University Press, 2005:84–90; *Cognitive Therapy: Basics and Beyond,* Beck J. New York: Guilford Press, 1995; *An Introduction to Cognitive Behaviour Therapy Skills and Applications,* Westbrook D, Kennerley KJ. London: Sage Publications, 2007; *Mind over Mood: Change How You Feel by Changing the Way You Think,* Padesky CA, Greenberger D. New York: Guilford Press, 1995; *Cognitive-Behavioral Therapy for Adult ADHD: Targeting Executive Dysfunction,* Solanto MV. New York: Guilford Press, 2001.

CHAPTER 7

1. "A laboratory driving simulation for assessment of driving behavior in adults with ADHD: a controlled study," Biederman J, Fried R, Monuteaux MC, Reimer B, Coughlin JF, Surman CB, Aleardi M, Dougherty M, Schoenfeld S, Spencer TJ, Faraone SV. *Annu Gen Psychiatry.* 2007 Jan 30;6:4.

2. "Manual transmission enhances attention and driving performance of ADHD adolescent males: pilot study," Cox DJ, Punja M, Powers K, et al. *J Atten Disord.* 2006;10(2):212–5.

3. "Prefrontal cortex and impulsive decision making," Kim S, Lee D. *Biol Psychiatry.* 2001 Jun 15;69(12):1140–6. DOI:10.1016/j.biopsych.2010.07.005

4. Reviewed in "Neural hyporesponsiveness and hyperresponsiveness during immediate and delayed reward processing in adult attention-deficit/hyperactivity disorder," Plichta MM, Vasic N, Wolf RC, Lesch KP, Brummer D, Jacob C, Fallgatter AJ, Grön G. *Biol Psychiatry.* 2009;65:7–14.

5. "Willpower over the life span: decomposing self-regulation," Mischel W, Ayduk O, Berman MG, Casey BJ, Gotlib IH, Jonides J, Kross E, Teslovich T, Wilson NL, Zayas V, Shoda Y. *SCAN.* 2011;6:252–6.

CHAPTER 8

1. "Acquisition and performance of goal-directed instrumental actions depends on ERK signaling in distinct regions of dorsal striatum in rats," Shiflett MW, Brown RA, Balleine BW. *J Neurosci.* 2010 Feb 24;30(8):2951–9.

2. "Neurobiology of skill and habit learning," Salmon DP, Butters N. *Curr Opin Neurobiol.* 1995;5:184–90.

3. "How are habits formed: modelling habit formation in the real world," Lally P, Van Jaarsveld CHM, Potts HWW, Wardle J. *Eur J Soc Psychol.* 2010;40: 998–1009.

4. "Alcohol has a dose-related effect on parasympathetic nerve activity during sleep," Sagawa YY, Kondo HH, Matsubuchi NN, Takemura T, Kanayama H, Kaneko Y, Kanbayashi T, Shimizu T, Hishikawa Y, Shimizu TT. *Alcohol Clin Exp Res.* 2011 Nov 1;35(11):2093–100.

5. "Physical Activity Guidelines for Americans," U.S. Dept. of Health and Human Services. 2008. http://www.health.gov/paguidelines/guidelines/summary.aspx

6. There's an excellent summary and list of references on the Harvard School of Public Health's website: http://www.hsph.harvard.edu/nutritionsource/staying -active/staying-active-full-story/index.html#references

7. "Exercise influences hippocampal plasticity by modulating brain-derived neu-rotrophic factor processing," Ding Q, Ying Z, Gómez-Pinilla F. *Neuroscience.* 2011 Sep;192:773–80.

8. "Association between attention-deficit/hyperactivity disorder and sleep impair-ment in adulthood," Surman CBH, Adamson JJ, Petty C, Biederman J, Kenealy DC, Levine M, Mick E, Faraone SV. *J Clin Psychiatry.* 2009;70(11):1523–9.

9. Division of Sleep Medicine at Harvard Medical School website, http://healthysleep.med.harvard.edu

10. "The Sleepless Elite: Why Some People Can Run on Little Sleep and Get So Much Done," Melinda Beck, April 5, 2011, http://online.wsj.com/article/SB100 01424052748703712504576242701752957910.html

11. Personal communication from Daniel Buysse, University of Pittsburgh Medical Center, September 5, 2011, and from Christopher R. Jones, University of Utah, September 22, 2011.

12. "Food additives and hyperactive behaviour in 3-year-old and 8/9-year-old chil-dren in the community: a randomised, double-blinded, placebo-controlled trial," McCann D, Barrett A, Cooper A, Crumpler D, Dalen L, Grimshaw K, Kitchin E, Lok K, Porteous L, Prince E, Sonuga-Barke E, Warner JO, Stevenson J. *Lancet.* 2007;370(9598):1560–7.

13. Some studies related to whole/refined grains and health: "Whole-grain con-sumption and risk of coronary heart disease: results from the Nurses' Health Study," Liu S, Stampfer MJ, Hu FB, et al. *Am J Clin Nutr.* 1999;70:412–9; "Whole grain intake and cardiovascular disease: a meta-analysis," Mellen PB, Walsh TF, Herrington DM. *Nutr Metab Cardiovasc Dis.* 2007; "Whole grain, bran, and germ intake and risk of type 2 diabetes: a prospective cohort study and system-atic review," de Munter JS, Hu FB, Spiegelman D, Franz M, van Dam RM, *PLoS Med.* 2007 Aug;4(8):e261; "White rice, brown rice, and risk of type 2 diabetes in US men and women," Sun Q, Spiegelman D, van Dam RM, et al. *Arch Intern Med.* 2010;170:961–9; "Whole-grain intake and cancer: an expanded review and meta-analysis," Jacobs Jr DR, Marquart L, Slavin J, Kushi LH. *Nutr Cancer.* 1998;30:85–96; "Dietary fiber and whole-grain consumption in relation to colorectal cancer in the NIH-AARP Diet and Health Study," Schatzkin A, Mouw T, Park Y, et al. *Am J Clin Nutr.* 2007;85:1353–60; "Dietary carbohydrate,

glycemic index, and glycemic load and the risk of colorectal cancer in the BCDDP cohort," Strayer L, Jacobs Jr DR, Schairer C, Schatzkin A, Flood A. *Cancer Causes Control.* 2007;18:853–63; "Whole-grain consumption is associated with a reduced risk of noncardiovascular, noncancer death attributed to inflammatory diseases in the Iowa Women's Health Study," Jacobs Jr DR, Andersen LF, Blomhoff R. *Am J Clin Nutr.* 2007;85:1606–14.

14. "Food sources of energy among U.S. population, 2005–2006." Risk Factor Monitoring and Methods. Control and Population Sciences. National Cancer Institute. 2010. http://riskfactor. cancer.gov/diet/foodsources/

15. "New frontiers in cardiovascular behavioral medicine: Comparative effectiveness of exercise and medication in treating depression," Blumenthal JA. *Cleve Clin J Med.* 2011 Aug;78(1):S35–S43. DOI: 10.3949/ccjm.78.s1.06

16. "Exercise as an augmentation treatment for nonremitted major depressive disorder: a randomized, parallel dose comparison," Trivedi MH, Greer TL, Church TS, Carmody TJ, Grannemann BD, Galper DI, Dunn AL, Earnest CP, Sunderajan P, Henley SS, Blair SN. *J Clin Psychiatry.*

CHAPTER 9

1. "Understanding ADHD in girls," Grskovic JA, Zentall SS. *Int J Spec Ed.* 2010;25(1):171–84.

2. "Patterns of friendship among girls with and without attention-deficit/hyperactivity disorder," Blachman DR, Hinshaw SP. *J Abnorm Child Psychol.* 2002 Dec;30(6):625–40.

3. "The social competence of children with attention deficit hyperactivity disorder: A review of the literature," Nixon E. *Child Psychol Psychiatry Review.* 2001;6:172–80.

4. "Differences in heterosocial behavior and outcomes of ADHD-symptomatic subtypes in a college sample," Canu WH, Carlson CL. *J Atten Disord.* 2003 Apr;6(3):123–33.

5. http://www.eeoc.gov/policy/docs/accommodation.html

6. "Stephanie Sarkis, Ph.D.: A Lot of Education and a Bit of Technology," http://www.everydayhealth.com/add-adhd/stephanie-sarkis-a-lot-of-education-and-a-bit-of-technology.aspx, July 26, 2011.

7. "Friends: A Natural Treatment for Adult ADHD," Kessler Z, Additude Magazine online. http://www.additudemag.com/adhd/article/8390-2.html

CHAPTER 10

1. A sampling of research on safety of ADHD medications: "Long-term safety and effectiveness of mixed amphetamine salts extended release in adults with ADHD," Biederman J, Spencer TJ, Wilens TE, et al. *CNS Spectr.* 2005;10(20):16–25; "Long-term treatment outcomes with lisdexamfetamine dimesylate for adults with attention-deficit/hyperactivity disorder stratified by baseline sever-

ity," Ginsberg L, Katic A, Adeyi B, Dirks B, Babcock T, Lasser R, Scheckner B, Adler LA. *Curr Med Res Opin.* 2011 Jun;27(6):1097–107; "Long-term safety of OROS methylphenidate in adults with attention-deficit/hyperactivity disorder: an open-label, dose-titration, 1-year study," Adler LA, Orman C, Starr HL, Silber S, Palumbo J, Cooper K, Berwaerts J, Harrison D. *J Clin Psychopharmacol.* 2011 Feb;31(1):108–14; "Twenty-four-week treatment with extended release methylphenidate improves emotional symptoms in adult ADHD," Rösler M, Retz W, Fischer R, Ose C, Alm B, Deckert J, Philipsen A, Herpertz S, Ammer R. *World J Biol Psychiatry.* 2010 Aug;11(5):709–18; "Long-term, open-label safety and efficacy of atomoxetine in adults with ADHD: final report of a 4-year study," Adler LA, Spencer TJ, Williams DW, Moore RJ, Michelson D. *J Atten Disord.* 2008 Nov;12(3):248–53; "Two-year outcome of treatment with central stimulant medication in adult attention-deficit/hyperactivity disorder: a prospective study," Bejerot J, Rydén EM, Arlinde CM. *J Clin Psychiatry.* 2010 Dec;71(12):1590–7.

2. "ADHD drugs and serious cardiovascular events in children and young adults," Cooper WO, et al. *N Engl J Med.* 2001 Nov 17;365:1896–1904.

3. "ADHD medications and risk of serious cardiovascular events in young and middle-aged adults," Habel LA, Cooper WO, Sox CM, Chan KA, Fireman BH, *JAMA.* Published online December 12, 2011.

4. "Representativeness of participants in a clinical trial for attention-deficit/hyperactivity disorder? Comparison with adults from a large observational study," Surman CBH, Monuteaux MC, Petty CR, Faraone SV, Spencer TJ, Chu NF, Biederman J. *J Clin Psychiatry.* 2010;71(12):1612–6.

5. "Two-year outcome of treatment with central stimulant medication in adult attention-deficit/hyperactivity disorder: a prospective study," Bejerot S, Rydén EM, Arlinde CM. *J Clin Psychiatry.* 2010;71(12):1590–7.

6. "Functional magnetic resonance imaging of methylphenidate and placebo in attention-deficit/hyperactivity disorder during the multi-source interference task," Bush G, Spencer TJ, Holmes J, Shin LM, Valera EM, Seidman LJ, Makris N, Surman C, Aleardi M, Mick E, Biederman J. *J Arch Gen Psychiatry.* 2008 Jan;65(1):102–14.

7. "A comparison of the efficacy of medications for adult attention-deficit/hyperactivity disorder using meta-analysis of effect sizes," Faraone SV, Glatt SJ. *J Clin Psychiatry.* 2010 Jun;71(6):754–63.

8. "Impact of stimulant pharmacotherapy on sleep quality: post hoc analyses of 2 large, double-blind, randomized, placebo-controlled trials," Surman CB, Roth TJ. *J Clin Psychiatry.* 2011 Jul;72(7):903–8.

CHAPTER 11

1. "Cognitive behavioral therapy vs relaxation with educational support for medication-treated adults with ADHD and persistent symptoms: a randomized

controlled trial," Safren SA, Sprich S, Mimiaga MJ, Surman C, Knouse L, Groves M, Otto MW. *JAMA.* 2010 Aug 25;304(8):875–80.

2. "Efficacy of meta-cognitive therapy for adult ADHD," Solanto MV, Marks DJ, Wasserstein J, Mitchell K, Abikoff H, Alvir JM, Kofman MD. *Am J Psychiatry.* 2010 Aug;167(8):958–68.

3. "Editorial: Coaching as a treatment for ADHD," Goldstein S. *J Atten Disord.* 2005;9:379–381.

4. "Does mindfulness training improve cognitive abilities? A systematic review of neuropsychological findings," Chiesa A, Calati R, Serretti A. *Clin Psychol Rev.* April 2011;31(3):449–64.

5. "Mindfulness-based stress reduction and mindfulness-based cognitive therapy: a systematic review of randomized controlled trials," Fjorback LO, Arendt M, Ornbøl E, Fink P, Walach H. *Acta Psychiatr Scand.* 2011 Aug;124(2):102–19; "The effect of mindfulness-based therapy on anxiety and depression: a meta-analytic review," Hofmann SG, Sawyer AT, Witt AA, Oh D. *J Consult Clin Psychol.* 2010 Apr;78(2):169–83.

6. "Mindfulness meditation training in adults and adolescents with ADHD: a feasibility study," Zylowska L, Ackerman DL, Yang MH, Futrell JL, Horton NL, Hale TS, Pataki C, Smalley SL. *J Atten Disord.* Published online November 19, 2007. http://www.wcbsthailand.com/download/c1_pdf/Mindfulness%20ADHD-Zylowska%20et%20al.pdf; "Comparing the effectiveness of mindfulness-based stress reduction and multidisciplinary intervention programs for chronic pain: a randomized comparative trial," Wong SY, Chan FW, Wong RL, Chu MC, Lam YK, Mercer SW, Ma SH. *Clin J Pain.* 2011 Oct;27(8):724–34; "Mindfulness-based stress reduction for stress management in healthy people: a review and meta-analysis," Chiesa A, Serretti A. *J Altern Complementary Med.* 2009 May;15(5):593–600; "Sahaja yoga meditation as a family treatment programme for children with attention deficit-hyperactivity disorder," Harrison L, Manocha R, Rubia K. *Clin Child Psychol Psychiatry.* 2004;9(4):479–97.

7. "Reduced ADHD symptoms in adults with ADHD after structured skills training group: results from a randomized controlled trial," Hirvikoskia T, Waaler E, Alfredsson J, Pihlgren C, Holmström A, Johnson A, Rück J, Wiwe C, Bothén P, Nordström AL. *Behav Res Ther.* 2001 Mar;49(3):175–85.

8. "Attention-deficit/hyperactivity disorder: is it time to reappraise the role of sugar consumption?" Johnson RJ, Gold MS, Johnson DR, Ishimoto T, Lanaspa MA, Zahniser NR, Avena NM. *Postgrad Med.* 2001;123(5):39–49.

9. "Food additives and hyperactive behaviour in 3-year-old and 8/9-year-old children in the community: a randomised, double-blinded, placebo-controlled trial," McCann D, Barrett A, Cooper A, et al. *Lancet.* 2007;5:5.

10. "Effects of a restricted elimination diet on the behaviour of children with attention-deficit hyperactivity disorder (INCA study): a randomised controlled

trial," Pelsser LM, Frankena K, Toorman J, Savelkoul HF, Dubois AE, Pereira RR, Haagen TA, Rommelse NN, Buitelaar JK. *Lancet.* 2011 Feb 5;377(9764): 494–503.

11. "Association of attention-deficit/hyperactivity disorder and celiac disease: a brief report," Niederhofer H. *Prim Care Companion CNS Disord.* 2011;13(3).

12. "Effects of caffeine on cognitive, psychomotor, and affective performance of children with attention-deficit/hyperactivity disorder," Leon MR. *J Atten Disord.* 2000;4(1):27–47; "Tea consumption maybe an effective active treatment for adult attention deficit hyperactivity disorder (ADHD)," Liu K, Liang X, Kuang W. *Med Hypotheses.* 2011;76:461–3.

13. "Acute effects of a glucose energy drink on behavioral control," Howard MA, Marczinski CA. *Exp Clin Psychopharmacol.* 2010 Dec;18(6):553–61.

14. "Complementary medicines (herbal and nutritional products) in the treatment of attention deficit hyperactivity disorder (ADHD): a systematic review of the evidence," Sarris J, Kean J, Schweitzer I, Lake J. *Complementary Ther Med.* 2011 Aug;19(4):216–27.

15. "Omega-3 fatty acid supplementation for the treatment of children with attention-deficit/hyperactivity disorder symptomatology: systematic review and meta-analysis," Bloch MH, Qawasmi A. *J Am Acad Child and Adolesc Psychiatry.* 2011 Oct;50(10):991–1000.

16. "Essential fatty acids and attention-deficit-hyperactivity disorder: a systematic review," Raz R, Gabis L. *Dev Med Child Neurol.* 2009;51(8):580–92.

17. "Association of fatty acid desaturase genes with attention-deficit/hyperactivity disorder," Brookes KJ, Chen W, Xu X, Taylor E, Asherson P. *Biol Psychiatry.* 2006;60(10):1053–61.

18. "Complementary and alternative treatments of attention deficit hyperactivity disorder," Kilincaslan A, et al. *Arch Neuropsychiatry.* 2011;48:94–102.; "Zinc in attention-deficit/hyperactivity disorder," Arnold LE, Disilvestro RE. *J Child Adolesc Psychopharmacol.* 2005;15(4):619–27.

19. "Alternative treatments for adults with attention-deficit hyperactivity disorder (ADHD)," Arnold LE. *Ann N Y Acad Sci.* 2001;931:310–41.

20. "Iron deficiency in children with attention deficit hyperactivity disorder," Lahat E, Heyman E, Livne A, Goldman M, Berkovitch M, Zachor D. *Isr Med Assoc J.* 2011 Sep;13(9):530–3.

21. "Complementary and alternative treatments of attention deficit hyperactivity disorder," Kilincaslan A, et al. *Arch Neuropsychiatry.* 2011;48:94–102.

22. "Efficacy of neurofeedback treatment in ADHD: the effects on inattention, impulsivity and hyperactivity: a meta-analysis," Arns M, deRidder S, Strehl U, Breteler M, Coenen A. *Clin EEG Neurosci.* 2009;40:180–9.

23. "The effectiveness of EEG-feedback on attention, impulsivity and EEG: a sham feedback controlled study," Logemann HN, Lansbergen MM, Van Os TW, Böcker KB, Kenemans JL. *Neurosci Lett.* 2010 Jul 19;479(1):49–53; "A review of

neurofeedback treatment for pediatric ADHD," Lofthouse N, Arnold LE, Hersch S, Hurt E, Debeus R. *J Atten Disord.* 2012 Jul;16(5):351–72.

24. "Biofeedback and neurofeedback treatment for ADHD," Lofthouse N, McBurnett K, Arnold LE, Hurt E. *Psychiatr Ann.* 2011 Jan;41(1):42–48. http://www.psychiatricannalsonline.com/showPdf.asp?rID=79275

25. "Training of working memory in children with ADHD," Klingberg T, Forssberg H, Westerberg H, Benninger J. *J Clin Exp Neuropsychol.* 2002 Sep;24(6):781–91; "A controlled trial of working memory training for children and adolescents with ADHD," Beck SJ, Hanson CA, Puffenberger SS, Benninger KL, Benninger WB. *J Clin Child Adolesc Psychol.* 2010;39(6):825–36.

26. *The Relaxation Response,* Benson H, Klipper MZ, New York: HarperTorch, 1976.

INDEX